Case Studies in Personnel

Management Studies Series

The IPD examination system provides a unique route into professional personnel practice. The Management Studies Series provides the essential core texts.

Management Studies 1
Series Editors: Michael Armstrong and David Farnham

Finance and Accounting for Managers
David Davies

Management Information Systems and Statistics
Roland and Frances Bee

Management Processes and Functions
Michael Armstrong

Managing Human Resources
Jane Weightman

Management Studies 2

Employee Development
Rosemary Harrison

Employee Relations
David Farnham

Employee Resourcing
Derek Torrington, Laura Hall,
Isabel Haylor and Judith Myers

MANAGEMENT STUDIES

Case Studies in Personnel

Editors

Diana Winstanley
Jean Woodall

Institute of Personnel and Development

To Rob, Nick and Victoria

First published 1992
Reprinted 1995

Phototypeset by Falcon Typographic Art Ltd, Fife, Scotland
and printed in Great Britain by the Bath Press

British Library cataloguing in publication data

Case Studies in Personnel. – (Management
Studies Series)
  I. Winstanley, Diana II. Woodall, Jean
  III. Series
  658.3
  ISBN 0–85292–475–5 ✓

The views expressed in this publication are the authors' own, and may not necessarily reflect those of the IPD.

**INSTITUTE OF PERSONNEL
AND DEVELOPMENT**

IPD House, Camp Road, London SW19 4UX

Registered office as above. Registered Charity No. 1038333
A company limited by guarantee. Registered in England No. 2931892

Contents

I   Employee resourcing

II   Employee development

v

III Employee relations

IV Integrated human resource management

Acknowledgements

A very big thank you to Maureen Beard for all her dedicated work, efficiency and professionalism in typing the manuscript which made the final stages of editing run much more smoothly than we had any right to hope! We are also very grateful to the IPD for encouraging us to embark on the book, and especially to Anne Cordwent for liaising with us over its production and for planting our feet firmly on the ground when our ideas overstretched our capacities. Thirdly, we are indebted to all the authors who made it possible, for writing the cases, getting approval of them from the organizations concerned and for tolerating our frantic telephone calls and illegible amendments – thanks. A big thank you also to all the organizations (named and unnamed) who allowed our investigations and opened themselves to our scrutiny. Without their help the book could not have been written. Finally, we would also like to express our thanks to our partners, for putting up with us, and giving us support through the project. Also to baby Victoria, whose timely arrival in January, did not totally wreck the project and whose close inspection of the text produced perhaps some of the more lighthearted but incisive editorial interventions.

D.W.
J.W.

List of contributors

Alan Arthurs, BSc, MA, PhD, is Lecturer in Industrial Relations and Personnel Management at the University of Bath School of Management and an Independent Expert on equal pay.

Paul Banfield, BA, MA, MIPD, is Associate Head of New Ventures at Sheffield Business School, Sheffield Polytechnic.

Ian Beardwell, BSc, MSc, PhD, MIPD, is Professor and Head of the Department of Human Resource Management at Leicester Business School, Leicester Polytechnic.

Will Blandamer, BSc, MSc, is a researcher at UMIST School of Management and is involved in research on behalf of the North West Regional Health Authority.

Michael Brocklehurst, MSc, is a Lecturer in Organizational Behaviour at the Management School, Imperial College, University of London, and has published a number of articles on home working and tele-working.

Carole Brooke, BA, is Lecturer in Computer Studies and a Company of Information Technologists Research Scholar at the Centre for Personnel Research and Enterprise Development at City University Business School. She is a member of Women in Management and of the European Women's Management Development Network and has conducted research into training opportunities and human resource issues.

Nicola Cawley, BA, DPM, GradIPD, is a Personnel Officer with the Wellcome Foundation Ltd.

Tim Claydon, BSocSci, MSc, PhD, is Principal Lecturer in Industrial Relations at Leicester Business School, Leicester Polytechnic.

Marjorie Corbridge, BA, MIPD, is Senior Lecturer in Human Resource Management at Portsmouth Polytechnic Business School and has been a Personnel Manager within the Wessex Regional Health Authority.

David Farnham, BA, MSc, FIPD, is Principal Lecturer in Industrial Relations at Portsmouth Business School and has been a member of the IPM's National Education Committee since 1988. His publications include *Personnel in Context* (IPM, 1990), *The Corporate Environment* (IPM, 1990) and (as co-author with John Pimlott) *Understanding Industrial Relations* (Cassell, 1990).

Patricia Fosh, BA, PhD, is a Lecturer in Industrial Relations at the Management School, Imperial College, London; she is co-editor with

Craig R. Littler of *Industrial Relations and the Law in the 1980s* (Gower, 1985) and co-editor with Edmund Heery of *Trade Unions and their Members* (Macmillan, 1990).

Philip Frame, MSc, PhD, is Deputy Head of the Management School at Middlesex Polytechnic. He has worked for the Race Relations Board as researcher/conciliator and as a training officer. He has written on learning in teams and is author of *Management Responses to Expenditure Cuts* (Gower, 1991).

Thomas Garavan, BBS, LLB, MBS, LLM, FIITD, is Lecturer in Employee Development at the University of Limerick, College of Business, Ireland. He is author of *Training and Development in Ireland* (Gill & Macmillan and the Irish Institute of Training and Development) and *Employee Relations and Employment Law in Ireland*, with Gunnigle and Fitzgerald, Plessey Maint and Tech Centre, University of Limerick.

Rosemary Harrison, BA, FIPD, is Lecturer in Human Resource Management and Development at Durham University Business School. Her books include *Training and Development* (IPM, 1988), *Employee Development* (IPM, 1992), and she is co-editor of *Strategic Human Resource Management* (Addison-Wesley, 1992).

Edmund Heery, MIPD, is Reader in Industrial Relations at Kingston Business School, Kingston Polytechnic, and is co-editor with Patricia Fosh of *Trade Unions and their Members* (Macmillan, 1990).

Terence Kenny, BA, BLitt, CIPD, is Personnel Adviser to Baxter Gruenhut Management Ltd, a subsidiary of the Harper Group Inc, and is editor with David Guest of *A Textbook of Techniques and Strategies in Personnel Management* (IPM, 1983).

Alexander Lord, PhD, is Lecturer in Applied Psychology and Human Resource Management at Henley – the Management College. He manages Henley's Thames Valley Business Survey and is also a Project Manager for the Thames Valley TEC.

Ann McGoldrick, BA, MA, CertEd, PhD, MIPD, is a Senior Lecturer in Human Resource Management at the Department of Management, Manchester Polytechnic, and is author of *Early Retirement* (Gower, 1989).

Ian McLoughlin, BA, PhD, is Lecturer in Industrial Relations at the Centre for Business and Management Studies, Brunel – the University of West London, co-author (with Jon Clark) of *Technological Change at Work* (Open University Press, 1988) and co-author of *The Process of Technological Change* (Cambridge University Press, 1988). He has also written numerous articles concerning various aspects of industrial relations.

Hedley Malloch, BSc, MSc, PhD, MBIM, is Director of Management Development Programmes at Teesside Business School, Teesside Polytechnic.

Roderick Martin, MA, DPhil, is Professor of Organizational Behaviour and Director of the University of Glasgow Business School. He is author of a number of books, including *Bargaining Power* (Oxford University Press, 1992).

Sarah Moore, BA, MBS, is Lecturer in Organizational Behaviour at the University of Limerick, Ireland.

Michael Morley, BBS, MBS, AIITD, MIPD, is a Research Assistant at the Graduate School, College of Business, University of Limerick, Ireland.

Huw Morris, BSc, MSc, MIPD, is Senior Lecturer at Kingston Business School, Kingston Polytechnic.

Paula O'Brien, BSc, MSc, is a Lecturer in Human Resource Management at Loughborough Business School, Loughborough University of Technology.

Alan Peacock, MSc, DMS, MIPD, MMS, is Head of the Department of Human Resource Management at Portsmouth Polytechnic Business School. He was employed for many years as a personnel specialist in both public and private-sector organizations. He is a director of an employers' organization and regularly presents cases to industrial tribunals.

David Preece, BA, MPhil, MIPD, MIOP, is Senior Lecturer in Organization Analysis at Portsmouth Polytechnic Business School and author of *Managing the Adoption of New Technology* (Routledge, 1989).

Ivor Roberts, BA, FIPD, is Principal Lecturer at the Business School, Polytechnic of West London, and co-author with Professor T. McIlwee of *Human Resource Management in the Corporate Environment* (Elm, 1991).

Paul Smith, BA, CertEd, MA, PhD, is Lecturer in Industrial Relations at the University of Nottingham.

Paul Sparrow, BSc, MSc, PhD, CPsychol, Affiliate to the IPD, is Lecturer in Organizational Behaviour at Manchester Business School, Manchester University, and has been a consultant with PA Consulting Group. He has also written widely on human resource strategy and has published a book on 'competences'.

Roger Undy, MA, is Acting President and Dean at Templeton College, University of Oxford, and joint author of *Change in Trade Unions* (Hutchinson, 1981) and *Ballots and Trade Union Democracy*, (Blackwell, 1984).

David Walsh, BA, MIPD, is Principal Lecturer in Human Resource Management at Nottingham Business School, Nottingham Polytechnic, and was a co-opted member of the IPM National Education Committee and member of its Course Approvals Panel. He has also had a one-year secondment as consultant to the Head of Personnel with a leading UK retailer.

Jane Weightman, BA, MSc, PhD, is Honorary Lecturer in the School of Management, University of Manchester Institute of Science and Technology. She is author or co-author of seven books on management, including *Managing Human Resources* (IPM, 1990).

Brian Willey, BA, MA, MIPD, is Senior Lecturer in Industrial Relations at Kingston Business School, Kingston Polytechnic. He has worked in the past for the GMB trade union and in the Industrial Relations department of London Transport, and has produced a *Survey of Union Recognition* for the Engineering Employers' Federation (1986).

Diana Winstanley, BSc, PhD, MIPD, is Lecturer in Human Resource Management at the Management School, Imperial College, London, and has conducted and published research on recruitment in high-tech industry, and on managing and organizing engineering design.

Jean Woodall, BA, PhD, is Reader in Human Resource Management at Kingston Business School, Kingston Polytechnic, and is involved in research and consultancy on education and industry links, work-based assessment and management development.

Introduction

The need for case studies in personnel management

This collection of case studies originated in discussions over the revisions of the IPM Professional Education Scheme which took place in 1990. The new scheme placed greater emphasis upon skill development to enhance the knowledge and understanding gained. The entry of the concept of 'competence' into the language of management training meant that exercises, role-play and case studies were now to take an even more prominent place in the learning and assessment process. Also, there was a growing feeling that more effort should be made to integrate the study of employee resourcing, development and relations into a broader study of human resource strategies and policies as a whole.

The need for case studies was seen by us as presenting a particular challenge. To date, only three collections of case studies appropriate to the education and training of personnel managers have been published (Clegg *et al.*, 1985; Tyson and Kakabadse, 1987; and Mulvie and McDougall, 1991). Other collections of cases were not specific enough either in their personnel or human resource application or else because of their North American context (Foulkes and Livernash, 1990; Hilgert *et al.*, 1990; and Schuler and Youngblood, 1986), or were culturally inappropriate to the basic education and training of UK personnel management professionals.

What is a case study?

The case study is not a new method for the study of human behaviour, and its prominence in management education and training owes much to Harvard Business School. What is a case study?

> A case is a written or filmed description of an actual or imaginary situation which is presented in some detail. [Huczynski, 1983]

> an intensive or complete examination of a facet, an issue, or perhaps the events of a geographic setting over time. [Denny, 1978: 2, quoted in Clegg *et al.*, 1985]

> . . . a description of a situation . . . [consisting] of a few pages of written description of an actual situation facing an organisation . . . [describing] how the current position developed and what problem a key personality in the case is currently facing [Easton, 1982]

Within the framework of these simple definitions there are possibilities for considerable variation. Cases in HRM are usually situated in organizations

– but not always; they can vary in length from a few pages to, say, fifty pages; they can be used to highlight one aspect of a situation, or several; they can illustrate the underlying importance of one set of HRM theories, or the interrelatedness of several specialist business functions; they can be 'dead' (all the relevant information is presented to a student at the outset) or 'live' (where further information is injected during the course of analysis). The possibilities are limitless.

Using case studies

Using and learning from case studies is a skill. Like most skills it can be acquired with guidance, practice and respect! Just as we are not proficient in driving a car the first time we sit in the driving seat, it would be unreasonable to think that we can 'crack' the case study method from day one. At least one author of this text admits to having floundered when first handed a few pages of text, told that it was a case study, and to 'solve' it. While most introductions to collections of case studies focus upon justification of the case study method, only occasionally (Easton, 1982) has sufficient attention been devoted to the student's perspective.

In general, a step-by-step approach to complex problem-solving is advocated. There appears to be some slight difference in the number of steps involved, but the theme is the same:

1 Problem definition	1 Understanding the situation
2 Analysis	2 Diagnosing problem areas
3 Generating solutions	3 Generating alternative solutions
4 Evaluating solutions	4 Predicting outcomes
5 Presenting/implementing solutions	5 Evaluating alternatives
	6 Rounding out the analysis and planning for contingencies
	7 Communicating the results
[Tyson and Kakabadse, 1987]	*[Easton, 1982]*

Easton's approach is by far the most thorough, and it is not possible to do full justice to it here, except to indicate some basic 'dos' and 'don'ts':

- *Do* spend sufficient time reading the case study and trying to absorb the information before anything else. This will involve more than one reading, and the first attempt is best devoted to a quick 'skim'. It takes time to organize the information (viz. to work out what is missing; what is fact and what is opinion; and thus the extent to which we can establish clear facts, or will need to resort to more tenuous inferences, speculation and assumptions).

- *Don't* jump to conclusions or form any judgements at this stage!

- *Do* spend time identifying the problem(s). These may be present now, or may be indicated as future threats and opportunities; they may be explicit or they may be implicit and apparent only after the details of the case have been absorbed; problem areas may also be interrelated.

- *Don't* jump to conclusions about solutions. The problem areas need to be analysed in terms of symptoms and causality. At this point it is often useful to make use of visual techniques such as algorithms (Figure 1) or mind maps (Figure 2). Hypotheses may need to be tested against the evidence, and the problem itself may need to be reformulated. It can be useful to summarize your analysis in a short statement about the problem area, with supporting evidence, and some attempt to prioritize (in terms of importance to the organization, urgency and ease of solution).

- *Do* be as creative as possible in formulating solutions! If the case study involves group work, then it is important to observe the rules of 'brainstorming': let everyone make their contribution; treat all contributions as of equal merit; avoid judgement of new ideas. While the formal knowledge acquired during the course will be a major resource to draw upon, it is unlikely that it will be confined to precise topic areas, and experience and imagination can be as valid as formal knowledge here! Solutions can sometimes be presented as solution trees (see Easton, 1982).

- *Do* follow the solutions through by endeavouring to predict possible outcomes. This can be attempted by listing the solutions in terms of the key areas where they are likely to have an impact, and placing a value on the probabilities.

- *Don't* go for the most appealing solution until all the others have been systematically eliminated. It is important to clarify the criteria of choice between solutions (including the values of individuals/organizations, the importance and probability of effective outcomes).

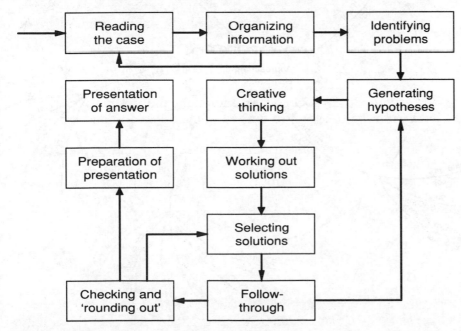

Figure 1 Algorithm of how to use a case study

- *Don't* just stop here! Once a solution has been agreed upon it is tempting just to sit back. However, 'rounding out the analysis' means that checks need to be made to ensure that the proposal is sufficiently detailed with respect to recommendations on decisions and implementation, and that there is a contingency plan in case of failure. Drawing up an action plan (Figure 3) can be helpful.

- *Do* give some thought as to how you will present the results. If the solution is the outcome of group work, this should be reflected in the presentation. There should be no room either for 'prima donnas' or for a shambling 'Greek chorus'! The nature of the presentation requires careful thought in relation to the role of participants, its purpose, audience, the timing and the level of feedback desired.

The intention is for this step-by-step approach to be helpful but not too prescriptive. Indeed, there is reason to believe that methods of complex problem-solving can be over-rigid as well as rigorous. They are often 'trapped' in a mechanistic, rationalistic way of thinking. The history of scientific discovery abounds with anecdotal evidence of the great inventions and discoveries that were made on a flight of the imagination or in the depths

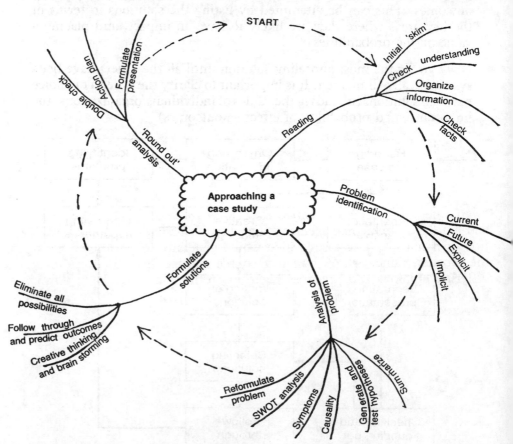

Figure 2 An example of a mind map for approaching case study analysis

16

Objective / problem	Action required	By whom	When	Outcome desired
Out-of-date appraisal process	1 Set up working party	Personnel plus representatives of line management, unions, etc.	Immediately	Consensus on what is needed and approval of new scheme
	2 Select consultant to advise	Personnel plus key line managers	Immediately	
[etc.]	[etc.]	[etc.]	[etc.]	[etc.]

Figure 3 The beginnings of an action plan

of dreams. The mind is a powerful tool of creativity (T. Buzan, *Making the Most of your Mind*, 1977), and there has to be a place for the intuitive and instinctual as well as the intellectual dimensions of the human psyche.

Structure and content

We have called the book *Case Studies in Personnel* because it is intended to complement other texts published by the IPM which support the training for graduate membership of the Institute. However, as most readers will be aware, there is considerable debate over the distinction between 'personnel' and 'human resource management'. Our use of the word 'Personnel' in the title does not preclude cases which would generally be positioned within the broader framework of 'human resource management'. Because of the differing opinions and practices regarding terminology, we have allowed the contributors discretion to use the wording which in their opinion best suits the subject matter of the case and the practice of the organization.

The case studies included in the book have been chosen for their authenticity and research vigour. They are essential training material for the IPM Professional Education Syllabus, stage 2, but are also valuable for use in general management education – on MBA, DMS and other business studies courses. All the cases are based on real companies and situations, although in many cases it has been necessary to disguise their identity. All the contributors are either experts in personnel or human resource management at leading polytechnics and universities or personnel practitioners of considerable experience.

As well as covering the main areas of personnel and human resource management, we have attempted to focus on topical issues and subject areas that in our view will become more important as the twenty-first century approaches. There are cases which, for example, cover new working practices, such as tele-working and home working, various aspects of flexible employment patterns, health issues at work, such as no-smoking policies, and, perhaps more pessimistically, cut-back management at work.

Finally, the cases have been ordered into sections relating to the traditional components of employee resourcing, employee development and employee relations, as well as an integrating section of cases. However, it is our intention to highlight the need to produce coherent human resource management policies and practices, and to appreciate the ramifications of one area on to others. Despite the dedication of a specific section to cases where the holistic approach is more marked, we believe it is necessary to adopt this wider approach in analysing *all* the case studies in the book.

Using this book

Finding the right case study

The book is not designed to be read sequentially from beginning to end. Instead readers should jump around, choosing cases to suit their particular needs. To help both tutor and reader to choose an appropriate case study, the accompanying table offers a simple classification of all the case studies in the book.

In Table 1 (pages 20–21) all the cases are listed by their number down the left-hand side. The four columns then identify:

(1) the industrial sector of the organization(s) in the case study,

(2) the size of the organization(s) in the case study,

(3) the level of difficulty of the case,

(4) the subject areas covered in the case.

Industrial sector

In order to help locate case studies covering a particular industrial sector the labels used under column 1 are as follows:

(A) identifies private-sector organizations;
(B) identifies public-sector organizations.

These categories are broken down alphabetically as:

A1 Banking, insurance and finance
A2 Brewing
A3 Chemicals and pharmaceuticals
A4 Computing and IT

A5   Construction
A6   Distribution
A7   Electronics and avionics
A8   Manufacturing and engineering
A9   Retail
A10 Public relations/marketing services
A11 General

B12 Civil service/quango
B13 Education
B14 Health
B15 Local authority

Organization size

Case study organizations are labelled in column 2 according to their size by number of staff as follows:

(L) large organizations with over 1,000 employees,
(S) small organizations with under 1,000 employees.

In some cases small organizations operate independently of a large parent firm. When these organizations are highly independent their plant size is taken as the indicator rather than the size of the parent company.

Difficulty

The case studies are labelled in column 3 according to their level of difficulty. We have identified three levels of difficulty:

(1) introductory,
(2) intermediate,
(3) advanced.

Clearly the introductory cases are more appropriate at the beginning of a course, leading to advanced cases once familiarity with the subject area and with using case studies has increased. In general, the cases that link together a variety of personnel issues and examine human resource management at the strategic level tend to be rated as more advanced than the cases dealing with specific issues at the operational level. However, we have provided some intermediate cases that do act as integrators, because the implicit philosophy behind this book is that to understand and practise human resource management requires an appreciation of the links between different human resource areas, and an ability to produce cohesive human resource plans and packages.

Subject area

Column 4 indicates the subject areas covered in the book. Further guidance on how the cases relate to the IPM professional education

Table 1 Choosing the right case study

Case study		1 Industrial sector	2 Organization size	3 Level of difficulty	4 Subject area
1	Aero Ind Software	A7 A4	L S	2	(4) 15, 20, 22, 23, 38, 46, 48, 52, 53
2	A-B-Zee	A9	L	1	(5) 20 (30) 38, 45, 52
3	Warner's	A8	S	1	(2) 15, 21, 23, 25, 46., 52
4	Bigcity Bank	A1	L	2	15, 20. 21 (32) 36, 50
5	Merlham	B15	L	3	3 (19) 23, 44, 50
6	Wellcome	A3	L	1	(8) (12) 28 (36) 51
7	Network	A4	L	1	(6) (13) (20) 23, 29, 33
8	Quench	A2	L	2	8, 12, 14, 30 (33) (35) 47, 49
9	United Ind Leason	A3 A8	L L	3	(30) 43, 47, 49
10	Barratt	A5	L	3	(2) (10) (13) 14, 18, 22 (23) 30, 31, 45, 56 (57)
11	Beckett	A8	S	2	(2) 18, 56
12	PRA	B12	L	1	2
13	Baker	A7	S	1	17, 56
14	Midland Kingston	A1 B15	L L	1	17, 38, 56
15	Joiner	A5	L	3	(2) (6) 18, 35, 42 (56) (57)
16	Kingsbury College	B13	L	1	15, 18, 20, 32, 37

17	IDL	A6	L	3	(2) 5, 9, (18) (19) 30, 34 (44) (46) 50 (52) 54, 56
18	Pinta	A8	L	2	4, 7, 8 (11) 19, 23 (25) (27) 40, 55, 58
19	PCFC	B13	L	3	7, 19, 40 (50) 58
20	Century Co.	A11	L	2	7 (19) (40) 50
21	Engineering Co.	A8	L	2	7, 11, 19, 37, 40, 58
22	Branch 11	B12	L	2	7, 11, 19, 40, 58
23	Kingston	B13	L	2	8, 12 (19) (40)
24	Wellbeloved	B14	L	1	1, 16 (19) 25
25	PRL	A10	S	1	15, 20 (46)
26	Hutton	B15	L	2	(20) 23 (27) 31 (46) 53
27	Engindorf	A4/A8	L	3	5 (9) (13) (18) (21) 23, 30, 31, 33 (34) 38 (45) (46) (49) (50) 53 (55) (57)
28	Venture	A8	L	2	5, 8, 12 (18) 19, 23, 24, 30, 31 (33) 35 (45) (46) 50, 52 (56) 58
29	Metaphorics	A4	L	2	13, 45, 56
30	Able	A7	S	3	5, 6, 8,
	Jones	A7	S		13, 14, 31
31	Leeway	A4	L	2	6, 23, 26, 35, 41, 42, 55 (56)
32	Dorefleet	B15	L	3	(6) 11, 13, 14, 26, 41 (47) 55

syllabus is provided in the tutors' manual. However, we provide here an alphabetically ordered index of subject areas which are labelled numerically and correspond to the numbers identified in column 4. Where the numbers are in brackets in column 4 it implies that the subject area is peripheral rather than central to the case.

Subject area code

Absenteeism, 1
Appraisal, 2
Balloting, *see* Unions
Benefit packages, 3
Brownfield sites, 4
Business strategy, 5
Career development, *see* Employee development
Change (organizational change), 6
Collective bargaining, 7
Communication, 8
Competence (and managerial competence), 9
Computers in personnel (*see also* IT), 10
Conflict management, 11
Consultation, 12
Corporate strategy, *see* Business strategy
Culture (organizational culture and sub-culture), 13
Cut-back management, 14
Development, *see* Organizational development *or* Employee development
Disciplinary procedures, *see* Dismissal
Discrimination, 15
Dismissal (and disciplinary procedures), 16
Disputes, *see* Conflict management
Education, 17
Employee development, 18
Employee relations, 19
Employment law, *see* Law)
Equal opportunities, 20
Equal pay, 21
Evaluating the personnel function, 22
Flexibility (flexible working patterns), 23
Greenfield sites, 24
Grievance, 25
Group working (*and see* Team building), 26
Harmonization, 27
Health, 28
Home working (and tele-working), 29
Human resource planning, 30
Human resource strategy, 31
Industrial action, *see* Conflict management
Industrial relations, *see* Employee relations
Industrial tribunals, 32
Information technology, 33
International personnel, 34
Involvement, *see* Consultation)
Job design, 35
Job evaluation, 36

Recommended reading

BUZAN, T., *Making the Most of your Mind*, London, Pan, 1977.
CLEGG, C., *et al.* (eds.), *Case Studies in Organisational Behaviour*, London, Harper & Row, 1985.
EASTON, G., *Learning from Case Studies*, London, Prentice Hall, 1982.
FOULKES, F. K., and LIVERNASH, E. R., *Human Resources Management: Cases and Text*, London, Prentice Hall, 1990.
HILGERT, R. L., *et al.*, *Cases and Experiential Exercises in Human Resource Management*, Massachusetts, Allyn & Bacon, 1990.
HUCZYNSKI, A., *Encyclopedia of Management Development Methods*, Aldershot, Gower, 1983.

MULVIE, A., and McDOUGALL, M. (eds.), *Human Resource Management in Practice: Selected Cases*, Bromley, Chartwell-Bratt, 1991.

SCHULER, R. S., and YOUNGBLOOD, S. A., *Case Problems in Personnel and Human Resource Management*, St Paul, West Publishing, 1986.

TYSON, S., and KAKABADSE, A., *Case Studies in Human Resource Management*, London, Heinemann, 1987.

I
Employee Resourcing

Poachers and gamekeepers: two approaches to recruitment and selection

Diana Winstanley

A paired comparison of two case study companies is presented here, Aero Industries and Software Services. They have been chosen to demonstrate two very different approaches to managing the recruitment and selection process as applied to technological staff in general and software engineers in particular. Both plants are part of large conglomerates in the private sector, and are based in the 'Golden Triangle' in the south of England (the corridor bordered by the M3 and M4 to the north and south, and Bristol and London to the west and east).

Despite some similarities in their position, there are also a number of features which separate them: their plant size, unionization, age, historical development and industrial sector. Aero Ind represents a firm which errs towards the 'poacher' orientation, whereas Software Services is more representative of the 'gamekeeper' approach to the recruitment, selection and retention of staff. A *poacher* can be defined as: a recruiter whose efforts are spent in 'poaching' or stealing the trained staff of competitor, neighbouring or other firms. A *gamekeeper* can be defined as: a recruiter whose efforts are spent in meeting human resource needs both in the short and in the long term by developing the company's own staff through nurturing, socialization, training and a 'golden cage' of benefits and promotion packages.

Table 1.1 Poacher and gamekeeper orientations towards recruitment and shortage labour markets

Indicator	Company orientation	
	Poacher	Gamekeeper
Internal mobility, career structures and development	Low	High
External mobility and staff turnover	High	Low

Table 1.1 continued

Indicator	Company Orientation	
	Poacher	**Gamekeeper**
Career orientation of staff	Cosmopolitan	Local
HRP horizon	0–2 years	2+ years
Planning outlook	Short-term	Long-term
Level of cohesion of personnel policies	Low	High
Ideal type of recruit sought	Experienced staff	Fresh graduates
Recruitment source	Other companies	Educational establishments
Recruitment channels used	Agencies, walk-ins	Sponsorship, milk round
Recruitment orientation	Aggressive, reactive	Proactive
Rigour of selection procedures	Low	High
Level of selection criteria: technical	High	Low
Level of selection criteria: behavioural	Low	High
Extent of non-functional selection criteria	High	Low

Background to the case

Aerospace Industries (Aero Ind for short) are part of a mature British unionized firm supplying equipment to the aerospace industry, and much of their work is defence-related (approximately 50 per cent). The plant which forms the case study employs 950 staff, 200 of whom are in the engineering department, where the design and development of products takes place. Each year the numbers recruited vary considerably, with MoD contracts, and the current target for the year is about thirty engineers.

Software Services is a small non-unionized British software house which is part of a highly decentralized conglomerate. Its core business is consultancy and the customization and installation of software systems. The plant which forms the case study employs about fifty staff, of whom about thirty are graduates working in the technological area. This year it is recruiting six new staff.

The situation: a comparison of recruitment strategies in a shortage labour market

Recruitment responsibilities

Both Aero Ind and Software Services have their own board, and the recruitment budgets are set and the strategies carried out independently of their parent companies.

At Aero Ind an engineering manager, who works in concert with the plant's own Personnel Department headed by a personnel executive, is in charge of the recruitment of engineering staff. There is considerable disagreement between the two over how to manage the recruitment process. The engineering manager was moved sideways into recruitment towards the end of his career in engineering. He favours the use of informal mechanisms and practices and likes to use his contacts in the industry, including his Masonic contacts. The personnel executive, on the other hand, is more concerned with formalizing the recruitment practices and bringing them into line with the rest of the firm. However, although he has a position of authority, he is relatively new to the post and is finding it difficult to assert his views, owing to a lack of tangible information on the current practices.

Unusually, the person in charge of the recruitment of technological staff at Software Services is the financial director. The reason is that, as a small company in a fast-changing environment and market, Software Services place a lot of emphasis on functional flexibility. In fact every engineer at the firm is encouraged to take on a managerial position, and this is reflected in a very flat organizational hierarchy, with job definitions being highly fluid. In this sense candidates are recruited to the organization rather than to a particular job, and the skills developed are fairly fluid and flexible.

Staff turnover

Both firms have a general level of voluntary labour turnover of less than 10 per cent but encounter a considerably higher turnover of young engineers and technological staff involved in software development.

Aero Ind face shortages in the labour market for highly skilled, experienced technological staff and the best engineering graduates, yet are shedding older apprentice-trained staff with obsolete skills. There is a policy of natural wastage in some areas to achieve this 'downsizing'. However, as well as producing unmanageable holes in the organization it is causing demoralization among staff working in these areas, with some of the best staff leaving as a result.

Software Services place the emphasis on flexibility to avoid skill obsolescence. The training is more cultural than procedural, and socialization into flexible working practices and a flexible attitude is seen as vital. All staff are encouraged to take on one management responsibility and rotate through a number of different ones.

Use of contract staff

Despite a general contraction in size the minor fluctuations of work load at Aero Ind have resulted in the utilization of over thirty contract engineers. As the engineering manager put it, 'It's to give us flexibility and give us a buffer. We've only had contract staff for the last three or four years, and it has built up to quite a peak in the last two years . . . lots of jobs that we do are fairly short-term projects, so we really need to have a bit of flexibility . . . although some subcontractors have been here for four years, which is silly.'

A different view prevails at Software Services. They use no temporary or contract staff and, as one manager said, 'We don't use contract staff, as we cannot get adequate control over them. You don't know what you are getting, and you don't know their standards of working. You have no control over them because . . . they can up and go somewhere else. On the whole the standard of the people is not that high.'

Software Services recruit only full-time permanent staff, who come in as trainees and then become junior analysts/programmers. From there they can become either a team leader, doing technical work and running a team of staff, or senior analyst/programmers who do a more technically oriented job. Staff are expected to work flexible hours to suit the customer, if necessary working late at night or over weekends when 'going live' with a new system.

The recruitment process

One disadvantage that Aero Ind face in recruitment is the image. They are not a 'household name', as they do not supply end-products to consumers. They operate from aging 'brownfield' industrial buildings. From a survey of engineers attending their walk-ins Aero Ind were seen in comparison with their main competitors as being technologically on the 'second rung of the ladder'. An advertising agency had been employed to change this image and had produced adverts based on research into potential candidates. The adverts showed a picture of a rebellious-looking young man as a typical recruit.

Aero Ind activate and drop recruitment channels in an *ad hoc* fashion. They target experienced candidates through occasional national advertising campaigns and have started using hotel walk-in presentations on competitors' doorsteps, which are advertised in the local press. At these walk-ins candidates can browse round a display of the company's activities, talk informally to Aero Ind engineers, read the recruitment literature, take refreshments and possibly be given a preliminary interview.

Recently the engineering manager has been experimenting with using recruitment agencies. In one case he paid for access to the agency's recruitment register, based on engineers it had placed in firms two to five years previously. The director of another local agency, a personal friend, has offered to organize the hotel walk-ins, on the proviso that the agency could recruit for other clients as well as for Aero Ind.

For recruiting fresh graduates Aero Ind used to operate the milk round, and the personnel executive is considering reintroducing it, despite opposition from the engineering manager. They are also currently overhauling their sponsorship programme of undergraduate engineering students, which has fallen into disuse without any clear programme for contact with or the development and utilization of sponsored students. The scheme is still operated from the firm centrally, and lack of communication, co-ordination and information between the corporate and local staff has meant that it is hardly used at all.

Software Services recruit only graduates into technological positions, and most of these are fresh graduates. All their fresh graduate recruits are from the local university, or from universities with similar characteristics, or are people who have lived in the district. This is because the managers believe it is important for a recruit to fit in with life in the surrounding countryside. The intake of computer programmers/analysts is fifty-fifty arts people and scientists. The biggest difficulty, the financial director believes, in recruiting arts graduates for such jobs is getting them to apply at all, and educating the career service that these graduates are what they want. The company tries to overcome this prejudice by putting up posters on the arts notice boards.

They prefer to recruit fresh graduates, feeling that if people have not worked elsewhere they are easier to train. As one manager said, 'you're not starting with any preconceptions of the work and the atmosphere, so they're more amenable to our culture and way of working'. The financial director believes that the main reason for people choosing to work at Software Services is the working atmosphere.

Selection criteria

The engineering manager at Aero Ind sums up the ideal engineering candidate as follows:

> Ideally they'd have a degree in electronics (or possibly physics, aeronautical science or electrical engineering), and preferably they'd have a few years' experience in engineering, particularly in an area compatible with our technology base. They're also selected for their personal qualities and attributes, their suitability for us . . . We then look for motivation and whether we think he'll fit in with our working relationship . . . It's obviously a bit subjective, but we haven't got time to spend hours doing psychological profiles; we have to make a judgement on the individual's suitability, and how he would interface with other people, and fit in with the team, knowing their personalities, attributes, strengths and weaknesses.

One candidate defined it in a nutshell as 'the right stuff'.

Software Services' main selection criteria are not technical. They seek out people who are 'relatively bright', combined with 'the willingness to work and work hard'. Attitude and motivation are stressed as being vital. This is reflected in the firm's willingness to train candidates from scratch, offering a comprehensive induction programme followed by a continuous education programme composed of:

- Individual tutorial sessions with a manager or mentor.
- External courses.
- Internal classroom sessions.
- Evening class fees, college and distance learning course fees paid by the company.
- Two days' study leave prior to the taking of external exams.
- Self-study course, with computers freely available.
- Management courses provided.
- Cassette tape/programmed instruction courses on applications provided.

Selection mechanisms

The main selection mechanisms and 'hurdles' used by Aero Ind are:

- The job description/person specification.
- The application form.
- Interviews.
- References.
- A test.

In addition to their own 'hunches', recruiters are provided with a one-paragraph summary of the job description and person specification. Candidates are asked to fill in an application form and are given brochures on the company. To help document the selection process, recruiters conducting interviews are given record forms. The one used for walk-ins, headed 'Informal interview record', includes the following headings:

- Name.
- Address.
- Telephone number.
- Qualifications.
- Current employer and telephone number.
- Current role.
- Salary: current/anticipated.
- Physical make-up (dress, manner, speech).
- Summary: exceptional/acceptable/not recommended.
- General comments. (Sum up candidate and compare him to someone known to us if possible.)
- Interviewed by: . . .
- Date: . . .

If candidates are recruited through the walk-in procedure, they have preliminary interviews with the engineering manager, personnel representatives or technical managers and engineers, depending on who is available at the time. New junior engineering managers are commonly used for the screening of candidates as a way of familiarizing them with the company. None of those involved has received any training in recruitment and interviewing techniques. If at this stage candidates are considered a possibility for various vacancies by the engineering manager, from his assessment of the interview reports, they are invited for further interviews on the company premises. At that stage line managers are more actively involved in the interviewing. When a job offer is made the references are taken up.

The engineering manager is experimenting with using a short ipsative personality test based on Marsden's personality types. He believes the advantages of this test are threefold: the recruiter needs only one day of training, the recruiter is provided with a comprehensive manual on interpreting the test scores, and the test takes less than half an hour for the candidate to complete and can be quickly interpreted. He himself found the results of the test 'fascinating' and 'illuminating'.

In order to identify the best candidates Software Services use the following selection mechanisms:

- Application form.
- Computer aptitude test.
- Interviews.
- References.

The application form and associated brochure give a good flavour of the culture and needs of Software Services. For example, the question on the application form that provides the greatest space asks, 'Tell us about something interesting you have done.' Although there are generic job descriptions for the technical roles, the brochure emphasizes flexibility in the job, with a summary of responsibilities and objectives for all technical candidates, including:

- To provide an excellent technical service . . .
- . . . to be helpful to customers, to be professional in appearance, and pleasant in manner . . .
- To help colleagues and cover tasks for them if they are away or in difficulties.
- To keep colleagues and management informed of successes, mistakes and new ideas.
- To enjoy your working hours as much as possible.
- To do anything out of the ordinary that you discover a need for.
- To maintain a high level of business ethics.
- To do whatever you can within your working hours to contribute to a high standard of excellence, and a friendly and profitable company.

The computer aptitude test reflects the emphasis on ability to learn and trainability rather than experience. The interviewing is shared out among the senior people, with most candidates having at least two interviews conducted by one or two people. The interview technique, questions and assessment are left to the subjective judgement of the person conducting the interview. Co-ordination of the interview data is left to the financial director.

Equal opportunities in recruitment?

Software Services have no formal Equal Opportunities policy, nor do they monitor for gender and race, but the financial director claims that, although slightly more men than women apply for positions with them, their recruitment is roughly fifty-fifty.

At Aero Ind inside each application form there is an ethnic monitoring sheet which states:

> This organization operates a policy of equal opportunities for employment and advancement; and it will assess applicants for jobs without regard to sex, physical handicap, marital status, race or ethnic origin.

However, when asked about the form, the engineering manager said, 'We're using the form because we're told to . . . We don't bother with monitoring, we have enough work to do as it is.' A personnel officer said, 'It just isn't feasible, particularly in our area . . . We'd be very unlikely to take on a foreigner or even a British person who had a foreign history – for instance, Indian grandparents – because of the difficulties involved for the screening process. It takes too long . . .'

When asked about the causes of the shortage of candidates with 'the right stuff', the engineering manager and a personnel officer launched an attack on the education system, blaming the shortage on the take-up of places by foreign and even British black students. 'Now you know this argument about a fair mix, but I think personally . . . that if you're in a shortage situation, which is clearly the case, we ought to be cutting back on our foreign students.' Asked whether he meant overseas students who took their skills back to another country the engineering manager said, '. . . and even the ones that don't, clearly there is all the problem of getting clearance and that sort of thing. So having an unbalanced distribution, when you're in very short supply, seems to be absolute lunacy. . . . If a university has fifty places, we'll say, and forty of those are from ethnic communities, this seems to be lunacy to me.' To which the personnel officer replied, 'And this isn't encouraging your own kith and kin to go down that avenue in any case.'

It is perhaps not surprising that among the 200 technological staff there were only two black people. The process by which this happens is perhaps illustrated by following a sample of thirty-five people attending a series of walk-ins. Of the sample, four were ethnic minority applicants. Of the four, two were Afro-Caribbean, and both were screened out in a personnel 'chat' before receiving a technical interview; only one was given an application form to fill in. This despite the fact that one had qualifications comparable with those of other candidates, as shown by entries marked on the interview form by the personnel representative. Only two other candidates failed to receive a technical interview; one was a manual worker, the other was an elderly man who had come in for the drink! The other two non-white candidates were oriental and neither was recommended for further interviews, although one was interviewed by a technical manager, who judged him to be 'acceptable', having sound technical qualifications and experience, 'smart', 'intelligent' and 'a good communicator'. This was despite a personnel assistant commenting as the man approached, 'Oh no, he's coming in. I can't tell the difference between these oriental types. They all look the same. I hope he speaks English.'

Of the same sample of candidates only one was female. She was eventually offered a job in the technical marketing area but turned it down, as the remuneration package was inferior to that of another job she had been offered. In the company there were only one female engineer and two female apprentices in technological positions. The common feeling among the recruiters was that they just did not get women applying for jobs.

Activity brief

1 (a) Summarize the main aspects of Aero Ind's and Software Services' recruitment strategy and philosophy in staff acquisition and retention.
   (b) How far do either Aero Ind or Software Services exhibit 'poacher' or 'gamekeeper' characteristics?
   (c) In what ways do their differing approaches reflect differences in their organizational characteristics and environment?
2 Assess the approach each firm adopts towards staff flexibility.
3 What are the advantages and disadvantages of using contract staff in the engineering industry?
4 How effective do you think *either* (a) the hotel 'walk-in' *or* (b) the recruitment agency is as a recruitment tool, and in what circumstances is its use most appropriate?
5 Critically assess the use of *either* (a) interviews *or* (b) tests in the case study companies' selection procedures and suggest how their use could be improved.
6 (a) Identify potentially discriminatory aspects of Aero Ind's or Software Services' recruitment and selection practices and outline ways in which discrimination could be avoided in each case.
   (b) If you were the new personnel executive at Aero Ind, how would you deal with the attitudes of the engineering manager, the personnel officer and the personnel assistant?
   (c) In what ways do you think the process of discrimination applies differently in the areas of gender and race?
7 Taking the role of a personnel consultant brought in to help *either* Aero Ind *or* Software Services, outline a plan of action to improve their recruitment and selection practices.

1

Recommended reading

IPM publications:

The IPM Recruitment Code.
The IPM Equal Opportunities Code.
The IPM Code on Occupational Testing.

ATKINSON, J., 'Manpower strategies for flexible organizations', *Personnel Management*, 16, 8, 1984, pp. 28–31.

ATKINSON, J., 'Four stages of adjustment to the demographic downturn', *Personnel Management*, August 1989, pp. 20–4.

BARTRAM, D., 'Addressing the abuse of psychological tests', *Personnel Management*, April 1991, pp. 34–9.

FLETCHER, C., *et al.* 'Personality tests: the great debate', *Personnel Management*, September 1991, pp. 38–42.

JENKINS, R., *Racism and Recruitment: Managers, Organisations and Equal Opportunities in the Labour Market*, Cambridge, Cambridge University Press, 1986.

JEWSON, N., and MASON, D., 'Modes of discrimination in the recruitment process: formalisation, fairness and efficiency', *Sociology*, 20, 1, 1986, pp. 43–63.

LEWIS, C., *Employee Selection*, London, Hutchinson, 1985.

POLLERT, A., 'The flexible firm: fixation or fact?' *Work Employment and Society*, 2, 3, 1988, pp. 281–316.

STRAW, J., *Equal Opportunities: the Way Ahead*, London, IPM, 1989.

WOOD, S., 'Recruitment systems and the recession', *British Journal of Industrial Relations*, 24, 1, 1986, pp. 103–20.

Recruitment for new superstores: A-B-Zee

David Walsh

This case explores the ramifications on recruitment of a business decision to launch a new chain of superstores. It enables a comparison to be made between two strategies for recruiting sales assistants, one in a shortage labour market for a London superstore and one in a surplus labour market in the north of England.

A well established leading UK retailer, Homewell & Sons, conducted market research into its own high street stores and branches. As a result the company decided to set up an independent subsidiary, A-B-Zee, to launch a new-concept superstore, specializing in children's products and based on edge-of-town sites. The independence of A-B-Zee was important to the development of an operation and work force that is, and is perceived as, distinct from its parent company.

A new company opening new superstores across the country means that recruitment is an early major concern. Responsibility for it fell to the personnel director, based at A-B-Zee headquarters in Bristol. As the first stores were to be located in both the south-east and the north of England, the personnel director had to tackle local labour markets characterized by either a critical shortage or a huge surplus of suitable people.

Locations for the new superstores are chosen primarily for commercial reasons, with less consideration being given to the availability of labour. As a member of A-B-Zee's executive board the personnel director does have a strong input in the choice of new sites, but the criteria of customer affluence and site access weigh far more heavily than the ease of getting the best staff. Nevertheless, A-B-Zee's recruitment objectives are unequivocal.

Background to the case

The recruitment challenge

The recruitment objectives for the new superstores were:

- It is an absolute requirement that the company recruits only those who fully meet its minimum standards.

- Each store should recruit a 'balanced work force across gender, age and ethnic group to reflect the company's policy of equal opportunity in each locality'.
- Recruitment must be cost-effective.
- Recruitment must serve the company's public relations interests in relation to both its prospective employees and customers.

Recruitment of sales assistants

A store manager's position is generally filled from the national labour market and well before the recruitment of sales assistants from the local catchment area. Each store manager has responsibility for the personnel function in-store, and is supported operationally by three full-time sales managers.

The personnel director decided to devise and co-ordinate the early recruitment campaigns centrally. Her specialist expertise would be invaluable in setting A-B-Zee policy and procedures, and her involvement would take considerable pressure off newly appointed store managers. Nevertheless, she recognized that local management would need to have 'ownership' of the recruitment and selection process. They would need to take responsibility for *their* staff. Consequently, both store and sales managers were heavily involved in the process initiated and run centrally by the personnel director.

Each store's staffing structure is planned for predominantly part-time workers, able to cover the extended trading hours typical of edge-of-town/retail park sites. While minimum standards of literacy and numeracy are regarded as essential, A-B-Zee's preference is for staff with a mature outlook, good communication skills and specific personal qualities rather than experience of the product range. Furthermore, parental experience or a responsibility for children is considered a real advantage when helping customers, whether adults or children.

The nature of the work, A-B-Zee's product range and the part-time hours generate far more applications from women than men, the company's equal opportunity policy notwithstanding. This outcome is supported by the rewards package on offer, which is less than competitive outside this area of work. Rates of pay are one of several constraints facing A-B-Zee's recruiters.

Constraints on recruitment

First, the rates of pay still follow those of the parent company. This causes few problems in areas of labour surplus, but prohibits any wage improvements that might help combat problems of serious labour shortage.

Secondly, not only is A-B-Zee new to each labour market, it is also a new company with an unfamiliar name. As such it has no reputation to call upon in its search for quality recruits.

Thirdly, it is company policy to refuse to recruit second-best. The company expects to adhere to the minimum standards outlined above.

Finally, each recruitment campaign is invariably faced with a demanding timetable for store opening. 'You've got to hold your nerve; as it gets closer to opening, the pressure increases. Operations management will be pressing you to get people by a certain date, in time for training and ready for trading' (personnel director).

The situation: recruiting in shortage and surplus labour markets

A-B-Zee is a company undergoing a step-by-step learning experience, and no more so than in the area of its new store recruitment. In London and the south-east the company has battled to meet its recruitment targets for new stores, where a 'sellers' market' has prevailed and competition from the retail giants such as Sainsbury's, Boot's and Tesco is fierce.

The strategy here has been to develop every avenue to generate applications, including a variety of innovative recruitment channels for communicating with candidates. At the same time, in the north of England a surplus labour market characterized by high unemployment undoubtedly favours the 'buyer', but A-B-Zee soon found that even here its recruitment efforts brought problems of a different kind.

Recruiting for a south London store

Experience in London earlier in the year had confirmed that the traditional process of a newspaper advertisement inviting requests for application forms, followed by an interview for those shortlisted, was woefully inadequate in meeting the staffing target of sixty part-time sales assistants who fully met A-B-Zee's criteria. Although the full-page display advertisements were imaginative and attracted attention, the recruitment process as a whole was found to be relatively slow in terms of (1) sustaining a candidate's interest in the vacancy and (2) the impending store opening.

This shortage labour market, combined with the constraints outlined above, very much centred the personnel director's attention on supplementing the existing recruitment practices with more innovative methods. In order to obtain enough applicants of the right quality the company had to take more of the initiative and be more accessible to potential employees. In other words it was obliged to adopt a more proactive recruitment strategy in this competitive job market.

Newspaper advertisements now invited candidates to telephone a 'hot line' number that was emblazoned across the page. This method provides immediate contact with the company and encouragement to those who might otherwise be disinclined to request an application form. The phone-in enabled A-B-Zee to arrange immediate interviews for those evaluated as suitable on the evidence of the telephone interview. In addition, the application form was simplified to make its completion more convenient and acceptable to candidates.

An alternative to the 'phone-in' was the 'walk-in', where candidates were invited to call at a local hotel and meet company staff. Where parents seemed likely to cancel the visit because they were unable to arrange for someone to look after the children, they were invited to bring their offspring with them. Staff were on hand to provide children with appropriate care, activities and the usual 'freebies', while the visitor/candidate had an informal interview. The emphasis was initially on selling A-B-Zee as an organization, with its 'fun' image and 'friendly' culture.

A-B-Zee successfully used the 'walk-in' to increase the number of applicants and then to influence those deemed suitable to join the company. In this respect the speed of the company's response to candidates is considered crucial, and so application forms and letters of offer were readily available. This also met the company's needs, since the 'walk-in' was initially introduced when the timetable to store opening was extremely tight and speed was of the essence.

While a phone-in or walk-in increases the lines of communication with applicants, the personnel director soon appreciated that such methods are limited by the circulation/readership of the newspaper and the effectiveness of the advertisement. Not every reader, for example, will look at the job adverts, however large or well designed they are. Consequently, with the assistance of its recruitment consultant, the company produced leaflets which were distributed to every house in those areas which (1) were relatively close to the new store and (2) would assist towards the objective of recruiting a 'balanced work force' in terms of the ethnic composition of the locality.

It was reasoned by the personnel director that the 'leaflet drop' would not only act as a recruitment channel but at the very least would publicize A-B-Zee's new store opening. Furthermore, leaflets, by their very nature, have to be dealt with in some way by their recipients. Even if they are eventually treated as waste paper, they cannot simply be avoided or ignored, as can newspaper advertisements.

All these supplementary recruitment methods were seen by the personnel director as making life more convenient for applicants: 'We've turned things right round. Now we are there to serve our potential employees.' For this difficult campaign things were certainly not as convenient for the team of recruiters, who were required to be available to applicants during the evenings and at weekends.

Finally, and inevitably, the company had to consider making its working hours more convenient for some of its prospective employees. Its model pattern of working hours needed to be modified to accommodate individuals' requirements. In a sellers' market applicants felt able to ask, for example, for term-time contracts and school-time hours.

These methods were designed to combat the problems set by a severe labour shortage without compromising A-B-Zee's recruitment objectives. Invariably, however, some applicants meeting the minimum required standards for personal qualities lacked certain skills and knowledge. This issue was tackled by a more intensive training programme, which itself increased the strain on already stretched training resources.

Recruiting for a northern store

After the recruitment challenges of London the personnel director was more relaxed about recruiting for A-B-Zee's new retail-park store in a Yorkshire town. The closure of several manufacturing companies was signalled by the high level of unemployment in the locality, and the eagerness of the local Job Centre to help with the distribution of application forms and the organization of interviews.

The personnel director was justifiably confident that a display advertisement in the regional press, inviting requests for application forms, would comfortably provide enough good applicants to meet her target of sixty part-time sales assistants. She also looked forward to recruiting a work force that reflected the composition of the locality, including members from the sizable Asian community.

The large display advertisement proudly announced the forthcoming launch of A-B-Zee's exciting new store and invited applications from those who felt they could contribute to its success as sales assistants. Application forms were available from the town's Job Centre, where staff were ready to respond to written, telephone and personal requests.

On the morning after the appearance of the advertisement, Job Centre staff arrived to find a queue snaking its way around the building and into the adjoining street. Several hundred people had called for A-B-Zee application forms. Within two weeks Bristol headquarters had received nearly 3,000 applications for their sixty vacancies. A total of 5,000 forms were eventually received. Disappointingly, only a handful appeared to be from Asians, an outcome inferred from the names on the application forms.

The interest generated by this campaign had now created severe problems for the personnel director. Firstly, the task of screening or shortlisting for interview was daunting: how to identify accurately and quickly 300 applicants for interview from the first wave of 3,000? It soon became evident that very few could be rejected on the basis of the essential requirements in the person specification and that there was often little to choose between people.

The sheer size of the task can clearly influence the quality of shortlisting decisions. The danger of subjectivity is very real, with the largely irrelevant factor of handwriting, for example, having an unwitting influence over decisions.

A second issue related to the resources that had to be directed to the screening process. The layout of the application form, for example, slowed the process down considerably. The most pertinent information ought to have been grouped together on the front page.

Considerable resources had to be devoted also to responding to all the applicants. In line with the objective related to public relations, the personnel director accepted that it is vital to any company to initiate and retain goodwill among its potential customers. In her view it was just as important, therefore, to respond quickly and courteously to unsuccessful as well as shortlisted applicants. By identifying in her letter the enormous response to the advertisement, the personnel director was able to (1) explain an applicant's lack of employment success on this particular occasion and (2) convey the enviable popularity of the new A-B-Zee store.

The glow of satisfaction created by the huge response was eventually replaced by acceptance that the whole exercise had been very resource-intensive and costly. There also lingered the disappointment in attracting so few applicants from the town's ethnic community.

Getting it right

A company setting up a factory or business in a new district usually has only the one chance to establish its reputation as an employer and to recruit the people needed for its future prosperity. A-B-Zee, however, will be continuing to establish its new-concept stores in locations all over the country. It at least has the opportunity to learn from and improve upon the recruitment experiences outlined above.

Future strategy is to devolve responsibility for recruitment to each store manager, who will benefit from the handbooks, training and advice to be provided by the small, centralized personnel function. Whether faced by a shortage or a surplus labour market, each store manager will be expected to get it right.

Activity brief

After reading this case discuss in groups the following questions:

1 What does the case tell us about the link between business strategic decision-making and human resource planning at A-B-Zee?
2 On the basis of the recruitment experiences at A-B-Zee, outline the characteristic features of a shortage labour market, and explain why the traditional recruitment process, a newspaper advertisement inviting requests for application forms and followed by shortlisting for interview, was found wanting by the personnel director.
3 Developing your analysis in question 2, explore the two-way nature of the relationship between A-B-Zee and its potential recruits in this shortage labour market, and the evidence that the balance of 'power' to some extent favours the candidates.
4 Identify some of the likely advantages of the 'phone-in' as a recruitment method, and the measures that A-B-Zee will need to have taken to ensure its success.
5 List the ways in which recruitment at A-B-Zee can serve the company's public relations interests.
6 Assume you are a member of an independent recruitment consultancy engaged by A-B-Zee to provide advice on the company's next store opening in a Lancashire town, an area of high unemployment and labour surplus. Your assignment is to deliver a brief report and/or formal

presentation to the company's personnel director recommending how, in relation to the company's recent recruitment for a northern store, the company's next campaign might (a) be made more cost-effective and (b) ensure a greater response from members of the town's ethnic minority community.

Recommended reading

ATKINSON, J., 'Four stages of adjustment to the demographic downturn', *Personnel Management*, August 1989, pp. 20–4.

CAMERON, K., 'Retaining retail staff through "star" treatment', *Personnel Management*, July 1991, pp. 38–40.

PADDISON, L., 'The targeted approach to recruitment', *Personnel Management*, November 1990, pp. 54–8.

PLUMBLEY, P., *Recruitment and Selection*, fifth edition, London, IPM, 1991.

TORRINGTON, D., and HALL, L., *Personnel Management: a New Approach*, Hemel Hempstead, Prentice-Hall, 1991, pp. 263–80.

WATSON, T., 'Recruitment and selection', in K. SISSON (ed.), *Personnel Management in Britain*, Oxford, Blackwell, 1989, pp. 125–37.

Case 3

Responding to racism: Warner's Bottling Company

Philip Frame

This case provides an opportunity to consider how personnel managers should respond to workforce racism. In particular, it focuses attention on the recruitment aspects of employee resourcing at Warner's Bottling Company. The implications of the case, however, and the lessons learned, are relevant to all aspects of equal opportunities provision at the workplace and to the delivery of professional personnel practice.

The concept of racism comprehends the ability to exert power and influence, and to do so in ways that subordinate individuals or groups, where action is based on racial prejudice. Racial prejudice means judging members of a racial group by their membership of that group rather than on the basis of their skills and qualities as individuals.

Background to the case

Warner's Bottling Company is a long established business which has been manufacturing and bottling alcoholic drinks, principally beer and cider, since the middle of the last century. The manufacturing base is on the outskirts of a large city. Overall, the company employs approximately 560 staff in a variety of departments, including the bottling department, which is the focus of this case.

Demand for alcoholic products is to a large extent seasonal, with the highest demand experienced in the run-up to Christmas. In the light of this predictable variation in demand, a high proportion of temporary staff are employed. The company is an example of a flexible firm, with a core of permanent, full-time staff and a peripheral grouping of non-permanent employees. Until recently recruiting, retaining and exiting members of the latter group had been unproblematic.

Of the 120 workers employed in the bottling department, about 50 per cent are permanent employees and 50 per cent temporary. All shopfloor workers are female, though the departmental supervisor and eight out of the ten foremen/women are male. Of the sixty permanent members of staff, fifty-five are white and the remaining five are either Asian (one) or Afro-Caribbean (four). In the main, shopfloor work is fairly routine and semi-skilled, although a degree of care is needed to tend the machines effectively.

Temporary staff are recruited throughout the year, using the channels of 'word-of-mouth' (existing employees tell their friends and relatives) and a 'vacancies' board at the factory gate. Recruitment of temporary staff is the job of the departmental supervisor. Potential employees present themselves to him for a fairly cursory interview which covers previous experience and a character reference. If successful, they are employed initially on one month's probation, during which time the rudiments of the task are taught 'on the job'. Nearly all probationers are successful and are recruited for the remainder of the year.

By the time of peak demand the department's full staff complement of temporary workers has usually been reached. In order to fill permanent vacancies which have fallen vacant during the year, it is the firm's policy to offer such vacancies to the best of the temporary staff at the end of each year. At this stage all temporary staff are laid off; 'the best' are subsequently offered permanent posts.

The performance criteria which are used to determine 'the best' of the temporary staff are concerned with timekeeping and attendance, willingness to do overtime as required, standard of job performance and general 'attitude to the work'. Foremen/women are in theory required to provide a brief written report to the supervisor on each temporary member of staff. The supervisor discusses the reports with the personnel manager; the latter has the final say in deciding who will be offered full-time work. No one is interviewed. Selected candidates are invited to apply. The selection system is based to a large extent on custom and practice; little or nothing on procedures is documented.

The situation: recruitment of permanent staff from a temporary pool

Towards the end of December there were four permanent vacancies. The number was fewer than normal, but not unexpected in the light of a contraction in the job market. On the basis of the foremen's/women's reports, and in conjunction with the bottling department's supervisor, the personnel department decided to offer the posts to four women of Afro-Caribbean origin. In the light of the department's performance criteria they were all deemed effective workers, the best of the year's temporary staff, and felt to have made a significant contribution to the department's productivity.

Somehow the permanent staff in the bottling department got to hear of the proposal and there was resistance. It took the form of a petition which

3

was reportedly signed by all the white full-time employees, to the effect that they wanted the permanent posts in question to be offered only to white women. The department was unionized and the petition was given to the shop steward. Whether she was involved in organizing the resistance is unclear.

The petition and its contents were then the subject of discussions with management. The steward took the position that she was expressing the views of her constituents; she also happened to support those views. If the content of the petition was ignored, serious trouble, including the strong possibility of strike action, was forecast.

The personnel manager was surprised and perplexed by this turn of events. He had vacancies to fill, wanted the best people for the job, and was aware of the company's responsibilities under the Race Relations Act, 1976. As he remembered it, the Act defines unlawful racial discrimination as less favourable treatment on grounds of race, colour, ethnic or national origins. Discrimination was either direct, via acts against individuals, or indirect, via rules and regulations that unfairly penalized members of a particular racial group. There had, though, been little or no trouble of this nature in the past. Indeed, he had always regarded the company as generally operating in a socially responsible fashion, although it did not have a formal and explicit Equal Opportunities policy.

He was also aware that at national, and indeed regional, level the union in question supported a policy of Equal Opportunities regardless of race, colour or gender. He was unsure, however, of the degree of influence which the union's regional officials normally exerted at the local level, or indeed the extent to which this apparent contravention of policy would be vigorously pursued in the light of local opposition. At the same time, he wanted to avoid a confrontation with the department's work force, and to retain the good working relations that bottling had traditionally enjoyed.

The personnel manager was at a loss. What should he do?

Activity brief

Individually read the case and then in small groups address the following questions.

1 Define the specific and the wider issues raised in the case.
2 Discuss the options open to the personnel manager. Where possible, you should draw on your own experience.
3 In the light of your experience, select the options which your group considers the most appropriate. Speculate on the consequences of your recommended action and justify your selection.
4 Prepare an oral presentation of up to five minutes which summarizes the results of your deliberations.

Recommended reading

There is no recommended pre-reading for this case. You are, though, invited to draw on your learning to date, from Stage I or II of the IPM course and from your own work–related experience and practice. In addition, you should consult any material on racial discrimination which is available at your workplace, such as the Race Relations Act, 1976, the Code of Practice in Employment produced by the Commission for Racial Equality or the IPM's Equal Opportunities Code of Practice. After you have considered the case, your tutor will provide you with specific references for recommended reading.

Equal pay and job evaluation at Bigcity Bank

Alan Arthurs

Bigcity Bank is a large banking organization employing nearly 50,000 staff. It has been under severe commercial pressure for several years, owing to losses incurred in acquiring and then disposing of a US bank and the need to make large provisions for doubtful and bad debts on loans to developing countries. It has a higher ratio of costs to income than its competitors. There is an urgent need to innovate, yet staff costs must be tightly controlled and, where possible, reduced. The introduction of new technology has not yet made the expected impact on these costs.

This case concerns Bigcity Bank's approach to job evaluation and equal pay within the general context of its employment policies for women.

Background to the case: a history of women's employment and equal pay in banking

Women employees at Bigcity Bank

In the first half of the twentieth century banking employment was dominated by men, but the proportion of women has grown, so that now 60 per cent of Bigcity Bank's staff are women. Most of the expansion of women's employment has been in typing, secretarial and lower-graded clerical work. Typically in British banks in the mid-1980s more than nine out of every ten female employees were in the lowest three clerical grades or their equivalent, whereas only four out of ten men were in these grades. Only 3 per cent of women were in management positions, compared with 45 per cent of men. One reason for this distribution is that for many years women were often recruited with lower qualifications than men, since it was assumed that the men would want to progress into management whereas nearly all the women would leave to get married and have a family. In the 1960s the average female employee stayed with the bank for only four years.

Attitudes have been changing and the bank has been introducing initiatives to encourage the career aspirations of more of its female staff.

Further impetus was given by the Equal Opportunities Commission, which conducted an investigation into Barclays Bank, following a 1983 complaint about its different recruitment practices for males and females. As a result that bank agreed to change its practices, train recruiters in non-discrimination and provide the EOC with statistics on applications, interviews and job offers for the following four years. In the late 1980s new 'female-friendly' practices were also encouraged by the decline in the number of school-leavers and the realization that more emphasis must be placed on the retention of existing married female staff.

At Bigcity Bank a member of staff specifically responsible for equal opportunities for women employees was first appointed in 1978. The formation of an Equal Opportunities Working Party in 1983 led to a number of changes over the next five years:

- Recruitment literature was revised to show women in supervisory positions and men at clerical levels.
- Equal opportunities became a subject of negotiation with the unions, and they were provided with information on the male/female distribution in different jobs and on relative promotion rates.
- Workshops on equal opportunities were held, particularly for staff with recruitment responsibilities.
- A few women-only courses for supervisory and managerial staff were developed.
- A career-break scheme was instituted to encourage selected female staff to return to work following a break of up to five years to care for pre-school children.
- A programme for the provision of creches and nurseries for staff children was begun.
- The requirement of staff mobility was changed, recognizing that, although it was necessary for staff to be prepared to move to other branches or offices, it should normally be possible to arrange it within reasonable travelling distance of their home rather than forcing them to move house.

Women's pay at Bigcity Bank

For many years most women at Bigcity Bank were paid less than men carrying out the same work. Up to the age of thirty-one salaries were closely related to the age of the member of staff rather than determined by the tasks carried out. After the age of twenty-three men were paid on a higher scale than women, so that by the time he was thirty-one years old a man would normally be earning 40 per cent more than a woman of the same age, even though he might be doing less demanding work. By the time of retirement the gap would be even larger.

In 1971, spurred by critical reports from the National Board for Prices and Incomes, by problems due to high turnover of female staff, and by the passing of the Equal Pay Act, 1970, the banks introduced a job evaluation scheme for clerical staff. For the first time pay was to be related to the nature of the work and women were to be treated equally with men. Four basic clerical grades were established. Most female staff were assessed as being in jobs which carried the lowest grade or the one above it. Secretaries and typists, an overwhelmingly female group, did not have their jobs evaluated but were put into pay grade categories according to the grade and status of their boss.

In 1985 Bigcity Bank staff were separated into seven main groups for purposes of pay and conditions. These groups, the number of staff in each, and their respective pay systems, are shown in Table 4.1.

Table 4.1 Pay groups for Bigcity Bank staff

Group	No. of employees	Job evaluation scheme
Senior and executive management Managers and appointed officers	9,000	Hay system
Clerical staff Grades CG1–CG4	33,000	National clerical system
Technical and services Unappointed grades 1–4	1,600	Bigcity T&S system
Appointed grades 1–5		Bigcity T&S system
Domestic staff		No system
Typists and secretaries Grades T1–T6	3,700	Bigcity job ranking system
Electronic data processing Managerial grades 31–2 Appointed grades 21–4 Unappointed grades 11–14	700	EDP system
Engineers Unappointed	200	National job ranking system
Appointed		Bigcity supervisory engineers' system

Equal Value legislation

Under the Equal Pay Act, 1970, women were given the right to equal pay with men when they were carrying out the same or broadly similar work. Where there was a job evaluation scheme women were entitled to have their jobs assessed and paid on the same basis as men. However, this concept of equal pay was challenged as too limited.

It was argued that women's right to equal pay should be widened to include comparison with men carrying out dissimilar work in the same organization. Often there is no man doing the same job with whom women can compare themselves; moreover job evaluation schemes frequently cover only a limited range of male-dominated or female-dominated jobs. A case taken to the European Court of Justice ruled that the United Kingdom was not complying with Article I of the European Community Equal Pay Directive, 1975, which had stated that the principle of equal pay outlined in Article 119 of the Treaty of Rome was to be construed as implying equal pay for work to which equal *value* is attributable. The British government was obliged, reluctantly, to introduce legislation and put forward the Equal Pay (Amendment) Regulations, 1983, which gave a legal right to equal pay for work of equal value from January 1984.

What does equal pay for work of equal value mean? In summary the British legislation gives a woman the right to equal pay when she is 'employed on work which is, in terms of the demands made on her (for instance under such headings as effort, skill and decision), of equal value to that of a man in the same employment'. Where a woman's job is found to be equal in value to that of a higher-paid man, the employer may be able to justify the pay differential on the grounds of a 'material factor', i.e. that the anomaly has arisen for a reason which is not to do with the sex of the job holders.

Equal Value in banking

The banks had three main options:

- To ignore the legislation and hope that it would not affect them.
- To analyse the legislation and their own circumstances, devise contingency plans, but take no pre-emptive action.
- On the basis of their analyses, to take action to ensure that they were not vulnerable to claims of equal pay for work of equal value.

For more than two years the do-nothing approach appeared to be working, but early in 1986 some female print finishers working at a chequebook factory brought a case against Lloyds Bank. They claimed that their work was equal in value to that of male printers, and in 1988, after the appointment and report of an independent expert, the industrial tribunal found in their favour. Although this case showed that bank employees and their unions were prepared to use the legislation, and could win a case, the

4

jobs were not in the mainstream of banking. A much greater threat came from a further case brought against Lloyds Bank by six typist/secretaries and one clerk/typist in April 1986. They compared their jobs with different grades of messenger.

The situation: Bigcity Bank and equal pay

The Equal Value legislation prompted Bigcity Bank to undertake a comprehensive review of its compensation and benefit policies and practices in late 1983. It analysed the implications of the legislation and, in particular, carried out a detailed analysis to assess its vulnerability to Equal Value claims.

Job evaluation and equal pay: the legal threat

One problem lay within the existing clerical job evaluation scheme, where cashiers had been assessed as falling within grade 2 but were only one point below the grade 3 level. It might be argued that the break point between grades had been deliberately chosen to ensure that cashiers were in the lower grade and that the bank could be accused of sex discrimination, since most of the nearly 9,000 cashiers were women.

Of more concern was whether individual women might take up a case and, if they did, what would be the result. In order to assess which jobs might have a good claim to equal value the bank carried out a series of evaluations of male-dominated and female-dominated jobs. Using existing job descriptions, the bank's job evaluation specialists looked at eleven jobs which were being carried out by female members of staff: those of Branch Cashier, Foreign Clerk, Departmental Computer Operator, Supervisor of Clerical Staff, Typist, Senior Secretary, Manager, Computer Centre Messenger, Money Market Sterling Dealer, Correspondence Clerk–Clearing and Domestic Staff or Cleaners. Each job was assessed using three approaches: the job evaluation system applying to the predominantly male technical and services staff; the system used for the predominantly female clerical staff; and the Hay system used to evaluate managerial jobs in the bank. Then they compared these evaluations with those of jobs held by some men who might be used for comparison in an equal pay case. These cross-evaluations suggested that for eight of the eleven chosen jobs held by women the choice of the appropriate male comparator would probably result in a finding by an independent expert of equal value. Even for the other three jobs there would be a moderate risk of their being found equal in value to a higher-paid male comparator.

An attempt was then made to quantify the cost if an individual woman in one of the eleven jobs were to win an industrial tribunal case. For the majority of them the cost would be over £1,000 a year. Then it was assumed that all the other women with similar job descriptions would take a case to a tribunal. For three of the jobs, the Branch Cashier, the Typist and the Correspondence Clerk–Clearing, the potential overall cost of mass tribunal claims could be well in excess of £1 million per year for each job.

Although these cases would cost enormous sums of money in theory, what was likely to happen in practice? Would the women really take up such cases? The probability of cases being taken to a tribunal was examined, using the assumptions that the greater the pay difference and the greater the likelihood of support from her union and from the Equal Opportunities Commission the more likely a woman would be to pursue a case. This analysis suggested that the greatest risk of claims came from female Branch Cashiers and female Correspondence Clerks–Clearing. It was estimated that the overall cost of losing Equal Value claims could be a minimum of £20 million a year. This was consistent with the analyses of the other large banks – one of them had estimated a cost of £40 million a year, and for all the Big Four banks the cost was thought to be likely to exceed £100 million a year.

Although the legislation appeared to pose a major problem for the banks, the outcome of any cases was obscured by uncertainty surrounding the defence available. The drafting of the Equal Value legislation had left this issue extremely vague. Some of the banks believed there was a good chance that the tribunals would accept that any pay differences between men and women were due to their separate bargaining arrangements or differential bargaining power and that this justified the inequality. Bigcity Bank was less sanguine, but acknowledged the uncertainty of the situation.

Job evaluation and equal pay: the solution

The decision facing Bigcity Bank in late 1983 was what action, if any, should be taken to reduce the risk of successful equal pay claims against the bank. One option would be to introduce a job evaluation scheme covering all staff, so that all employees, whether male or female, could be seen to be treated equally. It was rejected for three reasons. First, the cost would be very high. It was estimated that to bring in such a scheme would add approximately one per cent to pay costs. In view of the bank's profitability and competitiveness this could not be justified. Secondly, the legal uncertainties, discussed above, made it unwise to jump prematurely. Thirdly, major changes in the bank's structure and the organization of jobs meant that any job evaluation exercise undertaken at that time would have had to be repeated two or three years later to take account of all the changes.

Instead of comprehensive changes the bank decided to make smaller incremental ones which would slightly reduce the risk of equal pay claims or would reduce the cost of introducing a new job evaluation scheme. These changes sought to ensure that the number of male-dominated jobs and their pay were controlled, and where possible reduced, relative to female-dominated jobs.

Job evaluation and equal pay: a reappraisal

In late 1985 the bank reappraised its stance. After a slow start, some equal pay cases were being decided by tribunals. Victories for the women

4

involved were receiving a great deal of publicity. The Equal Opportunities Commission appeared to be interested in equal pay in banking, and the unions were raising the issue. The risk involved in tribunal cases was judged to be even higher than it had been perceived two years earlier. There was increasing concern that the negative publicity which a case could engender might lead to Bigcity Bank being perceived as anti-women. The industrial relations and commercial consequences for a bank with a 60 per cent female work force and a large number of female customers could be serious. All the banks remembered the reduction in student accounts at Barclays Bank because, some argued, it supported apartheid in South Africa.

The bank decided that in principle the way forward would be to introduce common conditions and the same job evaluation system for all staff. In practice numerous problems would need to be overcome before an appropriate job evaluation scheme, which would satisfy equal pay laws, could be successfully introduced.

One problem was to find a job evaluation scheme which would meet important criteria. The first criterion was that the scheme must be capable of assessing a wide variety of disparate jobs at all levels in the organization. Job evaluation is still largely a technique to ensure that acceptable and appropriate differentials are maintained between jobs at similar levels or jobs which draw upon the same labour market. Often, blue-collar, white-collar and managerial staffs have separate schemes in which different factors are used to evaluate the jobs. Sometimes there is further segmentation, such as between office and technical staff. It is still unusual to find a scheme which covers all or even most staff in an organization, and there has been little experience of such schemes. More recently there have been some attempts to stretch schemes designed for one group to others, or to redesign schemes to encompass a wider range of jobs.

A second criterion for a comprehensive job evaluation scheme was that it must be free of potential sex discrimination in its construction and in its operation. One purpose of job evaluation is to reflect the accepted hierarchy of jobs in an organization. Therefore schemes are normally constructed in such a way that they reflect the value system of the organization. Since men's work was traditionally believed to warrant higher pay than women's, many job evaluation schemes have incorporated such values. The factors chosen for evaluation and the weightings given to those factors have tended to favour men. For example, physical strength, more often associated with men's work, may be given a high weighting, whereas dexterity, usually associated with women's work, may be given a low weighting. However, although it can be demonstrated that certain job evaluation schemes clearly favour men, it can be very difficult, some would say impossible, to know whether a scheme contains inherent bias against women.

A third criterion for choosing a new job evaluation scheme was that it must be acceptable to, and ideally have the confidence of, staff at all levels and in all kinds of work.

The bank looked at several options. The possibility of adapting the existing clerical scheme was rejected, primarily because it would have required wholesale changes and taken up an enormous amount of managerial time to develop. For similar resource reasons the idea of developing the bank's own in-house scheme was rejected. Three proprietary schemes were examined, from which the bank chose the Hay system.

A major reason for choosing the Hay system was that it had been used successfully since 1981 to evaluate managers and appoint officers in the bank. In deciding upon its extension to all grades of staff the bank took into account the ability of the Hay Guide Chart Profile method to incorporate Equal Value criteria. Not only had Hay responded to the legislation by publishing a code of practice on equal pay for work of equal value, but its system had been used in some 'comparable worth' studies in the United States and had not been found to be discriminatory by the courts.

On the other hand the Hay system had been the subject of some criticism, particularly as to whether a job evaluation system which had changed little over a period of more than forty years could adequately reflect contemporary views about the relative value of different kinds of work. Other doubts about the Hay system had arisen because of its origin as a system devised primarily to evaluate management jobs. Its extension to non-management, routine and manual jobs had not been without problems. An important feature of the Hay system is the assessment of the 'accountability' of the job holder. In jobs low down the organizational hierarchy the criteria for assessing accountability tend to become less sensitive to differences between job responsibilities. Hay responded by making modifications and by allowing 'results of work', rather than 'accountability', to be the basis of evaluation. In a similar way some manual-worker jobs have caused evaluation problems.

However, after testing the Hay system on a full range of jobs Bigcity Bank decided that it was suitable and was able to take account of Equal Value considerations. A further benefit was that the quite large steps which typically separate the grades allocated after a Hay job evaluation exercise would allow flexibility and changes in job content without the need for constant re-evaluation. Such changes were occurring at an increasing rate in banking, with new technologies changing the emphasis from book-keeping to customer servicing and selling. Greater flexibility and adaptability on the part of staff were needed without the necessity to be constantly reassessing job grades.

A second problem was the attitude of the other banks in the Federation of London Clearing Bank Employers. The existing clerical job evaluation scheme covered all the banks. The federation provided a mechanism for ensuring that similar basic pay and conditions were maintained between the banks in order to avoid pay competition. Bigcity Bank attempted to persuade the other banks to adopt the Hay job evaluation system as a joint approach to Equal Value pressures, but the other banks showed little interest in an integrated job evaluation system and had different ideas about a replacement for the clerical scheme.

There were other disagreements within the federation, particularly over the degree of autonomy that each bank should have in formulating and operating its pay system. Yet if Bigcity Bank pursued an independent approach and left the federation it would be exposed to the pressures of pay competition, and it might be perceived by its staff as seeking to reduce pay relative to competitor banks.

A third problem concerned the attitude of the staff to a new job evaluation

4

scheme. Would male staff feel threatened by the idea of Equal Value? Would the potential losers (mainly the messengers and others in the Technical and Services area) fight to preserve their existing differentials over the clerical staff? Could the changes be introduced without disruption and a loss of morale? Morale was already low among the messengers, because their numbers had been reduced from 2,500 to 1,600 in the previous three years.

Activity brief

1   Why do women now form the majority of bank employees?
2   Do female bank staff have equal opportunities with their male colleagues?
3   What are the limitations and difficulties of devising a job evaluation scheme free of sex bias? Is it possible, or are the problems insurmountable?
4   How successful has the UK Equal Value legislation been? What do you think are the main factors limiting its success?
5   Should the bank's secretaries be paid according to the work they carry out or according to the status of their boss?
6   Should the bank's board of directors agree to go ahead with an integrated job evaluation scheme? Why?
7   How might the expected opposition of male staff, in particular the messengers, be handled?
8   Outline the main steps involved in introducing a new job evaluation scheme which would be seen to be free of sex discrimination.
9   What recommendations would you make for monitoring and maintaining the new job evaluation scheme?

Recommended reading

EQUAL OPPORTUNITIES COMMISSION, *Job Evaluation Schemes Free of Sex Bias*, Manchester, EOC.

McCRUDDEN, Christopher, 'Equal pay for work of equal value: the Equal Pay (Amendment) Regulations, 1983', *Industrial Law Journal*, December 1983, pp. 197–219.

TORRINGTON, Derek, and HALL, Laura, *Personnel Management: A New Approach*, second edition, 1991, chapter 33.

WAINWRIGHT, D., 'Equal Value in action: the lessons from Laird's', *Personnel Management*, January 1985.

Case 5

Rewarding performance in the public sector: the London Borough of Merlham

Edmund Heery

Performance-related pay

An increase in pay flexibility

Performance-related pay (PRP) schemes, which link the annual salary award to an assessment of individual performance in the job, have spread rapidly in recent years and now form an important component of white-collar remuneration in both private and public-sector organizations. Virtually all the major banks, building societies and insurance companies have introduced, extended or radicalized pay-for-performance systems; a number of large manufacturers, such as Cadbury's and Nissan, have introduced schemes (occasionally extending them to the shop floor); and in public-sector industries, such as the civil service, NHS and local government, PRP has been widely adopted under ministerial pressure. A recent survey of local government (LACSAB, 1991) found that 39 per cent of local authorities had introduced performance-related pay for at least some of their non-manual workers, almost without exception since the beginning of 1987.

This shift towards the greater use of PRP can be viewed as part of a more general movement towards 'pay flexibility' in British industry which has embraced a number of changes:

- First, organizations have sought to give greater weight to market forces in pay determination and to tie pay increases more explicitly to measures of business performance, not just through PRP schemes but through other mechanisms as well, such as profit-sharing.
- Secondly, there has also been a devolution of pay determination away from the national and towards the local level, so that industry-wide arrangements have declined as organizations have brought decisions on pay in-house and, within firms, managers have been given greater discretion to match rewards to the circumstances of particular business units.
- Finally, there has been a new focus on the individual employee and rewards which reflect his or her performance and circumstances, which

57

has meant that collective methods of pay determination have diminished in significance.

Of course, none of these changes has been absolute, and tradition continues to hold sway over much of the pay-setting process, but innovation has occurred, and change in each direction is readily apparent where PRP has been introduced.

Types of PRP scheme

Performance-related pay schemes come in all shapes and sizes but the vast majority share a number of common features:

- They rest on a mechanism for reviewing individual performance, usually over a twelve-month cycle. This may take the form of (1) an informal assessment by a line manager, unconstrained by any explicit rules or procedures; but more typically will consist of (2) formal merit rating, or (3) comparison of performance against agreed objectives (see ACAS, 1988). The latter, also known as output or target-based review, is the most popular, largely because it is seen as a way of translating general business objectives into the work routines of individual employees.
- The end-product of performance review is generally the allocation of the individual to one of a limited number of performance categories, each of which will be defined. The 'excellent' performer, for instance, may be an individual who has exceeded all his or her agreed targets and produced work of a uniformly high standard, while the 'fully effective' performer might be an individual who has achieved, but not exceeded, the majority of targets and produced work which adequately matches the demands of the job. It is this allocation which determines the size of the performance payment, or whether a payment is made at all.
- The performance payment can also vary substantially, both in scale and in form. In some schemes, for instance, the performance payment may be a modest non-consolidated cash bonus or the award of additional increments to high performers above a merit bar. In others, in contrast, considerable sums may be at risk, with the entire salary award and progression through scales or ranges being dependent on the results of performance review. This latter kind of 'merit only' scheme, which makes explicit provision for punishing the poor performer by withholding salary increases, is the most favoured option among organizations currently introducing PRP.

Table 5.1 shows the link between overall performance rating and performance payment in East Sussex County Council. In this case the assessment of individual performance determines progression through a fixed incremental scale and can also lead to the payment of non-consolidated bonuses to high performers who have reached their scale maximum. Although the scheme provides the opportunity to earn substantial payments (up to 10 per cent of salary) and denies salary progression to poor performers, it is not a

**Table 5.1 Performance-related pay
at East Sussex County Council**

Performance level	Within-scale incremental movement	Above-scale % of salary
1	3	8–10
2	2	5–7
3	1	0
4	0	0

Source: IDS Public Sector Unit (1989b).

true merit-only scheme because the latter continue to receive cost-of-living awards.

Background to the case

This case study concerns a large local authority which has decided to introduce PRP for its non-manual work force. It invites consideration of the practical and theoretical issues which are raised when designing a payment system of this kind. Increasingly, however, it has been recognized that the successful operation of a new payment system depends not just on good design but also on the process of scheme introduction and the steps taken to monitor and control the system and minimize any adverse side effects. Accordingly, the case invites consideration of these 'process' or scheme management issues as well. Finally, the introduction of a new payment system can have important implications for other aspects of personnel management. Two areas where PRP has been identified as having significant repercussions, and which are highlighted in the case, are industrial relations and equal opportunities policy.

The London Borough of Merlham

The London Borough of Merlham is located on the outskirts of the capital and provides a wide range of public services, including education, planning, housing, environmental health, social services and leisure facilities, to a largely residential area. The borough employs a total of more than 5,000 staff, of whom 2,900 (2,050 full-time, 850 part-time) work in non-manual occupations, excluding teaching. It is this group of employees who have been selected for coverage by PRP. At present these non-manual employees form two separate pay groups: (1) the Chief Officer group, comprising thirty-five senior managers (directors of services and their deputies); (2) the Administrative, Professional, Technical and Clerical (APT&C) group, comprising senior professionals and middle managers (principal officers), junior professionals and managers (senior officers) and clerical, secretarial and technical support.

The second, and by far the larger, group embraces a very diverse set of employees. It includes occupations which require professional qualifications and commitment, such as lawyers and architects, as well as routine clerical jobs. It also includes jobs with unambiguous and measurable outputs (e.g. project engineer) and those, like social or community work, where outputs are less tangible. Finally, the APT&C group covers employees who work in closely integrated teams (e.g. residential social workers) and others, such as accountants and environmental health officers, who work for much of their time on their own.

Existing pay systems

For both groups pay systems and levels are currently set through industry-wide collective agreements negotiated by employer representatives and trade unions. These agreements establish chief officer and APT&C grade structures, with grades consisting of a relatively short number of fixed incremental steps. Progression through these scales is generally automatic, with increments being awarded with each year's service and, although there is formal provision, it is virtually unheard-of for increments to be withheld for inadequate performance.

Although these nationally negotiated pay structures appear extremely rigid, there is some scope for local flexibility, and Merlham has considerable discretion over where it will locate particular jobs within the grade structure. This scope for flexibility can be turned against the employer, however, and NALGO (National and Local Government Officers' Association), the main white-collar trade union, has enjoyed considerable success in securing the regrading of jobs through the job evaluation procedure.

The traditional justification of the existing system of pay is that local authorities should offer fair, stable and gradually rising rewards in return for loyalty and professional service from their work forces. The basis of this exchange has been eroded since the 1960s, however, owing to successive government income policies, cuts in services and privatization, the curtailing of promotion opportunities and the growth of militant town-hall trade unionism.

Industrial relations

Industrial relations in Merlham are relatively stable, and though white-collar workers have taken industrial action, the borough has been spared the turbulence which has been characteristic of other London authorities. Two white-collar unions have membership and are recognized locally. The main one is NALGO, which has 47 per cent of the white-collar work force in membership, stretching from chief officers to the most junior clerical position. NALGO, officially, is strongly committed to the preservation of national bargaining and improving the relative earnings of the lower-paid and is opposed on principle to PRP. However, its local branches have considerable autonomy, and representatives in Merlham have wide experience of local negotiation. The branch is dominated by Labour Party and other left-wing activists, and there is a preponderance of employees from the social services department among branch officers.

The second union is FUMPO (Federated Union of Managerial and Professional Officers), a non-TUC union which recruits among senior managers and has a membership of about fifty within Merlham. FUMPO competes openly with NALGO on the basis of its non-militancy, concern to represent the interests of senior employees and support for greater flexibility in the determination of local government salaries.

Personnel management policy

In terms of its broader personnel management policies, Merlham has not been particularly innovative. For example, there is no authority-wide performance appraisal procedure, though individual departments have intermittently experimented with their own schemes for senior employees. Furthermore, although the council has invested heavily in training, commitment to the development of specifically managerial skills among chief, principal and senior officers has not been particularly high.

One area, however, where Merlham has been innovative is in the field of equal opportunities, where a series of measures has been taken to increase the number of women and members of ethnic minorities employed at senior levels of the organization and to ensure that women receive equal pay for work of equal value. There has also been considerable innovation in the field of benefits, with relatively generous car leasing, relocation and mortgage support schemes being introduced for senior staff as a retention measure.

The situation: the decision to introduce PRP

The decision to introduce PRP had its origins in a number of recent developments both internal and external to the local authority. One important internal change concerns the political control of the authority. Merlham has long been ruled by the majority Conservative group on the council, but in recent years the character of Conservatism in the borough has changed significantly. The leader's position and chairing of key policy committees have passed to the right wing of the party, and this has resulted in the council's withdrawal from its traditional paternalist commitments to its employees. The new leader, for instance, has been quoted in a local newspaper as saying, 'There have been too many soft options in local government and too many staff who have been able to drift along without offering full value for money. In today's enterprise culture that can no longer be tolerated.' One expression of this shift has been the privatization of a number of services, such as refuse collection. There has also been a reduction in the number of councillor meetings with trade unions.

A second internal change has occurred within senior management. A new chief executive has been appointed who is strongly committed to the notion of 'customer care' and the need to focus management attention much more on the outputs and effectiveness of local authority services. As part of this commitment she has initiated an authority-wide review of services, designed to formulate indicators of service quality and 'value for money', and simultaneously has set in train a review of organizational structure and management decision-making. The object of the latter is to concentrate powers of decision and cost control in the hands of the line manager directly responsible for service delivery, who will be held to account through 'robust measures of performance'. The avowed aim is to secure a 'loose–tight' form of organization, in which the devolution of operational responsibilities occurs within the context of strongly stated corporate objectives and an effective control system.

The perceived need for these internal changes has increased because of mounting external pressures on Merlham. Central government controls over local authority expenditure have grown tighter and legislation has exposed services to competitive tendering. These developments, in turn, have forced a review of staffing levels and stimulated a search for greater productivity, both among direct service providers and among support services, such as personnel and finance. For example, the authority has established an arm's-length Direct Services Organization, which operates on a commercial basis and which buys services, like training, industrial relations advice and legal expertise, from other parts of the organization. Financial and legislative pressures, therefore, are reinforcing the focus on service outputs and are requiring a much tighter control of costs across the authority.

The final source of interest in PRP has been the external labour market and the fact that, despite recession and relatively generous benefits, the authority continues to experience shortages of skilled staff. This is particularly a problem for occupations like computer programming, accountancy and law, where Merlham competes for labour against private-sector employers in central London. The view has been repeatedly expressed within the senior management group that these recruitment and retention difficulties will continue 'until staff are given the opportunity to raise their basic salaries'.

Activity brief

The combined effect of these various developments, within and beyond the authority, has been a decision by the council's personnel sub-committee to examine the introduction of PRP, in the first instance for all staff on Principal Officer grades and above, with a possible extension to all non-manual employees in the future. Assuming the role of an advisory group within Merlham's personnel department, provide the following:

1 An assessment of the suitability of PRP as a response to the situation facing the authority's management.
2 Outline proposals on the form or forms PRP could take within Merlham, giving reasons for specific recommendations made. Proposals should cover:

   (a) The method of performance review.
   (b) Responsibility for carrying out performance review, including the possible involvement of politicians.
   (c) The number and definition of overall performance categories.
   (d) The form and size of performance payment.
   (e) Procedures for dealing with poor performers.

3 An outline programme for the introduction of PRP.
4 Measures to ensure that PRP is operated equitably, that labour costs are not inflated as a result of the scheme, and that PRP has a positive impact on individual and organizational performance.
5 A summary of possible trade union responses to PRP proposals and an assessment of the implications of PRP for the future of industrial relations within Merlham.
6 A review of the implications of PRP for the pursuit of equal opportunities within the borough and outline proposals for ensuring that PRP does not erode existing policy commitments.

Additional tasks

7 Provide a general assessment of the possible benefits and disadvantages for organizations like the London Borough of Merlham of introducing PRP, and reach a conclusion as to whether the spread of this kind of payment system is desirable or not.
8 It has been widely argued that managers have developed new approaches to the management of human resources over the past decade. How would you describe the emerging 'management style' in the London Borough of Merlham?

Recommended reading

ADVISORY CONCILIATION AND ARBITRATION SERVICE (ACAS), *Performance Appraisal*, London, HMSO, 1988.

ARMSTRONG, M., and MURLIS, H., *Reward Management: a Handbook of Salary Administration*, second edition, London, Kogan Page and IPM, 1991.

GRIFFITHS, W., 'Kent County Council: a case of local pay determination', *Human Resource Management Journal*, 1, 1, 1990.

IDS PUBLIC SECTOR UNIT, *A Guide to Performance Related Pay*, London, Incomes Data Services, 1989a.

IDS PUBLIC SECTOR UNIT, *Paying for Performance in the Public Sector: a Progress Report*, Incomes Data Services and Coopers & Lybrand, 1989b.

KESSLER, I. 'Workplace industrial relations in local government', *Employee Relations*, 13, 2, 1991.

LOCAL AUTHORITIES' CONDITIONS OF SERVICE ADVISORY BOARD (LACSAB), *Performance Related Pay in Practice: Case Studies from Local Government*, London, LACSAB, 1990.

LOCAL AUTHORITIES' CONDITIONS OF SERVICE ADVISORY BOARD (LACSAB), *Performance Related Pay in Practice: a National Survey of Local Government*, London, LACSAB, 1991.

Case 6

Developing a 'smoking at work' policy: the Wellcome Foundation Ltd

Ann McGoldrick and Nicola Cawley

'Smoking at work' policies

Fewer people in the United Kingdom now smoke and awareness has increased regarding the potential health hazards associated with passive smoking. It is hardly surprising, therefore, that the later 1980s should have seen action on the part of employers, unions and employees to promote the introduction of 'smoking at work' policies in many organizations.

Surveys have demonstrated that smoking has become a minority habit, while there has been much publicity about the effects of the inhalation of tobacco smoke by non-smokers. In March 1988 the Independent Scientific Committee on Smoking and Health, chaired by Sir Peter Froggat, concluded that several hundred of the 40,000 deaths from lung cancer each year might be the result of passive smoking. Other negative effects, such as the aggravation of bronchitic and asthmatic complaints, allergic reaction, heart disease and dangers to pregnant women, were also identified. The overall recommendations of the committee were that non-smoking should be the norm in public areas and the workplace, with special provision for smokers.

While the legal position is still unclear, it has been argued that the Health and Safety at Work Act, 1974, requiring the employer to pursue all practical means to ensure the health and welfare of employees, may apply to smoking and its effects. The Health and Safety Executive have endorsed this view, although case law has raised some complicating issues, and employers need to introduce policies with care if they are to avoid the pitfalls of unfair dismissal claims. Pressure from employees, however, as well as the acknowledgement of the statutory duty to protect their interests, has encouraged the growth in the number of companies initiating and developing such policies. The Institute of Personnel Management has introduced a guide for personnel managers responsible for smoking policies at work. It assists in the process of establishing the appropriate stages and procedures for a smoking policy which will '. . . treat fairly the needs and wishes of both non-smoking and smoking employees and provide a healthy and efficient working environment'.

Background to the case: the Wellcome Foundation Ltd, Crewe

The Wellcome Foundation is a major international pharmaceutical company engaged in the research, development, manufacture and marketing of human health care products. The company has five sites in the United Kingdom, based mainly in the south-east of England. The site at Crewe Hall in Cheshire is the location of the sales and marketing headquarters in the UK. It is based in twenty-five acres with a Jacobean mansion house in the centre, surrounded by a mixture of old army buildings, modern production units and warehouse facilities. Sales and marketing management, together with administrative staff, are based at Crewe, with all representatives also reporting here. In addition, the site houses a production and packaging unit, a printing division and the distribution network. The total work force reporting to the site is approximately 1,000, covering a diverse range of staff and including a large unionized manual presence.

The situation

Introduction of the no-smoking policy

The company is concerned to provide a healthy working environment for employees, promoting an efficient workplace. Taking all considerations regarding the risks now associated with passive smoking into account, management considered it incumbent upon the company to protect non-smoking individuals. Some other Wellcome locations had already begun to introduce policies in this respect. Management at Crewe, therefore, decided to develop and implement a no-smoking policy in the interest of non-smokers. At the same time, it was appreciated that the rights of smokers within the work environment had to receive consideration. It was therefore necessary to define the type of policy to be introduced, as well as establishing an appropriate strategy for its implementation.

It was recognized that the issue would be an emotive one and would require careful evaluation and discussion to establish agreement between all parties. In the recent past a great deal of discontent had been aroused when a ban was imposed on smoking in meeting rooms at Crewe, without consulting union representatives. A preparatory step, therefore, was to establish a joint negotiating procedure between management and unions. The Site Consultative and Negotiating Committee was seen as a suitable vehicle, being composed of management and staff representatives from the three main Crewe departments (Logistics, Production and Printing) and representatives of the major site unions, EETPU, UCCAT, T&G, AEU, MSF, NGA and SOGAT.

A presentation was prepared by the safety manager, assisted by the personnel department, which outlined the dangers associated with smoking on site and the risks of passive smoking. Having discussed the issues raised, the committee agreed that a working party should be established, which would be charged with the task of developing a site policy in respect of smoking on the Crewe site. A special group was deemed more appropriate than utilizing an existing committee in an attempt to provide a group representative of management and employees and of smokers, ex-smokers and non-smokers. This was recognized as being in line with the procedural recommendations made by the Health Education Authority.

Setting up a working party

The composition of the working party was determined by the Site Negotiating Committee and it was chaired by the safety manager. Four management representatives were selected and nominations were sought from the shop stewards for five members to represent the unions.

At the first meeting of the working party, however, problems were revealed. It was established that only two members of the group were smokers, although it did include some ex-smokers. At the request of the unions, it was decided to try to balance the composition by adding two additional nominated union representatives who were smokers. The group then met at least monthly over a six-month period to carry out its brief:

> To recommend a policy to the Site Negotiating Committee to protect employees from passive smoking. This policy will have regard to the criteria to be applied in establishing a smoke-free environment and the process by which this is achieved.

In its subsequent meetings the working party established that many parts of the site were already no-smoking areas. These included any building with a related health or safety need, such as production buildings, warehouses storing chemicals, and food preparation areas, as well as site meeting rooms. Discussion therefore focused upon the extension of provision rather than the introduction of a totally new policy.

Several members of the working party were selected to attend a seminar run by the local area health authority, entitled 'Smoking Policies at Work'. The seminar enabled the group to obtain direct information about the stance adopted in other companies in the area, learning from their approaches and the problems encountered. This complemented information obtained in respect of other Wellcome sites, as well as examples of procedures adopted in other organizations which were contained in published reports.

6

The survey

The working party decided that it was important to obtain a broad impression of the extent of the problem and the feelings of employees on the issues involved. They wanted to establish that the outcome accurately reflected the views of the work force, ensuring that the policy could be implemented and maintained successfully. They also sought to comply with 'best practice' as recommended by the Health Education Authority and the Institute of Personnel Management. A decision was consequently taken to carry out a workplace survey to obtain information on staff preferences from all who would be affected by the change. It was decided that a questionnaire would be widely distributed, rather than selecting a more limited sample of employees. There was concern that smokers should also be given the opportunity to comment, since the proposed changes would place restrictions on their behaviour in the workplace. It was hoped in this way to avoid the polarization of attitudes which the IPM warns may occur if 'martyred' smokers feel a need to insist upon their 'rights'.

The survey was organized and co-ordinated by the safety manager. Attention was paid to the design and phrasing of the questionnaire, in an attempt to obtain clear answers and to avoid bias. After several drafts the working party agreed upon the final format. Likewise it was considered appropriate to publicize the questionnaire well. It was announced at the Site Negotiating and Consultative Committee and in site notices. A letter was sent to all departmental managers explaining the aims of the exercise, requesting their assistance in raising staff awareness and encouraging completion. The questionnaire was ultimately distributed to the payroll list of 651 employees permanently working on-site, since representatives, who merely reported to the site, were not to be included. A letter accompanied the document, presenting the reasons for the survey, and it was returned direct to the safety department. A response rate of 450 was achieved, which was considered a positive outcome.

The questionnaire sought to establish the views of employees in relation to the proposed changes, also collecting details about current working areas, the practice adopted and more detailed views of smoking in various public areas on site. It also investigated any health and hygiene effects which employees felt they suffered or might suffer as a result of exposure to tobacco smoke, as well as assessing smokers' attitudes towards restriction and assistance in giving up smoking. Table 6.1 summarizes the major survey results, which were used to provide direction for the future meetings of the working party.

It was clear, for example, that the majority of employees were non-smokers or ex-smokers and that about a third of smokers wanted to give up the habit. The vast majority also felt that smoking should not be permitted on-site, or only in designated separate areas. Further details revealed that this view was held in respect of most communal areas (e.g. reception areas, corridors, dining rooms, toilets, etc.), and many wanted to see some restrictions even in the Sports and Social Club. There was strong support for retaining and even extending the ban on smoking at

Table 6.1 Summary of the main results of the survey (%)

All the sample (n = 450)

	First choice (n = 440)	Second choice (n = 325)
Smoking status		
Smoker	24.6	
Non- or ex-smoker	75.4	
Views on smoking at work		
Not permit	32.4	
Separate areas	51.9	
Permit	14.1	
Don't know	1.6	
Current workplace smoking arrangement		
Permitted	59.2	
Not permitted	40.8	
Preferred action		
No change	25.7	11.7
Smoking and no-smoking areas	23.4	37.6
No smoking except at breaks	9.3	29.8
Total ban	41.6	20.9
Bothered by tobacco smoke at work		
Yes	57.8	
No	42.2	

Smokers (sub-sample, n = 110)

Views on smokers' rights	
Right to smoke freely in the workplace	71.7
Not a right	28.3
Difficulty of not smoking at work	
Easy or very easy	28.4
Difficult or very difficult	71.6
Would use help if it were offered	
Yes	43.0
No	57.0

meetings, even though the manner of its introduction had previously caused discontent. A fair proportion of employees, in fact, declared that they were bothered by tobacco smoke and sometimes needed to move from where they were working as a result of it. Concerns expressed included long-term health effects, eye irritation, coughing and breathing problems, headaches and loss of concentration, as well as the smell of clothes and hair after exposure.

In terms of the desired outcome, employees preferred either a total ban on smoking in the workplace or restricting it to specific areas, rather than the option of permitting smoking at specific times. Smokers, in fact, generally agreed that non-smokers should have the right to work in smoke-free conditions, although some felt that restriction would make things difficult for them during working hours and did not wish to receive help to stop smoking.

6

The policy established

On the basis of information obtained, the working party produced a 'policy on smoking at work' for the Crewe site. Once agreed, the final document was presented by the chairman of the working party to the Site Consultative and Negotiating Committee for consideration and modification. A clear statement was made on behalf of the working party that the object was to protect non-smokers from the effects of passive smoking, not to engage in moral judgements in respect of the practice of smoking. Part of the policy, however, focused upon the positive support which the company would provide to those who wanted to give up smoking. After a brief discussion of the rationale of the introduction of a policy at Wellcome, the terms were defined and an indication was given of how they would be implemented. Extracts of major provisions are given in Appendix 6.1. The outcome was that smoking was prohibited in all buildings on the site, except in designated areas or open air spaces.

Implementing the policy

Copies of the policy were issued to members of the Site Consultative and Negotiating Committee, who were requested to communicate it through the appropriate channels. Various issues arising were:

Timing
It was agreed that implementation should be gradual. Workplace meetings were organized to explain changes and the policy was publicized on National No Smoking Day (the second Wednesday in March). They were followed by a 'settling in' period, with full implementation announced for 1 May.

Refuge areas
Line managers in each department were made responsible for designating 'refuge' areas, work permitting, for the use of smokers during break times where such areas were requested. Such provision had been considered a 'grey' area by the Site Consultative Negotiating Committee, since it would have to be supplied from departmental budgets and there was variation between potential facilities across the site. In production areas smoking had only ever been feasible during break times, but the ban represented a new restriction for many office staff. If smokers requested a refuge area and it was not provided, they had a right of appeal through the company conciliation procedure.

Single occupancy areas
Line managers also had the responsibility of determining whether a smoker in a single occupancy area could have that area designated for smoking. Pollution of adjacent areas and the need for others to enter the area were to be taken into account. It was clearly stated that non-smokers and visitors should not normally be expected to enter designated areas in the presence

of smoke. If this proved to be a recurrent problem the designation of the area would be reviewed.

Recruitment

Recruitment of smokers was not precluded, and the company seeks to appoint the best candidate for the post. Personnel officers were instructed to advise candidates of the smoking policy and its implications. A copy of the policy is provided during the induction programme.

Visitors

The policy was applied to visitors as well as to members of staff. A notice is displayed at security entrances informing all visitors to the site that smoking is permitted only in designated areas.

Restaurant and social club

In the restaurant a separate area was designated for smoking, with an extractor system fitted into the ceiling. While the Sports and Social Club was an on-site facility, provided by the company, it was not deemed to be the workplace. Attendance was at the employee's discretion and it was consequently not included in the policy.

Assistance for smokers

A statement in the policy indicated the availability of assistance for those wishing to cut down or stop smoking. Counselling and advice were made available 'on request' through the site occupational health service, either for groups or for individuals. A series of counselling meetings were held during working hours immediately after the policy was implemented and some of those giving up smoking entered a national 'Quit' campaign competition, with the opportunity to win a holiday.

Support services

Line managers were referred to the site occupational health physicians and the site safety officer for advice and assistance in relation to health, environmental and safety issues arising from smoking on-site. The personnel department was designated the appropriate source of information in respect of the interpretation and application of the company's personnel policies as regards smoking at work.

The review

A review of the policy was undertaken after it had been in operation for approximately a year. The review consisted of a questionnaire to divisional managers which elicited information about the provision of designated areas, problems encountered, needs for disciplinary action and any changes in work efficiency. The results were collated by the safety officer. They indicated that satisfactory smoking areas had been established across the site, although in a few cases it would be necessary to investigate the spread of smoke into adjoining areas. These included the canteen, where the electrostatic 'smoke eaters' which had been installed were not considered adequate to protect non-smokers. No disciplinary action had been necessary, and managers had not received many complaints from non-smokers.

6

Activity brief

1 Present a rationale for the introduction of a smoking policy at work.
2 What factors should an organization investigate before introducing a policy on smoking at work?
3 Assess the policy introduced at the Crewe site of the Wellcome Foundation and the implementation strategy adopted, considering 'best practice'.
4 Consider the alternative arrangements available to companies when introducing a policy, evaluating the benefits and problems of each of those identified.
5 What potential problem areas should the personnel function be aware of when a policy is being developed and implemented?
6 Investigate the legal implications of passive smoking at work and those which relate to the introduction of a policy on smoking at work.
7 *Either* (a) list the areas an organization might consider incorporating into a workplace questionnaire designed to provide the basis of decisions in respect of an appropriate policy on smoking. Use any available examples or questionnaires.
Or (b) design a questionnaire for an organization known to you.
8 Obtain copies of policies on smoking from organizations or published material, comparing the terms and any information available with regard to implementation procedures.

Recommended reading

ACTION ON SMOKING AND HEALTH, *How to Achieve a Smoking Policy at Work*, London, ASH, 1988.

HEALTH AND SAFETY EXECUTIVE, *Passive Smoking at Work*, London, HSE, 1988.

HEALTH EDUCATION AUTHORITY, *Smoking Policies at Work*, London, HEA, 1987.

INCOMES DATA SERVICES, *Smoking and Alcohol Policies*, Study 418, London, IDS, 1988.

INCOMES DATA SERVICES, 'Filtering out the smokers', *IDS Top Pay Unit Review*, 108, February 1990, pp. 2–5.

INCOMES DATA SERVICES, *Smoking at Work*, Study 474, London, IDS, 1991.

INSTITUTE OF PERSONNEL MANAGEMENT, *Smoking Policies at Work: an IPM Guide*, London, IPM, 1990.

JONES, T. H., and KLEINER, B. H., 'Smoking and the work environment', *Employee Relations*, 12, 6, 1990, pp. 29–31.

PAINTER, R.W., 'Smoking policies: the legal implications', *Employee Relations*, 12, 4, 1990, pp. 17–21.
UPTON, R., 'Has workplace smoking become a burning issue?' *Personnel Management*, 20, 1, 1988, pp. 44–8.

Appendix 6.1 Policy on smoking at work, the Wellcome Foundation Ltd, Crewe site: extracts and main provisions

To whom it applies

The policy applies to all persons, including visitors and contractors, on the Crewe site. It is the responsibility of all employees to take reasonable care of themselves and others.

The policy and rules

The Crewe site regulates smoking on its premises. It seeks to accommodate both non-smokers and smokers and will take reasonable measures to control smoking in work environments.

In all cases where non-smokers and smokers work together or are required to meet together, the protection of non-smokers and ex-smokers from the unpleasantness and health risks of passive smoking is the primary consideration and these areas will be no smoking areas.

This means that smoking is prohibited in all buildings across the whole site, including all communal areas such as toilets, cloakrooms, locker rooms, reception areas and corridors. Smoking is not permitted in company vehicles unless occupied only by smokers.

Smoking will be permitted in the following areas:

1   Designated smoking areas.
2   All open-air areas where smoking is not otherwise prohibited.

Facilitation

The company recognizes the danger and unpleasantness of smoking and has considered these within the context of its philosophy of being a responsible employer and a member of the community at large.

Site management is responsible for developing, implementing, maintaining and reviewing appropriate procedures and rules. The establishment of local arrangements such as the provision of separate smoking areas where necessary is the responsibility of local line managers.

Case 7

Managing flexible working practices: tele-working at Network Services

Michael Brocklehurst

This case describes how one firm introduced a pilot scheme to enable its sales trainers to work from home, using computers. Such work is usually termed 'new technology home working' to distinguish it from traditional home working and the people who do it are dubbed 'tele-workers' or 'tele-commuters'. The National Economic Development Office has estimated that 20 per cent of the UK work force will be working from an electronic office in the home by the year 2010 (NEDO, 1986) and, although most past estimates have proved wildly optimistic, the phenomenon does seem set to grow.

The case aims to establish some of the personnel implications of flexible working in general and tele-working in particular. The case will help to prepare personnel practitioners to give advice on the introduction of tele-working schemes, how the schemes will affect the home workers and their managers, and what the wider organizational implications are likely to be.

Background to the case

Network Services

Network Services are a UK subsidiary of Systems Inc, a US company which owns a wide range of businesses, all in the 'high-tech' field. Network Services sell the terminals which go with networked systems linked to a mainframe computer; other subsidiaries of Systems Inc sell the mainframe computers and associated software. Network Services enjoyed rapid growth throughout the 1970s and 1980s, although in 1990 they began to experience business problems, in common with much of the rest of the industry. The company employs nearly 5,000 people and its head office is situated about eighty miles to the west of London along the M4 'Silicon Valley'.

Network Services are almost a textbook example of a human resource model of personnel management (Guest, 1989). There is a 'strong' culture, part of which licenses and encourages individual initiatives, and this is matched by a 'flat' hierarchy. Indeed, there is no clearly prescribed and published organizational structure at all. The offices are open-plan, and very few individuals have an office to themselves. Appraisal is very much a matter of the manager and employee jointly agreeing the employee's goals and a broad strategy for achieving these goals; employees are then left free to work towards the goals, with the manager acting as a resource if required.

The 'Project 2000' working party on flexible working practices

Julia Taggart is a senior personnel manager at the company, part of whose job is to head a working party entitled 'Project 2000'. The working party's brief is to look at the likely changes in working practices which will become either desirable or essential in the run-up to the year 2000. Their brief covers issues of labour demand and labour supply, such as the ramifications of the 'demographic downturn' (Atkinson, 1989), as well as issues of work which may affect demand for the company's products. As with many organizations in this industry and in this region, the company has experienced difficulties in recruiting and retaining high-calibre staff; this in spite of its human resource employment policies and above-average rates of pay.

The sales training team at Network Services

Roger Dainton is the head of sales training for the company. There are twelve sales trainers in his team, who are divided into three teams, each with a manager who reports direct to Roger. There is also an administrator/secretary. (See Figure 7.1.) All the sales trainers (other than the Generic Skills group) are seconded to the department from regional sales teams, usually for a period of two years, after which they return to the field. Most of the trainers are in their late thirties. The average time with the company is eight years, and the most recent newcomer has four

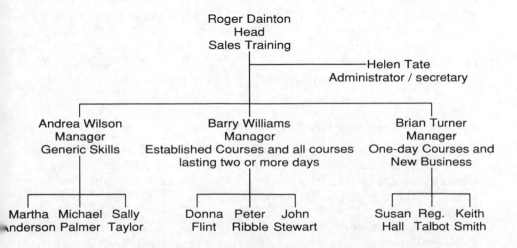

Figure 7.1 The sales training team at Network Services

years' service. A lot of the sales trainers' time is spent on the planning and delivery of training courses – usually at hotels scattered throughout the country. Some courses last only a day or two but some run for a week and there is even one two-week course. Roger Dainton was anxious that his trainers should become more proactive and start to try to uncover unmet training needs in the regional sales forces in order to generate more work for the group.

The situation

The problem: office space and relocation costs

Roger Dainton was under pressure to improve the quality of his group's service provision and, at the same time, to cut costs. Two of his biggest costs were office space and the costs of relocation. The problem of office space was not a small one. Each employee costs the firm £7,000 per annum in terms of office space. The second big cost arose because most sales trainers are seconded. Secondees who do not live within travelling distance of head office had to relocate (and then be relocated back at the end of the secondment). The cost was £10,000 per relocation and there was always at least one in any two-year period. The need to relocate also deterred many potential secondees from applying to join Sales Training in the first place.

The solution: tele-working?

Roger had just been reading about the attempts of other organizations to switch staff to tele-working, whereby some employees work from home, using terminals linked to the mainframe via the telephone network (Judkins *et al.*, 1985; Kinsman, 1987; Brocklehurst, 1989; Stanworth and Stanworth, 1991). Roger decided to call a meeting of his entire team to test the water with relation to introducing flexible working practices in the sales training team through tele-working. At the meeting Roger observed that the group seemed very enthusiastic, particularly Martha Anderson, who likes to make her views known at every possible juncture. Nobody spoke against the idea, although a number of people did not say very much.

The pre-pilot stage of tele-working in Sales Training

Roger decided to go ahead with a pilot scheme of tele-working. Sales trainers would no longer be expected to come into the office unless they needed to attend meetings. Instead they would work at home with computer terminals linked to the company's mainframe computer. Each trainer would have electronic mail and an electronic diary as well as the standard software packages used at work. The pilot would be on a voluntary basis. Roger reasoned that those who welcomed tele-working would benefit and those who wanted to remain office-based could do so and would not be affected.

There was thus bound to be a net gain. He also decided that both he and the administrator would need to remain office-based. In order to keep costs down he decided that people could have terminals and other equipment only as they became surplus to requirements in other parts of the company; this meant that the implementation of the pilot would be staggered. Some desks would still be kept in the office for use by the sales team but they would be reduced in number from twelve to three. Each person who opted for home working would be paid an extra £200 per annum to cover extra heating, lighting, etc.

The pilot would run for twelve months, when a decision would be reached whether or not to let sales trainers continue indefinitely as tele-workers. Roger was particularly concerned to assess the effects on costs and service delivery as well as employee acceptance.

At this stage Roger decided to contact Julia Taggart to tell her of his plans. Julia was familiar with the concept of tele-working, having carried out a survey of the literature when starting out with 'Project 2000'. She was happy to agree to Roger's request that she should assist in helping to monitor the pilot by interviewing all the team at the end of twelve months.

The post-pilot review of tele-working in Sales Training

Julia conducted her interviews and wrote up what she found as a series of 'vignettes'. Some of the most interesting are included below. The two extreme points of view are represented by Martha Anderson and Brian Turner.

Interview with Martha Anderson
Martha has two young children and had only just returned from maternity leave when the project started. Prior to maternity leave, Martha had been a trainer for five years.

> I have nothing but praise for tele-working. I save over two hours a day travelling. I avoid the wear and tear of the M4 and I save a small fortune in petrol. I see more of my children, although I still need a full-time nanny. When she was ill one day I got no work done at all. I can be with them when they come home from school for an hour and then catch up in the evening. I can also put in the occasional trip during the day, visit to school, trip to the dentist, etc. I was seriously thinking about going half-time until this pilot came up. The only problem I have had is when I wired up a plug incorrectly and singed some of my wallpaper! Silly! I really ought to get a fire extinguisher! My productivity has doubled because I can work without interruption. It's good for planning courses I am going to give by myself. I still come in to the office but only about once a fortnight, so I have to do some of my admin. which previously Helen used to pick up. I always arrange to meet one of the others for lunch when I do come in. The only problem I do have when coming in is people in other sections saying, 'Where have you been? I thought you'd left.' When I explain about being home-based I get a few quizzical eyebrows. But I feel a bit special, being part of something like this. It shows that the company mean it when they say they 'trust us to do the business'. Mind you,

I make more demands on Andrea Wilson than I used to, and I feel a bit guilty, because she has as much to do as ever.

Interview with Brian Turner

Brian is a young 'high-flyer' – in spite of his senior position he is the youngest member of the team. His perspective is that of a manager who has to cope with the implications of tele-working.

I can see tele-working makes sense for someone like Martha, but it's not for me. I work hard and I play hard but I like to keep the two apart. Indeed, I use the half-hour it takes me to drive to the office as a transitional period, 'switching on' in the morning and 'switching off' at night. I tried working at home for a few days but, frankly, I enjoy being in the office. I like the buzz, the bustle, the excitement. Mind you, it's not what it was since this project took off, the place is like a morgue now! I'm also a bit worried about the managerial aspects of tele-working. It's not that I don't trust my team, it's just that I am a hands-on manager, I suppose. I like to manage informally by 'walking around'. I think an informal word of encouragement, letting people know they are doing a good job, or a word of warning if it is needed, is much better than a formalized system of regular meetings and all the associated paperwork. Someone was visiting from the States the other day and he was a bit sceptical when I told him I manage people. 'Where are they?' was his response. I felt a bit foolish when I said they don't work in the same place as me. I also worry a bit about customer care. We preach that all the time on our sales courses. Yet I know one of our customers tried to contact one of my team at home at ten in the morning and was told she'd popped out to the shops! It doesn't give a good impression, does it? I'm also a bit worried about the team spirit. We had a meeting of the whole team the other day and it was noticeable how people only sat and talked to those they work with on courses. That never used to happen.

Interview with Michael Palmer

Michael Palmer is in his late forties and is a very experienced trainer with a background that goes beyond just sales. His wife works, and their grown-up children have long since left home. Michael is one of life's self-starters, with a high degree of internal motivation.

This pilot project has been a great opportunity for me. After about three months into the project I negotiated with the company to go half-time. That meant I could start my own consulting business, working from home, and it suited the company, who are trying to reduce head-count at the moment. Tele-working has taught me a lot about what you need to know to be an independent consultant, how to organize myself and make effective use of my time. I know if I come into the office for meetings I'm conscious of the cost: what I could be earning in my consultancy. I've honed my time management skills, believe me! My productivity is much greater, working at home. It also means I can time-shift activities. I can spend a day going to see clients and catch up on my Network Services work in the evening. Being at home during the day means I can walk our two dogs – they used to get a bit fretful when there was nobody at home all day. I suppose I'm not a great team player, although I like to socialize with the rest of the group, but to be honest I don't think there's as much of that as there used to be. Maybe it's because I'm half-time? But I could never have built up my business without the chance to tele-work.

Interview with Donna Flint

Donna is thirty years old. She lives alone and is very involved in her work. She has worked her way up from being a copy typist and has always felt a need to 'prove' herself.

Tele-working is a bit of a curate's egg, really – good in parts. There are some things about the office I'm glad I don't have to tolerate any more, but there are also some things I miss. I find the office stuffy and tiring. All that neon light. I like the windows open but others don't. It's nice not having to dress up for work, feeling you are 'on parade'. I'm also able to keep in touch with my friends more easily – they'll ring me at home for a quick chat in the day whereas they're reluctant to ring me at the office. I also like being around the house during the day. My neighbours, who are out all day, have been burgled twice. On the other hand I miss the office and the 'grape-vine gossip'. Also, at home there's nobody to bounce ideas off or help with an immediate problem. You feel reluctant about ringing people up unless it's something really serious. I also miss having my own space at work, my own desk. It feels strange coming in and having to find any old spare desk. It doesn't help when people in other departments say things like 'Oh! Working at home, are we? How cushy! I suppose you get to see all the daytime soaps, then?' I'm also a bit concerned about career development. You know the old cliche: 'Out of sight, out of mind'. Well, it may have a germ of truth. I feel I'd like to have more contact with my manager, Barry Williams, although he's a first-rate manager. I also have problems accessing the mainframe during the day because it's so heavily used; we all experience that. But it doesn't worry me. I can always access it at two in the morning if need be. In fact that's another good thing about tele-working. You don't have to stop working just because the office has closed.

Interview with Peter Ribble

Peter was with the northern area sales team before joining Sales Training on secondment. He is in his early thirties, with three children, all under six. His wife works two half-days a week, when her mother comes in to look after the children.

The big advantage of this pilot project is that it means I didn't have to relocate. In fact, if I'd had to relocate, I wouldn't have taken the secondment. It also means I don't have to put up with office life. I have a 'thing' about passive smoking. Being at home means I see more of my children. That's important to me, especially as I'm often away for days at a time, running courses. Mind you, the children can get in the way. Our house isn't that big, and I have to use the dining-room table. The company paid for us to have a business line but a couple of times my five-year-old has answered the phone! In fact the line has been a bit of a problem. We're still on an analogue exchange in this area, which presents problems transmitting data. Indeed, equipment has been a difficulty. It took two months to get a business line installed, and I've only just got my printer. Although I like working from home, it's not always easy. I'm not a particularly good self-starter, and I can easily spend the first hour of the day 'faffing about'. At the other end of the day, when my wife comes in she expects me to have the dinner cooked! It's good that Barry Williams, my manager, is also working from home, because he appreciates what it's like; but I was talking to John Stewart, who also reports to Barry, and we were both saying how we need more of Barry's time than we used to because we're home workers. But I think it says a lot about this company, about how it regards us as mature people, that they support a project like this.

Interview with Helen Tate

Helen, the administrator/secretary, is in her late thirties and is held in high regard by the sales trainers for her administrative skills. Roger Dainton had decided that her role was incompatible with working at home. She would need to be office-based in order to co-ordinate the work of the sales trainers.

There never was any question of my working from home, but I was worried how it would affect me when the others started to. The trainers used to give me bits of work to do when they were around the office which made my job more interesting. Now they're at home it's easier for them to do it themselves. I'm also worried about the sociability. When the trainers come in they do come and say 'hello' but they have to hover around, and it's a bit awkward. Also we don't seem to arrange to go out as a gang like we used to do. But I have to admit, my job has become more important in that I have to schedule a lot of the activities of the trainers. They've all found it easier to let me keep and manage their diaries for them, and that's made things much more interesting.

The post-review meeting between Roger Dainton and Julia Taggart

A week after Julia had concluded her interviews she met Roger to discuss the pilot. Roger was clearly very pleased and enthusiastic about how the pilot had turned out:

Look what we've achieved! Look at the savings we've made. [See Table 7.1.] There's also no question that we've increased productivity by at least 50 per cent in terms of additional courses we're running. I'm going to reorganize the team so each person is responsible for a particular area sales team. We can do that now my group are scattered throughout the country. They'll all be able to provide a better service and be more proactive in examining training needs. The people who are tele-working like it – you must know that if you've talked to Martha. I know Brian isn't keen, but he's carried on working in the office, so there's no difficulty there. I want the 'Project 2000' working party to support me when I argue that this pilot should be made permanent. In fact everyone should be encouraged to work from home. After all, we should be showing our external customers a lead, so that they've more reason to buy our products.

Table 7.1 Savings made during the pilot

Nine office spaces at £7,000 p.a. each	£63,000
Relocation expenses for Peter Ribble	10,000
Less £200 p.a. special payment for eleven people	2,200
Total savings	£71,800

After Roger had gone Julia reflected on what he had said. She knew that, from Roger's perception, the pilot *had* gone well, but that did not tell the whole story.

Activity brief

1 From your analysis of the interviews, what would you consider to be the major advantages and disadvantages of tele-working to (a) the tele-workers, (b) the managers?
2 Prepare a brief report to the 'Project 2000' working party, analysing the 'success'of the pilot project on tele-working and what Network Services have learned about such flexible working practices.
3 Appraise how best the organization can 'learn' from the experience of the pilot.
4 What advice would you be able to give to the next manager who approached you to set up a tele-working scheme along the lines of the Sales Training experiment? How could the company help Brian Turner develop the skills and style appropriate to managing tele-working staff?
5 Network Services chose a voluntary scheme whereby staff are still partly office-based and still retain all the conditions and status of full-time 'core' workers. Other organizations have made their tele-workers self-employed and entirely home-based on a non-voluntary basis. What are the personnel implications of this alternative strategy?
6 What other flexible working practices (Curson, 1986), besides tele-working, might Network Services consider? How might these alternatives help to meet some of the company's requirements?

Recommended reading

ATKINSON, J., 'Four stages of adjustment to the demographic downturn', *Personnel Management*, August 1989, pp. 20–4.

BROCKLEHURST, M., 'Home working and the new technology: the reality and the rhetoric', *Personnel Review*, 18, 2, 1989.

CONNOCK, S., *HR Vision: Managing a Quality Workforce*, London, IPM, 1991.

CURSON, C. (ed.), *Flexible Patterns of Work*, London, IPM, 1986.

GUEST, D., 'Personnel and HRM: can you tell the difference?', *Personnel Management*, January 1989, pp. 48–51.

JUDKINS, P., *et al.*, *Networking in Organisations*, Aldershot, Gower, 1985.

KINSMAN, F., *The Telecommuters*, Chichester, Wiley, 1987.

NATIONAL ECONOMIC DEVELOPMENT OFFICE, 'IT futures surveyed: a study of informal opinion concerning the long-term implications of information technology', *Technology for Society*, 1986, p. viii.

STANWORTH, J. and C., *Telework: the Human Resource Implications*, London, IPM, 1991.

Case 8

Cut-back management at work: Quench Ltd

Sarah Moore

Quench Ltd is a large brewing company, established in 1923. Its continued success resulted in rapid expansion, and by the late 1970s it employed some 3,000 people. The structure of the organization reflected that of a traditional machine bureaucracy, with a high division of labour, specific spans of control and a clear hierarchy. In terms of market performance the company experienced continuous large-scale growth which ended in the 1960s, plateaued in the 1970s and began to decline towards the end of that decade. The case concerns the company's response to market decline, with two programmes or plans for downsizing the firm and cutting back staffing levels. The programmes are accompanied by a shift in the company's personnel philosophy and policies as a whole.

Background to the case

The brewing industry

The brewing industry is one of the oldest types of business known. Historians suggest that the making of beer, in some form or other, dates back beyond Roman times, and in many respects the basic principles have changed very little over the years. The process itself is divided into six main stages:

- Grinding malted cereal grain (usually barley) into a coarse flour, or 'grist'.
- Producing a malt extract, or 'sweet wort', by transferring the grist into a mixer and blending it with water.
- Boiling the liquid with hops in order to 'bitter' the beer.
- Fermenting with yeast.
- Maturing the beer in large casks where secondary fermentation takes place and the beer acquires sparkle.
- Packaging the beer, either in kegs (75 per cent of all beer is packaged this way) or into bottles and cans.

8

The rigorous control and monitoring of each stage have always been emphasized; the slightest variation in temperature or quantity can have drastic effects on the final product. Traditionally, workers have had significant on-plant familiarity in order to monitor the process at different stages on the shop floor. However, recent years have brought changes and developments never before thought possible in the industry. Technological and biochemical innovations have resulted in the widespread sophistication of methods, aimed mainly at improving efficiency. The modernization of the industry has incorporated almost every part of the brewing operation. From genetic engineering (where specific genes are added to yeast cells in order to speed up the fermentation process) to the automation of cask handling and the complete information networking of whole brewing plants, the industry has moved forward, leaving behind any companies which fail to respond to or become part of the changes.

The emphasis on increased efficiency results primarily from a fall-off in demand. Consumption figures have decreased as alternative products such as wine, spritzers, etc., are becoming the centre of huge marketing campaigns. Also, as a result of increasing awareness of health and safety factors, as well as changing trends, overall levels of alcohol consumption are on the decline. The industry is facing some very real threats, but has also seen the emergence of definite opportunities for development.

The situation

The company's contraction

Even by the standards of the brewing industry Quench have been slow to change. Work methods and the design of jobs have been so firmly established and for so long that adjustment was originally seen as too complex, too costly and too much of an upheaval for the work force. Employees, from the start, enjoyed the benefits of job security and excellent pension plans. The company established a long-standing reputation for looking after its employees. Trade union activity and involvement, while not actively discouraged, tended to be low.

Up to the early 1980s there had been no lay-offs in the company, at which time it became evident that the organization would have to find ways of reducing costs if it was to remain viable. Since then the organization has implemented one major plan to reduce the work force and is now engaged in a second. The first plan took five years to implement and reduced the work force from 3,000 to 2,200. The second has a target time set at three years, two of which have already elapsed.

The aim of the current programme is to reduce the permanent work force by a further 1,000 people. Such a massive decrease in the permanent (or core) work force has in the past, and continues to, put enormous demands on the strategic and innovative capacity of management, particularly on the human resource function. Rationalization has required a huge amount of effort in terms of careful and appropriate implementation of human resource tactics such as job redesign, redeployment and retraining. In the process of reducing the work force the options and compensations offered to employees differed significantly between the two plans.

Plan 1

This involved the establishment of a policy of compulsory early retirement for anyone over the age of fifty-five years. At the outset the average age of the work force was relatively high, partly because very little hiring had been done over the preceding years. Twenty-six per cent of employees were over fifty years of age, 50 per cent were aged between forty and fifty years, and only the remaining 24 per cent were under forty. Also, at the time of this plan, union involvement was low and negotiations were kept to a minimum. Consultation with those who were to be directly affected by the cuts was practically non-existent. The plan took five years to reach its target of reducing the work force by 800. Not much changed on the technological front, but detailed job analyses were carried out so that, in the words of one manager, 'unnecessary jobs could be eliminated'. One real change did occur in that the general ratio between managers and workers became significantly narrower. Before the cuts there were four workers to every one manager, as against a three-to-one ratio at the end of the plan.

Plan 2

With the second plan came the realization that efficiency could no longer increase without a concentrated commitment to and investment in new technology. As a result some real and radical job restructuring took place. The wider range of alternatives, policies and issues that have been considered are outlined below.

Retraining and redeployment
A massive amount of money was allocated to retraining and redeployment activities for the remaining work force. Effort was directed towards identifying areas of overload and underload so that a more workable balance could be achieved through the reorganization of employees. Relocation within the company occurred on all fronts, to the extent that any individual at any level of the organization was likely to be 'shuffled around' to different areas or functions. Management found it necessary to enter into in-depth negotiations with regard to the implementation of these changes. As expected, middle managers and white-collar workers were least resistant and tended to have a positive attitude, especially with respect to retraining, which they saw as personally beneficial. In other sectors, however, there were varying levels of resistance, and by far the most difficult to reconcile were the craft workers whose jobs were traditionally focused on specific skills. New technology has been introduced, most notably over the last eighteen months, during which time the previously manual plant has been replaced by a highly automated system. The new system not only demands less staffing but also requires completely different kinds of skills. Thus the type and content of training

have had to be adjusted significantly. Investment in the new technology has amounted to approximately £20 million.

Voluntary or early retirement

A considerable amount of time has been devoted to establishing mutually acceptable agreements between unions and management regarding this point. It is the area in which most negotiation time is taken up, and from which the most satisfactory results have been reported. It is generally agreed that, as a method of achieving voluntary redundancies, the high monetary compensation was worth the investment.

Outplacement counselling

Management made the decision to include redundancy counselling as part of the new strategy. Again, a certain amount of investment was necessary in order to provide this service. The decision was made before trade unions were notified. Expertise in this area was bought into the company, with counsellors located in-house for a period of three months. The service was not used and is seen by management as having been a waste of time and money.

Job redesign

A significant element of the downsizing strategy has been to combine and reorganize different tasks, not only to make the system more manageable and controlled but also to facilitate definition and measurement of performance. Job redesign operates hand-in-hand with retraining and, like the latter, is primarily driven by the new technology. The following is an example of how some of the core jobs have changed.

Cask handling
While the loading and unloading of beer kegs has been a prime target for automation over the last few years, it is only relatively recently that the appropriate technology has become available. Quench have installed equipment which enables both full and empty kegs to be brought to their destinations completely automatically. Through the use of a conveyor system and a high-tech video recognition base, the long-term costs of time and labour have been eliminated. Instead of workers staffing the paths from the brewery to the trucks, one or two workers monitor the movement of the kegs from a computer control base where any problems can be detected quickly and dealt with immediately. This automation is also expected to reduce the accident rate drastically, as many of the reported injuries in the plant are caused by falling or rolling barrels.

Malting
The new technology will also change the methods of malting. The traditional method involves workers spreading barley over a flat area (floor malting) so that the grain can germinate. With the old technique batches of about thirty tonnes could be malted at a time. The new machine enables batches of up to 190 tonnes to be processed at one go. Again, the machine is completely computer-controlled, and variations such as temperature, humidity and ventilation can be monitored at a single computer terminal.

Keg tracking

A new keg tracking system has also been introduced whereby individual barrels can be traced to their current location so that it can be easily seen which barrels are being filled, which are in the warehouse and which are out with the distributors. Previous to the tracking innovation, this information could only be estimated. Now accounting personnel can base their figures on accurate and attainable data through the use of a VDU which is hooked up to the system.

Fermentation

Traditionally the fermentation process demanded skilful control of time and temperature in order to ensure perfection in the production process. Now fermentation is to be controlled and adjusted by machines, not people, with a manual fallback option in case the system breaks down.

In short, the entire brewing process can now be controlled, monitored and driven by computers. Thus many of the positions that traditionally involved manual inputs have been replaced by computerization. A significant proportion of the new positions involve a lot of basic data input. Productivity and performance on the part of many of these operators are seen as a problem.

Performance evaluation

Quench have planned to bring in a harmonized pay structure and total re-evaluation of jobs. At present, there are three separate categories in which performance is evaluated, and pay structures differ between all groups (see Table 8.1). It is hoped that the re-evaluation of jobs will be completed in less than a year and that, under the new structure, performance evaluation will be more accurate and perceived as more equitable across all categories. Also, the management to general worker ratio is to be narrowed again, and at the end of plan two there will be just two workers for every one manager.

Table 8.1 Categories and pay structures

Category	Male	Female
1 White-collar	70	30
Secretarial	0	100
Management	66	34
2 Supervisory	100	0
3 General worker/craft worker	90	10

Selection, recruitment and promotion

Owing to a complete hiring freeze, promotion is conducted exclusively from within the company. The only individuals who are hired from outside are highly specialized employees taken on to carry out a specific (usually highly technical) job. Individuals are hired on a permanent basis from outside only when there is no one from within the company capable of filling the position.

Information and communication

In comparison with the first rationalization plan, where top management maintained a policy of limited communication until after the announcement of the compulsory redundancies, the current policy encourages more open communication from both sides. Nevertheless, there still remains a very significant amount of private preliminary planning, especially on the part of the strategic managers. Because all redundancies are to be voluntary, communication of sufficient level and quality is more often encouraged. For example, if it is proposed that a team of six people is to undergo a 50 per cent reduction in force, it is hoped that three workers would not quit their jobs until (1) all remaining workers agree and accept the rationale for the reduction, and (2) feasible ways of restructuring the work had been decided upon.

Job security

High levels of job insecurity are evident throughout the organization, and it is generally recognized that much of the remaining work force is experiencing stress, anxiety and uncertainty as a result. Resistance to change is generally seen as a prime obstacle in the implementation of the restructuring process. There has been talk of establishing a job security policy whereby the remaining work force would be guaranteed full and constant employment with the company. However, management are reluctant to initiate such a policy too early and are unsure as to its immediate benefits even if it could be guaranteed.

Long-term staffing strategy

Departmental responsibility

In the early stages of the second rationalization plan it had been proposed that a specialist task force should be organized in order to deal with the on-going reductions of staff. In fact, although there was a lot of positive support for the idea, it was never implemented. Instead it was decided that the main responsibility for the cut-back programme should lie with the personnel department, along with co-operation and communication from all other areas.

Adaptation and maintenance

Once the work force has been reduced to its target level, effort is to be concentrated on the maintenance of a 'lean staff' policy. In future emphasis is to be placed on retraining at a non-specialist level, so that redeployment can be more easily accommodated throughout the organization and levels of flexibility can be increased.

Externalization

The use of contract workers has increased steadily over the last five years. The organization has adjusted its previously self-sufficient profile and now buys in several peripheral services such as in-house maintenance, electricians, fitters, builders, computer and data processors. Temporary workers are also employed in various departments throughout the company.

Organizational response to change

While, as previously noted, some sectors have responded favourably to the huge changes that are under way, the general atmosphere is one of mistrust and anxiety. As one worker put it, 'Everyone seems to be looking over their shoulder. No one really knows for sure what's going to happen next.' There are many who have expressed the concern that, even though redundancies are voluntary, those who remain with the company feel insecure about their ability to adapt to the new and fundamentally different structures which are emerging.

Activity brief

1 How would you assess the first plan's impact on the work force and on the organization as a whole? What are the most probable reactions to such a plan?
2 Suggest reasons why the outplacement counselling provided in the second plan was not used.
3 Identify any pitfalls with respect to the harmonizing of pay structures.
4 Outline some of the arguments for and against the establishment of a job security policy, with particular reference to this case.
5 Evaluate the second rationalization programme and state how you would assess its success in the longer term.

Recommended reading

ATKINSON, J., and MEAGER, N., 'Is flexibility just a flash in the pan?' *Personnel Management*, September 1986, pp. 26–9.

BIDDLE, D., and EVENDON, R., *Human Aspects of Management*, second edition, London, IPM, 1989, pp. 192–207.

BRAMHAM, J., *Human Resource Planning*, London, IPM, 1989, pp. 56–66.

CAMERON, K. S., *et al.*, *Readings in Organizational Decline: Frameworks, Research and Prescriptions*, Boston, Mass., Massachusetts Publishing, 1988.

EGGERT, M., *Outplacement: a Guide to Management and Delivery*, London, IPM, 1991.

ROBERTSON, I., *et al.*, *Motivation: Strategies, Theory and Practice*, London, IPM, 1992.

THOMASON, G., *A Textbook of Human Resource Management*, London, IPM, 1988, pp. 497–509.

Case 9

The introduction and implementation of early retirement programmes in two UK organizations

Ann McGoldrick

In recent years early retirement schemes and arrangements have been utilized in many organizations in the United Kingdom as a human resource planning mechanism. When a reduction in the size of the work force is essential to meet organizational objectives, they may in themselves be sufficient to generate the necessary contraction in numbers, although they have frequently been used in conjunction with a more general programme of redundancies. As well as assisting in overall reduction, they may be used as a flexible tool to deal with other human resource planning problems. Whether used alone or as part of a wider redundancy programme, the terms offered will normally be designed to meet the specific needs of the older employee, who is less likely than younger colleagues to re-enter the labour force. This case study provides the opportunity to assess and compare the early retirement procedures in two UK organizations, considering the reasons for their introduction, the terms and the implementation strategies.

Background to the case

Government surveys in the United Kingdom have demonstrated the substantial decline in the economic activity rates of older sections of the population, particularly among men. While ill health (disability) retirement obviously remains an important cause of early withdrawal from the work force, other developments at national and company level have contributed to the trend. In the United States, Europe and other industrialized societies the desire to provide job opportunities for younger workers has led to the operation of state schemes, which have been specifically designed to encourage older employees to leave the work force by offering them financial incentives. The Job Release scheme in the United Kingdom was part of this movement, although it was less extensive than many. The terms on offer were limited and confined to those approaching normal state retirement age, and it was necessary for the organization to replace a retiring employee with a registered unemployed worker. The scheme now no longer operates. Periodic surveys carried out by the Government Actuary Department and the annual surveys of the National Association of Pension Funds (NAPF) also demonstrate the expansion in occupational pension scheme cover in the UK, together with the gradual improvement of the terms offered. This development has also supported routes to early retirement and encouraged its use as a human resource planning mechanism within organizations.

Early retirement terms

In many occupational pension schemes the terms have been introduced and extended to provide for early retirement on grounds of ill health (disability), at the request of the employee and, when it occurs 'at the employer's request', as a redundancy provision. The terms offered are likely to differ according to the circumstances. The available options are outlined in Appendix 9.1.

The operation of schemes

Personnel managers facing recession are frequently at the sharp end of workforce cut-backs. Early retirement procedures have been seen as one of the innovative approaches which can be used in cutting labour force costs while avoiding redundancies elsewhere. Increasing numbers of pension schemes have included standard arrangements in respect of redundancy retirement, as well as in respect of ill-health early retirement. Temporary schemes, with added benefits, have frequently been utilized to directly support numbers reduction. The NAPF have in fact pointed out that occupational pension schemes have become a 'key weapon for managing early retirement and redundancies'.

Enhanced early retirement benefits can make compulsory retirement more palatable and can also encourage volunteers as part of redundancy schemes. Costs may be substantially met by the scheme, if the pension fund is healthy or in surplus. Severance payments can cushion the retirement, adding to the perceived generosity of treatment of those leaving. Benefits have been perceived by employers, by unions and by employees opting to retire. Problems have also arisen or can be expected, however, which need to be addressed if the trend continues. In the future, pension schemes may not have the funds to support these benefits or it may be necessary to limit the opportunity for other scheme improvements. Some unions have questioned the appropriateness of using pension funds to reduce the employer's redundancy costs. Employees may also come to expect generous benefit offers and an early or flexible retirement arrangement as a right, although demographic changes may reduce their attractiveness to employers.

While the terms of the scheme are of obvious importance, a successful outcome for the employee and the employer also depends upon the organization's implementation strategy. This again is usually the task of the personnel function. United Industries Ltd and Leason Machine Tools have both utilized early retirement arrangements, although the standard terms within their pension schemes and special benefits offered varied. The procedures they adopted to introduce, carry through and support the arrangements also differed in many respects.

Early retirement at United Industries

The human resource problem

United Industries Ltd (UIL) is a large British-based multinational corporation, with a diversified product base in manufacturing and chemical production. It operates as a series of relatively autonomous companies, each with its own board and a discrete geographical focus in the UK. The group head office is in London and the central board retains overall control, dictating major policy but usually permitting the subsidiary organizations to determine implementation strategies. World-wide UIL has 75,000 employees, approximately three-quarters of whom are based in the United Kingdom. It is a highly unionized organization, although it has generally maintained a reasonable record in employee relations, with an established reputation as a generous employer. Employee benefit levels, in terms of pay and pension scheme provision, are high for its sectors, and the organization has experienced no difficulties in recruitment and retention. After a fairly stringent cut-back in numbers in the early 1980s, most operations within the organization have remained profitable. Increasing competition in certain areas, however, detracted from UIL's market share, with serious effects on overall profit levels. The UIL (Chem) division was one which was losing market share. Investigations suggested the need for a staffing reduction at the production level and the establishment of a leaner management structure.

During the recession of the early 1980s UIL had been forced to engage in redundancy programmes across the entire organization. Overall workforce numbers are now just above half the previous total. UIL (Chem) division had not been seriously affected this time, with a significantly lower reduction rate than many other operations. Consequently many employees have been with the company for more than twenty years, and this aspect of the personnel profile also suggested causes of concern for the future. In the previous company-wide redundancy programme the terms had been considered generous, although unions had been discontented at the selection procedures operated, the use of compulsory redundancies and redeployment in some areas. It was also felt that line management had put pressure on older employees to accept the voluntary early retirement option which had been incorporated into the scheme. An agreement had subsequently been established with the unions, determining that the organization would attempt to avoid redundancies in the future and that there would be full consultation regarding terms and procedures in any subsequent initiatives.

The central board were aware that there would be strong resistance from union representatives to further staffing reductions. Examination of the workforce age profile also suggested that it might be sufficient to employ a generous early retirement arrangement. A decision was therefore taken to authorize the UIL (Chem) board to introduce and administer a special redundancy early retirement scheme, which would seek volunteers and attempt to obviate the need for further redundancies among younger employees. Details of terms and implementation procedures were delegated to the human resource director at UIL (Chem), under the direction of the local board.

Pension and early retirement terms

At UIL the normal retirement age is sixty years for both men and women. The pension scheme is a contracted-out contributory final salary scheme. The pension accrues at a rate of one-sixtieth of final earnings for each year of pensionable service. After forty years' service an employee is entitled to a pension equivalent to two-thirds of final salary. The scheme also includes terms for voluntary early retirement and retirement at the employer's request. In both cases the scheme provides an accrued pension, without actuarial reduction for members aged fifty years and over, after they have completed ten years' pensionable service. When the retirement is on a redundancy basis, it is also usual to receive a severance payment and a bridging pension equivalent to the state pension until normal retirement age, while life assurance (death-in-service) benefits are also continued.

Implementing the scheme

The financial problems which the division had been facing were already a matter of concern amongst the UIL (Chem) work force. There had been speculation that further reductions in numbers would be required, causing apprehension that some of the procedures utilized in the early 1980s might again be employed. Personnel had, in fact, been approached by a number of employees who feared that they might be forced to accept redeployment or be made redundant. The human resource director decided to set up immediate discussions with representatives of the seven unions involved, outlining the required workforce changes and the offer to be made. Assurances were given that compulsory retirement would not be employed, while all eligible employees would be treated equally and the option would not be indefinitely withheld from anyone who wanted to retire.

With the general consent of the unions, it was decided that the entire work force would be informed immediately of the impending early retirement programme. Eligible employees would then receive details of their specific terms, in writing, as quickly as could be arranged through the pensions section of the personnel department. Assurances were given that there would be no pressure and that employees would be given time for consideration, as well as assistance and counselling if they decided to volunteer. The local board had decided to offer the benefits which applied to redundancy retirement. In order to ensure that sufficient volunteers were obtained, they also offered employees with ten years' service and aged fifty-five years and over credit for potential years of service up to normal retirement age for the scheme.

Within two weeks the necessary information had been circulated to the work force, while within six weeks eligible employees had received a written statement of their personal terms for consideration. They were invited to seek an appointment with a representative of the personnel department. In addition, a series of seminars were held for line managers, to inform them of the details of the pension scheme and the terms established, as well as provide instruction in appropriate ways of dealing with staff should they be approached. They were required to try and ensure that eligible employees were not put under pressure by colleagues. The letter to eligible employees stated that the offer was to be open for six months and it was made clear that all who applied would be permitted to retire. Key employees might be asked to postpone the date of retirement while alternative arrangements were made, although this would be done as quickly as possible.

Follow-up procedures

The company normally runs a pre-retirement course in the year preceding retirement. Under the current circumstances, it was decided to arrange a set of 'early retirement meetings' for those opting to retire, although in some cases the meetings actually took place after their retirement date. Financial advice was provided as part of the meetings, although retirees could also opt to visit a private financial consultancy organization, whose services had been engaged by the company for their benefit. Other sessions were designed to attempt to meet the needs of those retiring at an earlier age, including advice on further work and part-time job options. After early retirement, former employees retained the same rights as current staff as members of the social club, they received company publications and, as with all 'pensioners', were contacted annually by a company representative or pension visitor.

UIL (Chem) monitored the application of the scheme over the time of its operation, utilizing their computerized personnel record system to provide an analysis of response rates and details of the take-up profile. They reached the target quite easily within the period, with slightly higher acceptance than required, particularly in areas of management and among shopfloor foremen/women. Some disruption was caused within departments owing to the uneven effects of the scheme, necessitating some changes in job responsibilities, retraining and a certain amount of recruitment. The personnel department was severely pressed in dealing with volunteers, making the arrangements for counselling and responding to the changes – a situation intensified by a reduction in its own numbers during the period.

An independent consultant was engaged to monitor the response to the scheme. All retirees were contacted twelve months after the date of their retirement through a postal questionnaire survey, while more detailed interviews were carried out with a selected sample. The results suggested that they were generally satisfied with the treatment they had received and with their retirement experience to date. Approximately a quarter referred to subsequent problems in respect of finances, health or adapting to retirement; rather fewer referred to indirect pressures they had experienced which had influenced their retirement decision.

Early retirement at Leason Machine Tools

The human resource problem

Leason Machine Tools has a head office and three local operating sites in the Midlands, with a work force of approximately 2,500. Employees are predominantly engaged in heavy engineering and are recruited locally. There has been a tradition of family members joining the organization when opportunities arise, and labour turnover has been low. The firm is a major employer in the district and has enjoyed a reputation as a secure and reliable employment prospect where the old 'family firm' tradition is maintained. The growth of the work force during the 1960s and 1970s necessitated the introduction of more formal central personnel procedures, although the retention of the 'family culture' was encouraged at the production sites. Personnel staff were expected to spend time in the production areas, and the personnel department encouraged the maintenance of the welfare role, with an open-door policy and assistance in respect of medical, personal and family problems. Leason's also prided themselves on their excellent employee relations record, which had left them generally free of strike action.

Through the 1960s and 1970s Leason's had expanded considerably and the work force had doubled as they operated in a secure market, with no direct competition in their specialist areas and a full order book. In the early 1980s, however, they had been hit hard by the recession. Increasing numbers of their customers had ceased trading, contracted or diverted funds previously utilized for investment in new equipment. The company had managed to avoid a major redundancy programme by a policy of no recruitment, natural wastage and internal job reorganization. A programme of voluntary redundancies had also been arranged, involving severance payments well in excess of the legal requirements. Employees over the age of sixty years had also been permitted to take their earned pension benefits immediately, with no actuarial reduction, if they elected to do so. The strategy caused a severe drain on company finances and had also affected the security of the pension scheme fund, although it was deemed to have been largely successful when business revived considerably in the middle of the 1980s. In the later 1980s there was again a significant fall-off of orders, which made it obvious that the organization could not sustain the existing workforce size. Management's diagnosis of the prospects for the next five years was pessimistic. Even if the recession were to end, it would be some time before customers would be likely to engage in significant capital expenditure and business might pick up for Leason's. A relatively drastic cut-back in numbers was therefore deemed essential for the survival of the organization.

Management decided to introduce a programme of redundancy/early

9

retirement at all three sites and at head office. After discussion with the union convenors, it was determined that it should be of a voluntary nature in the first instance, although management made it clear that compulsory redundancies would follow if sufficient numbers were not generated. The personnel department was required to implement the arrangements for the programme, commencing with the early retirement scheme.

Pension and early retirement terms

At Leason's a contributory final salary scheme is also operated. Traditionally contribution rates have been lower and the pension is based on an accrual rate calculated in eightieths. Service of forty years provides a pension equivalent to forty-eightieths of final earnings. Normal retirement age has remained in line with the state pension age, although legally women may now choose to work on until sixty-five years. This has not been directly encouraged. Employees over the age of fifty may request early retirement. In such circumstances the scheme provides benefits based on accrued pension rights, with an actuarial reduction to compensate for earlier payment. The percentage discounted operates on a scale in relation to years before normal retirement age. After negotiations with the unions in the mid-1980s the reduction factor was lowered and was not applied to those who had ten years' service and were within five years of normal retirement age. When retirement is as a redundancy at the employer's request, the actuarial reduction is still applied, although it is normal to provide a severance payment. Those with ten years' service and within five years of normal retirement age receive the full benefits accrued to date.

Implementing the scheme

While the work force had already ascertained that there were problems in respect of orders, there was an expectation that the company would again pull through, as it had done when it had previously encountered problems. Once the decision to implement a numbers reduction programme had been taken, the work force were notified by letter. The nature of the problems faced, the need for staffing cuts and an outline of the redundancy/early retirement procedures were briefly discussed. It was emphasized that the company would first seek volunteers and would attempt to minimize compulsory redundancies. The terms of voluntary early retirement, as defined for a redundancy situation in the pension scheme terms, were included as an enclosure with the letter. Members of the work force were invited to attend a series of meetings, when the situation and future implications would be more fully explained.

The unions had agreed to participate in the meetings, which occurred within the two-week period following the announcement. Management representatives outlined the company's problems and the difficulties for the future, survival being dependent upon a rationalization of workforce size. They again assured the work force that, as far as possible, it would be accomplished by voluntary means. Union convenors put forward the alternatives, including a discussion of the more generous nature of the early retirement option under these circumstances. Reference was made to the compulsory redundancies which might follow if sufficient volunteers did not come forward.

Letters had already been prepared providing the details of the offers for each employee. In the week following the meetings those eligible for the early retirement arrangements were notified of the specific terms available should they opt to retire early. They were required to reply in writing to the personnel department within three weeks of receiving the communication should they wish to accept the terms. The welfare officer of the personnel department at each site was designated as the contact point for those seeking any further information.

Follow-up procedures

The company has for some years operated an annual pre-retirement course. Since more employees were retiring than could be coped with in this way, several courses were set up in the following six-month period. Generally retirees attended after the date of their retirement and the course was more or less identical to that normally offered six months prior to normal retirement age, although it was adapted to include financial advice in respect of investment of lump sums from a financial adviser of a major building society. All those who retired received the monthly company magazine and became members of the Retired Employee Association, which utilizes the staff social club facilities once evening each month. Any problems arising in respect of pensions or retirement could be referred back to the welfare officer at the site on which they had worked.

A fair response was obtained in respect of the early retirement option and the redundancy scheme, although it was not entirely sufficient to Leason's needs at the time. A year after the initial programme was introduced the company again contacted eligible employees over fifty years of age, repeating the early retirement offer but adapting the terms for those now nearing normal retirement age. Men aged sixty-two years and over and women aged fifty-seven years and over who had ten years' service were informed of their eligibility for enhanced benefits. The new offer, again of a temporary nature, provided this age band with accrued service and credit for potential service to normal retirement age in the calculation of the pension. The age for obtaining an accrued pension without actuarial reduction was set at fifty years for both men and women, irrespective of service. Further volunteers were obtained, although the offer caused some tension with unions and discontent among employees.

While Leason's monitored the scheme in terms of numbers reduction, they did not obtain detailed statistical analyses of the take-up profile. The personnel department had difficulty in dealing effectively with all the implications of the introduction and running of the schemes, also suffering staff reduction themselves. Reallocation of staff duties proved significantly easier in respect of shopfloor jobs than at management level, where it became necessary to delay some early retirements in

9

order to make replacement arrangements. No particular follow-up had been planned in respect of those who had retired, although management later felt that it might be beneficial. The views of those who had retired early had subsequently been voiced by the unions, and the remaining work force were felt to be somewhat discontented at the procedures employed.

Activity brief

1 Evaluate the benefits of early retirement as a human resource management strategy.
2 Obtain copies of your organization's pension scheme booklet or member handbook and any material relating to special early retirement schemes which have been utilized. Assess the standard provisions for early retirement under differing circumstances and consider special scheme options which have been available, comparing the benefits offered to those in the two case organizations.
3 Compare the implementation process in the two companies and discuss the likely impact on employees.
4 Draw up a 'code of good practice' in respect of the implementation of an early retirement scheme as part of a redundancy programme, assessing the appropriate procedures to follow.
5 Consider the relevance of early retirement in the future, evaluating the pressure for changes in retirement policy.

Recommended reading

ATKINSON, J. *Early Retirement*, Brighton, Institute of Manpower Studies, 1985.
BEEHR, T. A., 'The process of retirement: a review and recommendations for future investigation', *Personnel Psychology*, 39, 1986, pp. 31–55.
EUROPEAN INDUSTRIAL RELATIONS REVIEW, 'Trends in voluntary early retirement', *European Industrial Relations Review*, 135, 1985, pp. 17–19.
EUROPEAN INDUSTRIAL RELATIONS REVIEW, 'Early retirement: an international comparison', *European Industrial Relations Review*, 145, 1985, pp. 20–3.
INCOMES DATA SERVICES, *Early Retirement*, Study 337, 1985.
INDUSTRIAL RELATIONS REVIEW AND REPORT, 'Redundancy and early retirement – pension terms and conditions', *Industrial Relations Review and Report*, 467, 1990, pp. 7–14.
MCGOLDRICK, A. E., and COOPER, C. L., *Early Retirement*, Aldershot, Gower, 1989.

PERSONNEL TODAY, 'It's time to prove your worth', *Personnel Today*, 19 March 1991, pp. 21–8.

In addition readers should consult publications produced by ABI (Association of British Insurers).

Appendix 9.1 Early retirement terms

Deferred pension benefits

After two years of pensionable service a member of an occupational pension scheme is entitled to a deferred pension payable at normal retirement age for the scheme. This is based on pensionable salary on leaving, increased by the retail price index up to 5 per cent per year up to normal retirement age from 1 January 1985.

As an alternative, the scheme must offer the option of a transfer payment to another scheme or, for example, as the basis of a personal pension. The transfer value will be calculated by the scheme actuaries.

Accrued pension with actuarial reduction

The scheme may offer an immediate pension based on current pensionable service. This will be calculated on the basis of actual years with the pension scheme, but it may be actuarially reduced to take account of the longer payment period. Normally, the earlier an employee retires the more serious the pension reduction incurred. A minimum age will normally be established within the scheme for when a member becomes eligible for benefits. Reduction factors may vary according to age or retirement circumstances. Unreduced pensions have often been offered to those close to normal retirement age in recent years, or according to resource planning requirements at the time. Different actuarial reduction factors have sometimes been applied to men and women within schemes, to take account of differing retirement ages and assumptions. Judgements by the European Court of Justice, in particular *Barber v. Guardian Royal Exchange Assurance Group*, brought such practices into question.

Accrued pension

In recent years more schemes have introduced more favourable treatment to permit or encourage early retirement. Schemes may offer an unreduced pension or accrued pension, based upon current pensionable salary and actual years of pension scheme membership, from the time of early retirement. While this can be an expensive alternative, it may be seen as more effective support in respect of enforced redundancies among older employees or as a way of obtaining volunteers. It may be offered on the basis of a minimum age or to those within a set period before normal retirement age; likewise a service criterion may be incorporated, when it can be interpreted as a reward for long-service employees.

Enhanced pension

An immediate pension may be offered which not only relates to actual years of pensionable service but also includes unearned credit for some or all of the remaining years up to normal retirement age. The generosity of the offer again may vary, for example on the basis of age or pensionable service. Organizations may utilize this mechanism to increase the attraction of early retirement for all or differing categories of employees, according to their human resource strategies.

Severance payment

When early retirement is treated as a redundancy a severance payment may also be offered by the organization, in addition to pension benefits. This should be distinguished from the option of commuting pension for a tax-free lump sum at retirement which exists within many schemes.

Temporary or bridging pension

Since eligibility for the state retirement pension does not arise until the age of sixty-five years for men and sixty for women, this can prove an obstacle to early retirement. Under some early retirement arrangements there has been provision for paying a temporary pension from the time of retirement or from a fixed age. The temporary pension might be paid until state pension age or the normal retirement age, and is frequently a fixed amount or a proportion of the single person's state pension. It has also been used in some schemes which operate a lower norm generally than the state age. It has been employed, for example, in some schemes which have equalized benefits at an age lower than sixty-five years or in which the age for male members has been reduced. There are now questions as to whether this is discriminatory, if benefits are not made available to both men and women on the same basis.

Life assurance

According to Inland Revenue regulations, it is permissible to continue death-in-service benefits up to normal retirement age for employees who are made redundant.

II
Employee Development

Case 10

Employee development at Barratt

Rosemary Harrison

The case illustrates many important points about human resource development (HRD). (In the text, following Barratt practice, the terms 'employee development' or, occasionally, 'training and development' are used in preference to HRD.) These points are:

- The need, if human resource development is to make a real contribution to organizational success and to 'the bottom line', for HRD goals and strategy to be an integrated part of the wider human resource strategy, serving human resource strategic objectives, and aligned with business goals.
- The need for the HRD manager to 'know the business' if he/she is to play an effective part in strategic decision-making and implementation.
- The need for informed, proactive, collaborative relationships between the HRD manager and the key parties in the organization, and for him/her to have a high level not only of technical expertise but also of analytical, political and interpersonal skills.
- The value of continually reviewing what is going on in employee development at various levels of the business; and the wisdom of never failing to question what is done, of always evaluating activities and outcomes, and of producing feasible, well costed alternatives when changes seem indicated.

The case also offers a fascinating insight into the many ways in which 'luck' or 'fate' can be seized and used to advantage by the expert human resource development manager.

Background to the case

Barratt Developments plc, an international house-building and construction firm with its headquarters in the north-east of England, decided in 1989 that it needed to start investing more heavily in the development of its work force. The trigger to this interest was its rapid growth as a company, and hence the importance that some in the company began to attach to securing and retaining high-calibre managers and other key staff. Others were influenced by comparisons with other firms: there was a feeling that 'if they do it, so should Barratt'.

The situation

A new position of Group Training Manager was therefore established, and Roy Hugman, an experienced personnel practitioner, was appointed to the post in January 1990. The task outlined to him was to identify the issues, define the needs and formulate a long-term corporate strategy to improve the strength of the contribution from the company's employees at all levels. Thereafter he was to implement and manage systems and programmes to achieve that aim. Behind these tasks lay the overall mission of developing a high-quality, flexible, committed work force which would stay with the company and enable it to maintain its leading position.

The initial strategy

Barratt had no specialist personnel/human resource function, nor did it intend that one should be set up – any form of bureaucracy was alien to the company's culture, and the various personnel activities were carried out by line managers according to informal custom and practice.

Realizing the need for a human resource strategy to be established before anything meaningful could be accomplished in the area of employee development, Hugman convinced the board that his first step must be to analyse the state of the work force. He needed to carry out an assessment of its strengths, weaknesses and potential; its productivity and performance levels; turnover, absenteeism and retention rates; how and from where it was recruited; how skills and knowledge were acquired; what kind of rewards and incentives were offered; what were the prevailing patterns of industrial relations, and what was the overall culture and structure of the company. From this information he could then recommend to the board the human resource goals and strategy, and the strategy for employee development, that would best serve business needs at corporate, unit and operational levels.

He spent his first five or six months on these tasks. His first objective was to establish strong links quickly with key directors of the company who were already aware of the importance of good human resource management and development. These directors would form a supportive, powerful group and were politically essential if employee development was to obtain the company's real commitment. Hugman was helped here by being able to operate freely, without the constraints of any existing personnel or training function.

He therefore began to visit directors and other personnel in the company's seventeen subsidiaries in Britain, spending on average a day a week out of his office for the purpose. His aim was not only to identify human resource issues and needs, and to promote collaborative relationships, but also to establish a proactive 'presence' in the company. He saw the importance of creating the image as well as the reality of a proactive, concerned and informed function, in touch with the real needs of the company at every level and committed to responding to them quickly and in relevant ways.

At the end of his first month, in January 1990, keeping up the momentum, and practising a style of interaction with key parties in the business that he was to follow consistently thereafter, Hugman presented a progress report to the board of directors summarizing his first impressions of the main human resource issues and employee development needs at Barratt, and outlining an initial strategy for their approval. The title page is reproduced below:

Group Training

A company-wide strategy to develop personal excellence and organizational teamwork, to create and then confidently meet the challenges of the nineties and beyond.

QUALITY PEOPLE TO IMPROVE A QUALITY COMPANY

This lead-in was astute: in effect it comprised both an employment development mission statement for Barratt, and an outline of goals and strategy for the function. As we shall see later, the imprint 'Quality people to improve a quality company' was to prove particularly well chosen. At this stage, together with the reference to future challenges, it was calculated to make an impact on those who were responsible for the running of an international organization which was a leader in the field but must always be alert to the need to retain its competitive edge through maximizing its key assets, notably its work force.

The paper was brief, eight pages, with short, punchy, fact-filled paragraphs and a wide-spaced layout that made for immediate impact. Its introduction summarized its content lucidly, aroused interest, emphasized that costs would be involved if benefits were to be achieved, and finally gave assurances of the relevance and feasibility of the subsequent proposals:

> The purpose of this paper is to seek agreement about the company's approach to training and employee development through the nineties.
>
> An integrated approach focusing on manpower planning and employee development; training and education; and careers and education liaison is outlined. This is capable, with commitment, of engendering an 'excellence' culture through personal development, getting the best from managers and their people and also aiding retention and growth.
>
> Considerable work needs to be done and the company will have to invest sustained time, budget and other resources. The way forward, though, is inherently clear with requirements for each level of the company.

This was followed by an analysis of the external labour market and training situation; the company's training situation; and Hugman's initial perceptions of the key human resource issues facing the company. A strategy for employee development was outlined, aimed at achieving three or four objectives. The report ended with recommendations for action to obtain the data necessary in order to produce a more detailed strategy. A diagram summarized the essence of the report and identified the processes that were to be used in order to ensure the success of the group training function – consultation, review, collaboration, planning with regions and subsidiaries, and direct assistance wherever it was needed.

Hugman's recommended infrastructure for the function was particularly interesting and his prescription for the company's approach to employee development has universal validity:

> The Company's approach should emphasize that training and education is:
>
> - Driven by the needs of the business
> - Planned and administered as close to the source of need as possible
> - Of the best possible quality
> - Easily accessible to . . . people at all levels and encourages people to continuously assess their own strengths and weaknesses
> - Actively promoted by managers at all levels

In February the main board approved the company-wide strategy for employee development proposed in the January paper, and agreed to the setting up of three working parties, each to be led by a director of a subsidiary. Their brief was to produce a report for the main board in May which would contain:

- An analysis of the strengths, weaknesses, opportunities and threats facing employee development in the company.
- Recommendations on three major issues that had emerged in Hugman's initial 'audit' of human resources; each working party concentrated on one of these:

    1   An appropriate infrastructure which would ensure systematic employee development throughout the company.
    2   The introduction of personal development reviews (annual appraisal) in the company.
    3   Corporate (i.e. company-wide) training programmes for the forthcoming year.

The collaborative report, with a brief introduction by Hugman, contained focused, practical, clearly costed recommendations relating to each of the three headings. It was put before the board in May, and was approved. Hugman then began to prepare all the systems, procedures and documentation needed to ensure that plans could be activated. He was clear about the need for brevity, clarity and the avoidance of any appearance of bureaucracy in all he did, and this was reflected in the size of the training function: himself and his secretary, aided by one temporary employee to help set up a computerized database for his operations.

The employee development database

In parallel with the work he had been doing on producing an employee development strategy, policies and plans, Hugman was also establishing a database on Barratt's work force in Britain. This was derived from questionnaires sent, through their senior executives, to all 2,000 personnel across the company's seventeen UK subsidiaries. The activity, again, reinforced the image of an active training department working to produce outcomes that responded to individual and company needs.

The aim (which was realized) was that by the end of his first year the database would be computerized and the first of a series of 'profiles' would be drawn up on the skills, performance and productivity levels, turnover, absenteeism and length of service rates, age and salary levels, etc. of each occupational group in the company.

The collaborative processes

When someone is in the early days of taking up a new position and creating a new function, they have to absorb a mass of data and become familiar with the primary culture of their organization – the set of attitudes, beliefs and typical ways of behaving that explain 'the way we do things here'. In his first round of visits to the seventeen subsidiaries Hugman gathered a wide range of information, and impressions of attitudes to and perceptions of employee development in the company, as well as an increasing understanding of the main human resource issues which were of concern in the business units. By the time he had reached the stage of repeat visits he found he was getting feedback on ideas and suggestions he had implanted earlier and an interchange of ideas on appropriate courses of action.

Although the process of 'walking and talking the job' was clearly paying dividends, it was not always easy to carry it out. In reality it is quite difficult for a new manager, in a function not yet really understood in the company at unit level, to create a relationship where it is normal practice to 'drop in' on the managing director of a subsidiary. So Hugman often used visits which were ostensibly for other purposes as an occasion also to see MDs and discuss human resource issues with them – particularly their views about employee development needs. Thus, gradually, his appearance about once a month in the MD's office of one or other of the subsidiaries became the 'norm', and so a new culture surrounding training and development began to build up in the company.

Summary: January to May 1990

By the end of May 1990 Hugman had:

- A great deal of data on the major human resource issues and, within those, on the employee development needs and problems facing the company at corporate and at business unit level.

- Reports and action plans from each of the three working parties which he had presented to the board, obtaining their approval of his proposed human resource goals and strategy.
- The foundations of a comprehensive and up-to-date database covering all the company's British work force, with the aim of producing detailed profiles related to each occupational group.
- A detailed employee development strategy which, together with proposals relating to a wider human resource strategy, was due to be presented to the annual managing directors' conference in October.

The four-day conference was to be held at Cannes. Hugman intended to launch there the package of training and development initiatives for the company that he had been putting together during the summer.

'Forward through quality'

During June 1990 two different employee development initiatives began to come together: Hugman's employee development strategy and plans, and a projected Total Quality Management programme which it was intended a firm of consultants should install across the company. Late in June, at a one-day board meeting, the two initiatives were discussed, and it was then that the directors and Hugman realized that, rather than continue to push forward on two separate fronts, the initiatives should be integrated within an overall employee development strategy whose mission would be to achieve total quality through people. In this way, employee development strategy and plans would have a meaningful context instead of perhaps appearing to rest on what Hugman called 'a generalized act of faith'.

Two weeks later, early in July, at a main board of directors meeting in Liverpool, Hugman made a presentation to the main board about this strategy (its title page is reproduced below).

An update on Group Training Strategy

January–June 1990

Two initiatives now linked to form one integrated strategy

FORWARD THROUGH QUALITY

The plan stated in clear terms the company's mission:

> The aim of Barratt Developments plc is to exceed customer expectations, by promoting and continuously improving standards beyond those of our competitors, through excellence in all our work, products and services.

Then came employee development strategic objectives:

> By linking the strategy for employee development with the business aim, to achieve competitive advantage through total quality.

We are now embarking on one integrated, understandable and clearly visible thrust for all Barratt people.

The strategy was to be achieved by:

- Building an effective infrastructure for employee development.
- Monitoring and reviewing work performance and identifying employee development needs.
- Organizing company-wide training and development initiatives to meet key corporate training needs.
- Facilitating Total Quality Management through appropriate forms of employee development.

The policies that had by now been established relating to these four strategic objectives for employee development were outlined, including information on costs and time scales.

The presentation was a success, and it was agreed that Hugman would do another at the directors' conference at Cannes in October, presenting the guidelines for training and employee development in the company, and launching all the initiatives that were now in their final stages of preparation.

That preparation was meticulous, and included a video explaining the Total Quality Management programme, and all the supporting paperwork – forms, manuals, information packs, and so on – for the various employee development initiatives (e.g. personal reviews and training courses to support the system; the introduction of specific employee development responsibilities into management jobs at unit level, and a directors' programme at Durham University Business School). Whilst Hugman was in Cannes, carrying out an extremely successful presentation which resulted in directors' support for the strategy, specific policies and operational plans, his secretary was preparing for every subsidiary a package of materials to progress each element of the overall programme, ready for the managing directors of those subsidiaries on their return.

October 1990: the recession bites

And then fate intervened. For some time it had been evident that the country, and the construction industry in particular, were moving into recession. What had not been clear was just how serious and long-lasting that recession was to be. During the Cannes conference the latest set of financial data was studied by the main board. Immediately word went out to the subsidiaries to embark upon a drive for greater efficiency, with the elimination of any unnecessary expenditure.

It is a familiar and threatening scenario for a training function, and in an industry not noted for high investment in employee development, and in a company where the specialist function was so new, it could have been a death knell. However, Hugman had prepared his ground well: he had already looked hard at his budget to see where, if necessary, cut-backs could be made. As soon as he returned from Cannes he wrote to his director with a detailed plan, involving some programmes being put on ice, others trimmed, and the introduction of various employee development systems (like personal reviews) being postponed. The aim was to cut costs in tactical areas whilst preserving the essential strategic thrust of employee development intact and maintaining the board's commitment to it. It was a wise proactive move. Hugman argued that what mattered, at this stage, was that the company should keep its custodianship of employee development, remaining committed to the principles behind the specific initiatives that had been agreed at Cannes, even if action on those initiatives had to be deferred for the time being.

November 1990: the cancellation of the sales marketing training programme

At this point, once more, fate intervened, although, on closer analysis, not so much fate as the happy result of some long-standing and careful work by Hugman as he went the rounds of the subsidiaries uncovering various important but often neglected employee development issues.

For some time he had been concerned about what was happening to sales training. On his arrival in January 1990 a training programme, run by external providers, had been running for a year. A successful sales force was, of course, crucial to the company, and so the programme had a very high profile. It consisted of sixty-seven training days, was broad in its focus, generalized in its content, ran in every region, and had an up-front cost of £110,000. It was evaluated, in a fashion, twice a year, with the external providers taking the lead in the process – not surprisingly, given that until Hugman arrived there was no training specialist at Barratt who could direct or carry out such an activity. A good relationship existed between the senior executive who had responsibility for the programme and the external providers who designed and ran it, and both parties were satisfied that the results were good.

By May 1990, when his second round of visits to subsidiaries was under way, Hugman was becoming increasingly concerned at some of the views being expressed to him about the sales training programme. In August 1991 one of the key external people involved in running the programme left, as did the senior executive within Barratt who had worked most closely with him in organizing the programme. When, after the October directors' conference and the efficiency drive that followed, Hugman agreed with the company not to renew the contract for the sales training programme until he had done a comprehensive evaluation of its results, there was little opposition. The contract, up for review in December, was not renewed, and all formal sales training was suspended. This immediately 'saved' Barratt £110,000 and gave Hugman the time he needed to take stock.

November 1990 to May 1991: evaluation of sales training

The review took in not only the group sales training programme but also sales training activities and needs throughout the whole of the company. This proved a beneficial activity from another viewpoint – it took Hugman legitimately out and about in the subsidiaries again, where, whilst looking at a specific and major area of training need in a consultative way, he could also talk to MDs on broader human resource management and development issues.

In his evaluation of the sales training programme, feedback sheets received from past and present participants, analysis of views of the programme obtained during his visits to subsidiaries, and an examination of other data began to yield a detailed appreciation of the strengths, weaknesses and outcomes of the training, and of the true scale of its cost. Hidden costs, in fact, were shown to total more than twice the apparent costs, bringing the overall figure to around £230,000–£240,000. The indirect costs related to factors like:

- Internal administration and clerical employment costs involved in running the programme.
- Material and equipment costs.
- Accommodation and running costs.
- Lost production time.
- Lost opportunity costs.
- Replacement costs for trainees.
- Supervision time by senior people both in relation to temporary replacements and to trainees back on the job and doing projects and other learning activities.

Hugman also discovered that the training programme only skimmed the surface of learning activities in the subsidiaries: most of the real 'training' was going on through a process of informal learning from peers and superiors; reviews from trainees and their managers showed very clearly that the need was for that process to be carried out in some formalized, effective and efficient way rather than the major thrust being to send people away on external courses. Training, it was clear, had to be closely related to the needs of the job and to the systems and procedures of the company. It also had to be timely, and designed in ways that would enable regular assessments of progress to be made and to be fed back to trainees and their managers. There must also be effective transfer of learning to the job, with the ability to measure consequent impact on job performance.

May 1991: the new sales training policy

By mid-1991, in the midst of much other activity related to employee development and human resource strategy at Barratt, Hugman had formulated what he believed to be an appropriate alternative sales training policy: a flexible learning scheme, fully job and company-related, rigorous and assessable. The scheme would comprise structured texts, audios and videos, to be produced by a consultancy firm working closely with key personnel in the company; workplace instruction; and some training courses, but only of a kind, and at a time, when they would be fully integrated with the rest of the programme and would respond to real and measurable training needs. His recommendations also covered recruitment policy and its integration with training and development policy, together with analysis of the kinds of terms and conditions of service that would be most likely to motivate and adequately reward the sales force. Account was also taken of the kind of supervision needed if new learning was to be successfully integrated into job performance. Finally, he recommended a proper training infrastructure, comprising on-the-job sales trainers, trained sales managers, and a new Group Sales Training Co-ordinator position.

Hugman produced a detailed set of figures showing the breakdown of costs of the present programme (£240,000) and of the alternative flexible scheme he was recommending. His figures included the cost of establishing a new Group Sales Training Co-ordinator position and making an early appointment to it. In all, these new costs totalled £174,000. He also produced data relating to practice elsewhere, in companies that were similar in important respects to Barratt and who were carrying out flexible learning schemes. He had looked with particular interest at the schemes of three building societies which, like Barratt, had a decentralized structure, and which were also driven by a strong customer orientation and commitment to high quality.

Finally, in May 1991, Hugman made a presentation to the main board. It comprised a concise evaluation of the external sales marketing training programme; a comprehensive breakdown of costs related to that programme and to its outcomes; and a fully costed alternative scheme that included an analysis of the wider human resource issues that lay behind sales training and a set of recommendations related to that analysis, together with comparative data collected from other companies.

The data were relevant, meaningful and impressive. They survived the most rigorous questioning and finally won Hugman the support of even the (initially) least convinced of the board's members. They approved the budget he requested, £174,000, to which he was able to add £74,000 of funding obtained under the government's Option 5 Business Growth Training Programme, for 'innovative solutions to training problems', another impressive achievement in the board's eyes; they agreed to the establishment of the new Group Sales Training Co-ordinator position, and they committed themselves to supporting the whole initiative for two to three years in the first instance, to ensure that it could be properly designed, installed, piloted and evaluated.

The time scale laid down was for the training co-ordinator to be recruited immediately, together with relevant administrative support; for detailed functional analysis of sales positions to begin in July; for the various learning packages to be designed thereafter, with an anticipated finishing time of late 1992; and for the training of sales trainers and sales managers to begin in the autumn. By mid-1992 the new flexible learning scheme for the sales force should be ready to be introduced into the units.

By then over a year would have passed without formal sales training in the company. However, given the information produced by Hugman's evaluation, that seemed an affordable cost. On the other hand, for far less than the cost of running that training, an entire new strategy would have been produced, with the real commitment and support of top and business unit-level personnel, supplemented by action related to those wider human resource policies and systems that must themselves be changed if the expected improved performance and motivation was to be reinforced and sustained.

May 1991: employee development at Barratt

By May 1991 recession was still biting. On the 'Forward through quality' front, things were slowly beginning to move again after the restraints of October 1990. One of the most significant advances was to introduce for the first time in Barratt's history a 'manpower and training plan' section within the 'business plan pack' which all the subsidiaries' directors have to complete and send back to headquarters before the start of each budget year (July). The data they had to supply on a pro-forma was very simple: a projection of the main staffing issues and needs, with a particular focus on anticipated training needs, in each occupational category. But this documentation meant that by the end of June Hugman would have similar data from every subsidiary, thus giving him a business unit database containing comparable information across all the subsidiaries.

Personal reviews, too, were due to be launched. They would operate on a self-appraisal basis, and as their aim was to achieve meaningful discussion of work performance, and joint target setting and work planning between managers and individuals, most of their content would remain in the hands of those two parties only. However, there was one part of each form that was to be sent to Hugman: an agreement on every individual's training needs, and that individual's statement of career aspirations. Soon, therefore, Hugman would have, side-by-side with his business unit database, an individualized database giving him the ability to identify common employee development needs across various groups as well as keeping track of each individual's progress.

Of other key initiatives, the directors' programme was set to start at Durham University Business School in September 1991, although the Total Quality programme was to remain on ice until the new employee development strategy as a whole had begun to take root and results had become evident in terms not only of improved performance but also, perhaps even more important, of changed attitudes and culture.

The year and a half following Hugman's appointment had thus seen the building up of a proactive employee development function and culture in a company where, apart from 'a generalized act of faith', nothing, early in January 1990, could be taken for granted. In an industry notoriously vulnerable to major adverse movements in the economy, and very prone, at such times, to cut back on training and development as an immediate survival tactic, 'Forward through quality' was a mission becoming linked in people's minds with the need for a systematic, business-driven approach to employee development, and a commitment to carrying it out not simply or mainly through the small specialist function but through the daily activities of supervisors, managers and their people in all the seventeen Barratt subsidiaries. Injecting employee development into the bloodstream of a company is rarely easy, but at Barratt the transfusion seemed to be working: a belief was taking root that employee development was essential, not only to survival but also to continuous healthy growth at all levels

10

of the company. How far that belief holds in an organization that will always, like the sector to which it belongs, be prone to sudden cut-backs whenever recession bites, remains to be seen; but whatever the future may hold, the story of that year and a half contains invaluable lessons for any newly appointed training manager.

Activity brief

1 Having absorbed the information in the case, what advice would you give someone setting up an employee development function in a company for the first time:

   (a) Where there is already a specialist personnel management function?

   (b) Where there is no specialist personnel management function?

2 Design a 'Manpower and Training Plan' form and accompanying instructions for directors of Barratt subsidiaries to fill in. The forms, when collated, should enable the group training manager to produce annual staffing plans and training plans for each subsidiary, and an integrated staffing and training plan for the company as a whole.

To help you in this task, the following are the categories of employee at subsidiary level in Barratt:

Office-based

Directors
Managers
Accountants
Other administrative functions
Clerical
Secretarial
Sales/Marketing
Sales/Management
Various construction workers
Architects/designers/surveyors
Other technical functions
Technicians

Development-based

Field supervisory sales staff
Sales negotiators
Contract/area managers
Site agents/managers
Foremen/women
Trades
Other manual workers
Technical construction workers

Trainees

Apprentices
Technical trainees
Business trainees

3 Taking a particular organization with which you are familiar, produce goals, strategy and an action plan for yourself covering the next year to eighteen months which should ensure that you achieve and retain support at corporate and unit levels for employee development in the face of sceptical managers and/or the genuine need for major cut-backs because of recession or other external or internal pressures.

4   In your opinion, what are the key factors that Roy Hugman should take into account to ensure that his policy for flexible training is implemented effectively during a recession?

Recommended reading

COOPERS & LYBRAND ASSOCIATES, *A Challenge to Complacency: Changing Attitudes to Training*, a report to the Manpower Services Commission and the National Economic Development Office, Sheffield, Manpower Services Commission, 1985.

FOMBRUN, C., *et al.*, *Strategic Human Resource Management*, Chichester, Wiley, 1984.

HARRISON, R., *Training and Development*, London, IPM, 1989.

HARRISON, R., *Developing Human Resources for Productivity*, Geneva, International Labour Office, 1992.

HENDRY, C., *et al.*, 'The forces that trigger training', *Personnel Management*, December 1988.

LEICESTER, C. 'The key role of the line manager in employee development', *Personnel Management*, March 1989.

SPARROW, P., and PETTIGREW, A., 'How Halford's put its HRM into top gear', *Personnel Management*, June 1988.

WEBSTER, B., 'Beyond the mechanics of HRD', *Personnel Management*, March 1990.

Acknowledgements

This case was produced with the generous help of Roy Hugman, then Group Training Manager of Barratt Developments plc, with whom I had many long and fruitful discussions, and who supplied me with a great deal of valuable written data. I must also acknowledge my thanks to the company, who have allowed me to have the case published with no editing of my original draft beyond the correction of a few minor factual errors.

Case 11

Managing the training and development process in a small company: William Beckett & Co. (Plastics) Ltd

Paul Banfield

This case study is concerned primarily but not exclusively with the relationship between the organizational and managerial development experienced by William Beckett's over a three-year period and the contribution that training made to the process. Central to this relationship is the belief that training, of the appropriate kind and degree, can be a powerful agent of change, facilitating and enabling a company's desire to extend and expand its manufacturing capacity and ultimately its profitability.

Background to the case

William Beckett & Co. (Plastics) Ltd employ approximately forty-seven people and are situated in a newly built factory on the Tinsley Industrial Park, Sheffield. The company was formed six years ago as a result of a merger between two independent companies. One was run by David Whittington, an engineer who had set up his own manufacturing business, and the other by William Beckett, who had managed his own marketing venture and had used David's company to manufacture for him. If David provided the technical know-how, William, who came from a sales background, contributed a vision and entrepreneurial flair which quickly came to define the managerial style of the newly formed company.

The two merged in 1985, and, after operating initially from Barnsley, moved to Sheffield in 1986, with William Beckett as managing director and David Whittington as works director and shareholder. The company grew rapidly in product range, market penetration and employees, and currently has a turnover of £2 million. It has recently invested heavily in new technology and in its strategic planning capacity, as well as embarking on a major commitment to market a new product range in Europe.

116

The situation: a problem of growth

William Beckett realized in 1988 that growth was creating problems for the management of the company – problems that were a consequence of its recent success but which could, if not addressed, undermine the company's long-term prosperity:

- Rapid expansion of staff had left little or no time for identifying longer-term training needs and often meant that low performance and quality standards were becoming more serious and costly.
- The two original senior managers were under sustained and growing pressure to control a range of production and administrative operations, to the point where both were overloaded. This led to a feeling that all they were able to do was play a 'fire-fighting' role, simply maintaining the necessary level of output to meet current orders and priorities.
- Because the managers were under intense pressure to 'keep the thing going' there was little, if any, opportunity to review systematically the performance and appropriateness of job holders and the existing job structures. In other words, questions such as 'Are staff performing in the way we expect them to?' and 'Do the jobs they are doing need changing to reflect new and different requirements?' were not being asked. As a consequence, what might be described as 'drift' in working practices, attitudes and expectations occurred over a period of time.

The company's response: bringing in consultants

The first expression of management's concern that more time needed to be given to improving the 'people' side of the business came in spring 1988, when it successfully applied for a grant from the Manpower Services Commission – then the central government agency providing vocational, educational and business training programmes – to carry out a training needs analysis. The analysis was carried out by a team of external consultants who recommended a series of training programmes to address the key issues of team building and management development.

On the basis of these proposals, Sheffield Business School organized a series of half-day workshops for management, foremen/women and most of the company's administrative staff. The general feeling of those who attended the workshops was that they had been extremely useful and enlightening. Training needs for production workers were also identified, and met through courses organized by the Plastics Processing Industry Training Board at Telford, now operating as a privatized training body for the plastics industry.

A consequence of Sheffield Business School's work with the company's management and administrative staff was the first systematic attempt to identify individual training needs. This led to the works director and his newly appointed production manager enrolling on management courses at local colleges and to the accounts clerk training to become a qualified accountancy technician. All three commitments were part-time and involved regular absence from work of one day per week for one or two years. A newly appointed production clerk also benefited from the local chamber of commerce's provision of training opportunities.

As a result of these initiatives the company was invited to apply for a Business Growth Training award (BGT), which offered sixty days of subsidized consultancy. The award allowed the company to consolidate and extend its training commitment to both office and production staff. Whilst it seemed an attractive way of improving the competences of both managerial and other employees, it was not without its difficulties. Hindsight made them clear to all concerned, but at the time they were by no means obvious.

The underlying concept of BGT was that company growth and improved performance were likely to be effective in the long term only if based on a qualitative improvement in the capacity of managerial and employee resources. Put another way, sustained growth was unlikely in the absence of such facilitating mechanisms.

The major, but not exclusive, inputs through the BGT programme were made by four academics who were also experienced consultants in their own right. Each had a particular expertise in the areas of strategic planning, financial information systems, human resource management and marketing. The idea was that an overall assessment of the company's financial and strategic position should first be made, followed by work on its information systems. Once these tasks had been completed, a marketing survey would be undertaken to support the planned movement into Europe. The final stage would involve an analysis of the human resource implications of the company's current operations and medium-term plans. Arising out of this, organizational, sectional and individual training needs would be identified and a range of training and developmental responses initiated.

The pressure on individual managers, particularly the managing director, to cope with their own training and at the same time to continue to manage the business, whilst the consultants were trying to highlight deficiencies in financial information systems and the interpretation of data, became acute. Sensitivity to what was considered at times to be misunderstanding of the company's trading position and prospects increased. There was also a feeling, on the part of at least one of the consultants, that their advice and suggestions were not always appreciated.

Despite genuine efforts on both sides to accommodate these pressures and resolve differing perceptions, relations deteriorated to the point where the consultants and management agreed that that part of the BGT programme should come to a halt and the phase involving human resource management and development should be initiated. Nonetheless, this initial work on strategic planning, marketing and information systems not only created the basis of more effective internal operating systems but succeeded in imposing a longer time perspective and a strategic vision on to the existing and less systematic approach to management. As a direct result of phases one and two of the BGT programme the company successfully applied to the European Community for a grant to fund new investment in machinery, product development and new staff, all of which was in support of the drive to exploit the European market.

Up to this point, many of the changes that had taken place in the management of the company had had little obvious impact on either administration or production. They had been concentrated rather on improving information systems and on the abilities and strategic thinking of senior managers. Now was the time to identify and implement the changes within the company, directly affecting what was done, how and by whom, and to support these changes with focused training for an increasing number of Beckett's employees, further supported by a clear policy and implementation strategies.

Diagnosing the problem and identifying strategies for change

The first priority was identified as the organization and control of the administration department, consisting of: an accounts clerk, a sales administrator, a sales representative, a production clerk, an office junior/receptionist and a part-time wages clerk. These staff occupied the office adjacent to the managing director and were nominally under his general direction. However, his involvement in marketing, new product development and production left little time for any systematic review of the way the office was operating.

A report submitted by the human resource development (HRD) consultant highlighted a number of important issues. Among these were:

- Lack of flexibility.
- Jobs which had evolved in ways to suit the 'comfort zones' of their occupants.
- Breakdown in personal relations to the point where co-ordination and communications were compromised.
- Lack of clarity in job responsibilities.
- Lack of a sense of teamwork and shared responsibility.
- More of an individual than a company perspective on work.

It was clear that training could not precede action to address these problems. Therefore action initially took the form of a thorough analysis by management of the changes that needed to be made to bring the contribution of the office in line with the existing and future requirements of the company. This led to a general appraisal of individual abilities, potential and functional contributions. Three of the six office staff caused particular concern.

The office junior, who had been taken on at seventeen, was now twenty. Whilst well liked and very accommodating, she had shown little sign of developing into anything other than what she already was. At the same time as the company was moving towards higher standards of performance and additional skill requirements, this employee was thought to have little or no potential.

The accounts clerk was in a different situation as far as technical competence and contribution were concerned. The job was important to the effective functioning of the company, she was good at it, albeit in terms defined by herself, but she was unco-operative, rather moody and inflexible. An additional factor affecting her appraisal was that she had recently started a year-long course which would qualify her as an accounts technician.

The sales representative, a personal friend of the managing director, was in his mid-forties and had worked for the company for two years. His problem was that, whilst he had been employed as a sales representative, he had in fact redefined his job as that of internal sales administrator. Quite simply, he himself recognized that he was not an effective sales person, but he did have considerable experience of the company's products and customers and, given the right support and direction, had an important contribution to make.

Of the three other staff, none represented significant problems; all were capable and efficient, but there were areas where certain changes in job responsibilities were needed.

In the light of this situation, management had to decide what action to take. Getting the office 'right' was the first priority. Once that had been achieved and training put in place to facilitate the changes, attention could be given to assessing the further training needs of the production department. Working through the options led to a collective decision on the part of the management team to resolve the problems through several interlinked actions which had short and long-term implications for the company's sales effort and administrative support functions.

Developing a company training policy

In addition to working closely with management in this difficult period, the HRD consultant was also involved in the preparation of a comprehensive and company-wide training policy. Central to this was agreement on a company 'mission statement' and, deriving from it, a formal written commitment to an on-going process of training and development in line with the company's operational and strategic needs.

A training matrix was then designed which allowed management to represent all the major training decisions on one three-dimensional diagram. This matrix contained details of the type of training, the participants, providers, location, time scale and resource implications and would represent the company's annual training plan. To supplement current information on training activities, a historical database was formed by designing and distributing a simple record form which required all employees to provide details of previous training activities and attainments at Beckett's and in previous employment.

Within a six-week period all the company's employees went through a development appraisal interview with one of the three senior managers and, on the basis of this, individual training needs were identified. At the same time, training priorities were being established and costings prepared.

Currently, the three production foremen have also been given the responsibility for analysing deficiencies in the competences of the plastics processing technicians and machine setters, against the National Lead Body's performance standards and with a clear remit from the production manager, Peter Stocks, to provide learning opportunities for these skilled workers to bring them up to the required standards. The foremen themselves were also committed to the improvement of their own supervisory skills through attendance at college-based courses in supervisory management. The intention was to extend this analysis and identification of training needs to all employees and to make recommendations for training on an annual and rolling basis.

Following these training initiatives, the company intends to apply for two national awards in 1992, based on its on-going investment in people and to gain formal recognition that will strengthen its reputation in the market. The experience of the past three years, despite difficulties and uncertainties, is now leading to real and prolonged improvement in staff capacity, flexibility and, above all, contribution. Much still remains to be done but a solid foundation has been established.

The secret, if there is one, of this company's ability to make such progress, and to acquire the capacity to go on planning and implementing its own training programmes, is not to be found solely in the context of training. Rather, the answer lies in the professionalism of its management and the recognition that only through their own learning and development would they be able to manage and develop the rest of their employees more effectively. Many others contributed, but without the will and achievement of those who manage at Beckett's little of lasting value would have resulted.

Activity brief

1 The managing director felt strongly that the training and development undertaken by senior management were an important foundation from which to extend these opportunities to the rest of the work force.

   (a) What is the relationship between improving the capacity of management and the success of broader training objectives?
   (b) What particular skills might management at Beckett's have acquired to support their long-term commitment to improve the skills and competences of all their staff?

2 What does the case tell us about the relationship between successfully managing a business and managing training?

3 Account for the difficulties in relations between certain of the external consultants and the managing director. What particular skills do training consultants need to increase the chances of success?

4 During the review of the organization and staffing of the office the managing director identified certain key skill deficiencies, particularly in the language and secretarial areas, in addition to staff whose performance and attitudes left much to be desired.

   (a) Consider the decisions that needed to be made and how they might be implemented.

(b) What do you think the managing director decided to do?
(c) What effect might these decisions have on the work and contribution of the HRD consultant?

5 One of the consequences of the company's training achievements was the need to develop its own internal capacity to manage and administer continuing training initiatives. The consultant suggested that one of the office staff, who worked twenty hours a week as a wages clerk, should be developed as a personnel administrator with specific responsibilities for training. What should have been done to achieve this?
6 What kind of difficulties do you think were experienced during the early phase of the BGT consultancy programme?

Recommended reading

COOKE, John, and KNIBBS, John, 'The manager's role in staff development', *Journal of European Industrial Training*, 11, 1, 1987.
LEICESTER, Colin, 'The key role of the line manager in employee development', *Personnel Management*, March 1989.
MEGGINSON, David, 'Instructor, coach, mentor: three ways of helping for managers', *Management Education and Development*, 19, 1, 1988.
MUMFORD, Alan, 'The role of the boss in helping subordinates to learn', in Bernard TAYLOR and Gordon LIPPITT (eds.), *Management Development and Training Handbook*, chapter 23, London, McGraw-Hill, 1975.
NEWBY, Tony, 'Strategy or reaction? You have a choice', *Training Officer*, January 1989.
SCHEIN, Edgar H., *Process Consultation*, II, Reading, Mass., Addison Wesley, 1987.

Appraising performance and identifying potential in a public research agency

Jean Woodall

Appraisal has a similar history to many other components of human resource management. Born in the UK, it was developed and applied in many US companies, where a great deal of attention was paid to the design of appraisal report forms. It is claimed that the current British trend is towards more person-centred skills-based approaches, while in the US the trend is towards more work-centred mechanistic systems, in which the importance of the interpersonal skill training necessary to support a staff appraisal scheme is de-emphasized (Randell, 1989). In the UK, despite recent survey evidence indicating the growing popularity of results-oriented methods (see Table 12.1), the move is away from using complex scaling techniques, towards the use of simple appraisal report forms. There is more interest in how managers arrive at their judgements and ensuring that the judgements are as valid as possible. More recently, performance appraisal has come to be seen as an essential ingredient in the performance management process. As the number of firms using merit pay and performance-related pay increases,

Table 12.1 Analysis of performance review forms

Methods	1977		1985	
	N	%	N	%
Results-oriented	102	57	155	63
Job behaviour-oriented	–	–	128	52
Personality trait rating	61	34	72	29
Alphabetical/numerical rating	19	11	68	28
Narrative:				
Free essay	2	1	6	2
Controlled written	10	6	108	44
Forced distribution global rating	–	–	24	10
Unclassifiable	24	13	–	–
Base	180		247	

Source. Phil Long, 'Performance appraisal revisited', Third *IPM Survey*, London, IPM, 1986.

and these mechanisms are extended to new groups of staff, so there is an increase in interest in appraisal as one mechanism used in the allocation of rewards.

Background to the case: the Public Research Agency

The UK government funds basic and applied civil research through five quangos which are supported by the Department of Education and Science. The five quangos conduct research through their own establishments, and by supporting selected research, study and training in universities and other higher education establishments. They also receive income from research commissioned by government departments and the private sector.

The Public Research Agency (PRA) is one of these quangos and employs around 3,600 staff, of whom about one-third are scientific specialists, another third research support staff, and one-sixth administrative staff (the remainder including maintenance and other miscellaneous groups). The Public Research Agency received a grant of nearly £191 million for 1989/90, but the effects were disappointing – the budget did not keep up with inflation, and units had to be closed. Plans for 1991/2 were based upon strict control of expenditure and a decline in the number of research projects.

This case concerns the performance management system for the administrative staff at PRA. Recruitment into administrative grades is at three levels: Administrative Assistant, Administrative Officer, and Executive Officer. The job holders carry out a wide range of work, including committee servicing, personnel administration, finance and accounting, data processing, public relations, the preparation of reports about the agency's work, and the administration of research grants. While appointments at Executive Officer level are made on the assumption that the candidates are willing to change their place of work if required to do so, Administrative Assistants and Officers are not required to transfer to a workplace that is beyond reasonable travelling distance from their home.

The situation

Appraisal of administrative staff at PRA

Being a quango, the Public Research Agency is very much influenced by government policy and conditions of employment. During the 1980s there were several initiatives to promote efficiency in the operation of public bodies, and to achieve a more effective deployment of staff, particularly those involved in administrative work. In the Public Research Agency they resulted in the adoption of a system of staff appraisal, but for the administrative staff only (scientific and technical staff were not covered). This resulted in the use of an appraisal process based on the documentation shown in Appendix 12.1.

The initial aims of appraisal were chiefly to provide feedback and improve performance, and to provide a way of comparing individuals for the purpose of promotion. The process would principally involve post holders and their reporting officers (usually the immediate line manager) plus a contribution from a countersigning officer (a superior line manager), a head of section and someone from the personnel section (see Appendix 12.1). The documentation was divided into several parts:

- Personal details and job description.
- Performance appraisal.
- Training needs.
- Job transfer.
- Endorsement by the job holder.
- Promotion appraisal.

Information contained in the final section would not be disclosed to the post holder.

The appraisal scheme (which was devised in the late 1970s) was introduced very carefully, with good training for the appraisers in respect of both report completion and interviewing. A reference manual was also supplied. The first people involved were section heads at Executive Officer grade, and the system was then introduced at progressively lower levels. By the early 1980s the scheme was fully in place. However, budgetary constraints led to pressure on staffing and consequently on the time available for both training and the conduct of appraisals.

A review of work organization at PRA

By 1989 it was clear that financial constraints would persist, and that there needed to be some wider-ranging review of work organization, not only at the level of administrative staff but at the level of technical staff. Consultations took place with the recognized unions through the Joint Negotiating and Consultative Committee. This process resulted in two initiatives: (1) the restructuring of the technical grades into one general category of research support staff, and (2) the introduction of performance pay. It was also agreed that the initiatives had implications for the use of appraisal, which should be extended to include both groups and should be revised so as to be more open. It was thought advisable to bring consultants in to assist with the redesign of the appraisal process.

12

Activity brief

1 Given the aims of the original appraisal process, critically evaluate the design of both the process and the content of the report form.
2 Comment on the appraisal report form, with particular reference to the methods used for the rating and assessment of the post holder.
3 Given the proposed introduction of performance-related pay, what factors should be taken into account in the design of a new appraisal process?

Recommended reading

BAILEY, D., 'Design for appraisal', *Training Officer*, March 1990, pp. 70–4.

FLETCHER, C., and WILLIAMS, R., *Performance Appraisal and Career Development*, London, Hutchinson, 1985.

FLETCHER, C., 'What's new in performance appraisal?' *Personnel Management*, February 1984.

FOWLER, A., 'Performance management: the MBO of the '90s?' *Personnel Management*, July 1990.

LONG, P., *Performance Appraisal Revisited*, London, IPM, 1986.

RANDELL, G., 'Employee appraisal', in K. SISSON, (ed.), *Personnel Management in Britain*, Oxford, Blackwell, 1989, pp. 149–74.

YEATES, J., 'Basing pay on performance', *Manpower Policy and Practice*, summer 1987, pp. 15–17.

Appendix 12.1 Annual Report form 'A' for administrative staff

Period of report: from _____ to _____

_____

PART 1 — PERSONAL DETAILS AND JOB DESCRIPTION

1.1 Personal details to be completed by the personnel section

Surname _____ Mr / Mrs / Miss / Ms / Dr

Forenames _____

Date of birth _____

Substantive grade _____ Date entered substantive grade _____

Periods of temporary promotion / substitution _____ (grade) from _____ to _____

Date appointed to present job _____

1.2 Details to be completed by the post holder

Academic, professional or technical qualifications obtained during period of report

_____
_____
_____
_____

Training courses attended during period of report

_____
_____

1.3 Job description (to be completed by the post holder)

Job title (if any) _____

(Summarize the purpose of the job, then set out, broadly in order of importance, the main duties performed during the period of the report; distinguish those of a continuous nature from particular projects and indicate where possible the approximate percentage of total time spent on each duty.)

Do you and the reporting officer agree the job description?   Yes ☐ No ☐

If 'No' please discuss with him / her and record any unresolved differences here. (A separate sheet may be used if required.)

PART 2 — PERFORMANCE APPRAISAL

The Notes for Guidance must be read *whilst* completing this section

2.1 Performance assessment by the reporting officer

Give a rating 1–5 for each relevant aspect of performance, using the following definitions and making full use of the space for your comments.

1 Outstanding
2 Performance significantly above requirements of the grade.
3 Performance fully meets normal requirements of the grade.
4 Performance not fully up to requirements of the grade, some improvement necessary.
5 Unacceptable.

Comments

Work Activity	
☐ Quality of work	
☐ Output of work	
☐ Planning of work	
Communication	
☐ Written communication	
☐ Oral communication	
Management	
☐ Management of staff	
☐ Effective use of other resources	
Working relationships	
☐ Relations with other staff	
☐ Relations with the public	
Knowledge / skills	
☐ Professional and technical knowledge	
☐ Application of knowledge and skills	
☐ Numerical ability	

2.2 Rating of overall performance

| Write in box overall rating of performance using scale 1–5 defined in section 2.1. ☐ | Your rating should not make allowance for any special factors such as age, inexperience, ill health and unusually high turnover of staff, but they should be stated below. Also use this space to complete the picture of the individual so that the report presents a fully balanced and informative assessment. |

The job holder has worked for me for _____ years _____ months
Signature _____ Grade _____
Name in capitals _____ Date _____

2.3 Countersigning officer's comments on performance

Indicate how much you see of the person's work and how far you can confirm the comments and ratings given. Record any areas of disagreement which may remain after discussion with the reporting officer. Add any further relevant comments.

The job holder has worked for me for _____ years _____ months
Signature _____ Grade _____
Name in capitals _____ Date _____

2.4 Agreed objectives (to be completed by the reporting officer)

The job holder and reporting officer should discuss and agree a list of specific objectives for next year. The objectives may be either operational (i.e. setting targets in relation to particular duties or projects) or personal (i.e. aiming to improve or enhance the individual's own effectiveness in specific areas.) Changes from past year's job description should be highlighted here. A copy of this section should be given to the job holder, who may request its review in the event of major change(s) to the job during the year.

PART 3 — TRAINING NEEDS   Name: _____

Unit division: _____

(Entries in this section should relate only to training additional to that normally provided in the present job and should take account of any views expressed by the person reported on.)

(a)   If, as a result of the assessment made earlier in this report, you consider that performance or potential could be improved by training please specify the precise needs and, if possible, suggest ways in which those needs might be met, including on-the-job training.

(b)   Have you taken action to implement your recommendations (e.g. arranged on-the-job training, nominated for training courses)?   Yes ☐ No ☐

 If not, what action will be taken?

A copy of this page will be sent 'in confidence' to the MRC Training Group.

PART 4 — NEW JOB AT THE SAME LEVEL

Should he / she be considered for a transfer to a different job in the same grade in the next year?   Yes ☐ No
☐

If you have answered 'Yes' say what kind of job and give your reasons below.

PART 5 (to be completed by the member of staff)

I have noted the completed appraisal report.

Signed _____ Date _____

PART 6 — PROMOTION APPRAISAL

Name: _____

The Notes for Guidance must be read whilst completing this section

6.1 Assessment of personal qualities by reporting officer

Tick a box for each quality or ability; make full use of the space for your comments.

X	Y	Comments
Acceptance of responsibility Seeks and accepts responsibility at all times	□□□□□ Avoids responsibility wherever possible	
Judgement Fully thought-out sound decisions	□□□□□ Takes superficial or unsound decisions	
Ability to produce constructive ideas Full of ideas which provide fresh insight	□□□□□ Few ideas, does not innovate	
Foresight Anticipates problems and develops solutions	□□□□□ Notices problems only after they arise	
Penetration Gets straight to the root of a problem	□□□□□ Seldom sees below the surface of a problem	
Drive and determination Wholehearted application to tasks; determined to carry them through	□□□□□ Lacks energy; easily discouraged; wastes time	
Reliability under pressure Completely reliable at all times	□□□□□ Easily thrown off balance, not reliable	

6.2 Promotion assessments

Assess potential to perform the duties of the next grade (specify grade _____).
Please tick

	Not fitted	Likely to become fitted in the next two years	Fitted	Well fitted
(a) Reporting officer's assessment	□	□	□	□
(b) Countersigning officer's assessment	□	□	□	□

6.3 Comments on promotion assessment

(Comments on long-term promotion potential are *not* to be divulged to the reportee.)

6.3 (a) Reporting officer's comments

Please justify your assessment at 6.2. If relevant show how the reportee has demonstrated the ability for the next grade.

6.3 (b) Longer-term potential

Please comment on further potential and, if you think the reportee has exceptional potential, explain why.

In my judgement the reportee seems to have the potential to reach the career grade of
_____ (grade).

Signature _____ Grade _____
Name in capitals _____ Date _____

6.4 Countersigning officer's comments

Please comment on the assessments made in 6.2 and 6.3 above and confirm whether the reportee has demonstrated the potential for the higher grade. Would you accept the post holder on promotion into a post at the higher level within your section?

Signature _____ Grade _____
Name in capitals _____ Date _____

6.5 Endorsement by Director / Head of Division (where applicable)

I have read the above Performance and Promotion Appraisal and endorse the recommendations contained in it.

(If the Director / Head of Division wishes to add any comments these should be recorded below.)

Signed _____ Date _____

Case 13

Solving the mystery of NVQs: Baker Electronics

Paula O'Brien

Few would dispute the claim that Britain's training record is a poor one. The work force is underqualified in relation to other countries'. In terms of the training provided to managers and employees Britain falls behind its major competitors. This scenario is largely due to underinvestment in training and has been a matter of public concern over the last thirty years. It has resulted in a series of national government policy interventions since the passage of the Industry Training Act, 1964.

The British work force has had various mechanisms for the delivery of training, including Industry Training Boards, the Manpower Services Commission and, more recently, local Training and Enterprise Councils (TECs).

Considerable confusion has been generated by the structure for awarding vocational qualifications. Over 300 different awarding bodies exist, many of whose qualifications are in the same occupational areas. Until recently there were no arrangements for mutual recognition and accreditation, and the system was perceived to be an obstacle to both employer and employee alike. For this reason, in 1986 a review of vocational qualifications was conducted, resulting, in 1987, in the creation of the National Council for Vocational Qualifications (NCVQ), whose task it was to effect a complete overhaul of all vocational qualifications up to technician level.

Background to the case

Baker Electronics

Baker Electronics was established in 1970, employing forty staff. Today it manufactures electronic transformers for use in television sets and microwave ovens, and employs 125 staff. It is not one of the largest electronic manufacturers, but considers itself to be among the leading companies with regard to the quality of its products. Baker Electronics has benefited from recent developments in manufacturing technology. Its factory now uses some of the most up-to-date equipment available. This heavy financial investment was undertaken in conjunction with a five-year human resource plan, which will mean a proposed reduction of 20 per cent in the labour force.

In 1990 Baker's board of management announced a commitment to a continuous quality process called 'Quality the Baker way'. A quality manager was appointed who undertook the task of striving towards the ultimate goal of 'zero defects'. The quality of work produced was subsequently expected to improve.

The key staff

The appointment of a personnel manager emerged from a situation where demographics, technological change and foreign competition had forced Baker's to recognize that investment in the work force was essential to success. Annette Evans was recently recruited to assist in the implementation of the 'quality improvement plan'. She was responsible for the long-term aim of developing in-house training programmes, initiating a staff development programme and improving liaison between the company and the local education service. One of her main priorities was to encourage employees to take advantage of the day release courses now available.

Investment in the work force is a belief which David Gray, the production manager, has held for some years. He has had a tough job persuading the other management team members that it is the way forward for the company. However, as Baker's has not experienced any real industrial disputes to date, it is believed by top management that the harmonization of terms and conditions for workers and management is an achievable goal. David joined the company in 1972 as a trainee apprentice and is now responsible for Baker's apprenticeship scheme. The only letters that appear after David's name are those of the City and Guilds electronics qualification, which he encourages his own staff to work towards. David is considered 'a hard taskmaster' but is highly respected by his staff and colleagues.

Eileen Black is in charge of the administration department. She has been with the company since it began and has seen her staff grow to a total of eight. Two of her staff attend evening classes in word processing and typing. The remaining staff in her department are quite happy with the skills they have acquired over the time they have worked for Baker's. A new addition to the staff is Hannah Green, recruited through the publicly funded programme of Youth Training (YT).

Management meetings are held on a monthly basis, usually on the last day of the month. The manager from each department attends, and ideally the meeting is seen as an opportunity for briefing on current issues and future plans. The norm is an oral report of the past month's achievements for each department.

The situation

Incident 1: the management board meeting

On her way to the Friday morning monthly meeting, Annette thought about her presentation. Ray White, the managing director, had spoken to her the previous day and requested that she give the board a run-down on her progress with the company's in-house training programmes. She reflected back on her previous job and could not help feeling frustrated with the slow progress that she was making at Baker's.

The monthly meetings were usually a time to catch up on what was happening in the rest of the company and to listen to other presentations. The personnel presentation was the last on the agenda, and Annette could not help thinking that there was some underlying significance in that fact. During her progress report on the development of in-house company training programmes she expressed her gratitude for the, albeit limited, response to her request for information on the training needs of each department. Annette asked whether anyone had anything to add to these requests. At this point, Eileen quite unexpectedly brought up the subject of her staff. Apparently, a few of her 'ladies' were concerned about rumours that they would have to attend college courses in the future. In her opinion they were competent enough in their work, and so far she had not received any complaints. As for Annette's request that she should devise a training plan for Hannah (the Youth Trainee), well, she had been just too busy.

Although she was exasperated, Annette responded diplomatically. She sensed that Eileen's comments were a direct challenge to her role. She began by arguing that, to the contrary, she felt it was appropriate for Eileen's staff to consider how to improve upon their skills. Baker's aimed to produce good-quality products, and that could be achieved only by having well trained staff. With regard to arranging a training programme for Hannah, Annette announced that she would have some free time the following week to discuss it with Eileen. Annette concluded by announcing that it was the responsibility of the personnel department to identify training needs and see that they were met and that she intended to report back to the board on her progress.

As Eileen chose not to respond, Ray thanked everyone for attending the meeting and asked Annette to stay behind. He thanked her for her presentation and asked her to keep him informed of any new developments. Annette agreed.

Incident 2: a meeting with the local Training and Enterprise Council

Annette had previously telephoned the TEC for a list of vocational courses available locally. She proposed using the information to tackle each manager at Baker's and to get them to indicate which courses they approved. She had received the leaflet and, anxious to proceed, browsed through it. Various City and Guilds and Royal Society of Arts qualifications were listed, but the leaflet contained several references to 'NVQs'. The abbreviation also appeared alongside the electronics and clerical courses being offered. She decided to ring Graham Jones, the contact named on the leaflet.

After Annette had explained the company's investment plan and how she had approached Graham's department for a list of courses, she went on to say that she had not come across the term 'NVQ' before and wondered whether Graham could explain. He suggested that the best thing for her to do would be to come in for a chat, as NVQs were a new type of qualification and there was not much literature available on them. A meeting was arranged for the following week.

At the meeting Graham explained that Baker's was the third company in the past two years to approach him for information on NVQs. He spent some time explaining NVQs. Annette noted the following points:

- The National Council for Vocational Qualifications was set up in 1986. It has two aims: (1) to create a set of standards based on what is needed in the workplace; (2) to create a comprehensive framework of qualifications.
- National Vocational Qualifications (NVQs) were introduced to provide a framework in which to achieve these aims, especially to reform and rationalize the system of vocational qualifications.
- NVQs require the co-operation of awarding bodies to establish clear standards of competence; participation is voluntary.
- The 'NVQ framework' has four levels of competence, and the deadline for the NCVQ to implement all four levels is the end of 1992, on government instruction.
- 'Units of competence' are a central theme of NVQs. The qualification is competence-based and employment-led. Competence to perform rather than competence to pass examinations is what is recognized. The specification of 'competence' and 'standards' required for successful performance must be made clear.
- There is no preferred training pattern or means of achieving a unit of competence. Open learning in the workplace is as valid as day release on a college course. Units will be assessed and credited separately, thus enabling the trainee to accumulate credits over varying periods and in different locations.
- Structured workplace learning will increasingly become a requirement, along with assessments in the workplace.
- In the local area, a few NVQ programmes had been introduced at Tollgate College of Further Education.
- There is an NVQ database, and a demonstration of it costs approximately £400. It stores all units, elements and performance criteria for every NVQ.
- Graham's comments on the database stressed that it did not include all qualifications.
- Graham also indicated that there were some teething problems with the NVQs.

Incident 3: a meeting with a lecturer at the college of further education

Rosemary Hyde, Senior Lecturer in Office Studies, explained that they had some experience of NVQs at Tollgate College. She had personally taken part in an 'NVQ Awareness Day'. They had contacted fifty companies in the district and invited the workplace supervisors to a presentation on NVQs, but only 10 per cent responded. She could not recall Annette being there. Annette explained that she was not employed by Baker's at the time.

The objective of the 'NVQ Awareness Day' had been to involve employers in course design and assessment procedures wherever possible. However, that had not happened, and one of the national retail stores in Tollgate town had set up its own scheme whereby trainees worked towards NVQ certificates. Rosemary had heard that it was even employing its own tutors for off-the-job training. This was a big change, as all trainees at the store used to come to the college at one time.

Rosemary felt that the new qualification would mean changes for both Annette and herself, especially as one of the aims of the NVQs is to introduce workplace assessment. Rosemary was pessimistic about how it could be achieved. On a more cheerful note, she informed Annette that the college was assisting local companies by offering the City and Guilds '929' course for training workplace assessors next September. She said she looked forward to seeing some of Baker's clerical staff on RSA courses in clerical procedures next term. Annette said she was certain this would happen and thanked Rosemary for her time. Finally, she asked to speak to someone in the electronics department before she left. But the lecturer was teaching his City and Guilds day release class and, as he had five new trainees starting that day, Rosemary thought that he would not be free. Furthermore, as the college was winding down for its Easter break it might be difficult to arrange an appointment over the next few weeks.

Incident 4: progress report to the managing director

Annette had prepared a report for Ray on what had happened. He was impressed with the work she had carried out and asked her to include it on the agenda of the next monthly meeting. He felt that if NVQs were likely to take off, then all Baker's managers would need to be accredited to deliver them.

Activity brief

1   Assuming the role of Annette Evans, personnel manager of Baker Electronics, how would you introduce the idea of NVQs to the other board members at the next meeting?

13

2   What would it mean for Baker's if they were to go ahead with implementing NVQs?
3   What do you think Rosemary Hyde was referring to when she said the new qualification would mean changes for both Annette and herself?
4   Why have employers been slow in supporting the NVQ framework?
5   What potential advantages should NVQs have over other qualifications for trainees?

Recommended reading

BURKE, J. W., *Competency-based Education and Training*, London, Falmer Press, 1989.

DEPARTMENT OF EDUCATION AND SCIENCE, *Business Administration Courses leading to National Vocational Qualifications in Further Education Colleges*, London, Department of Education and Science.

JESSUP, G., *Outcomes: NVQs and the Emerging Model of Education and Training*, London, Falmer Press, 1991.

LEITH, P., 'Training in the small company', *Training Tomorrow*, May 1991, pp. 13–15.

PUGH, S. C., 'Are you ready for NVQs?' *Adult and Youth Training News*, 1, June 1990.

ROWE, C., 'Training for tomorrow', *Education and Training*, May/June 1988.

THOMPSON, P., 'The meaning of vocational qualifications', *Education and Training*, May/June 1989, pp. 13–15.

THORNE, K., 'The workplace assessor', *Training Tomorrow*, September 1989.

Case 14

Collaboration over work experience placements: Midland Bank and the Royal Borough of Kingston upon Thames

Jean Woodall

This case concerns the development of education–industry links. It focuses upon links with schools (rather than higher education) and the provision of work experience placements for fourteen-to-sixteen-year-olds. This sphere of activity was relatively undeveloped in the UK until the mid-1970s. However, in the context of growing unemployment among school-leavers after 1975, and the need for job creation, work experience, and training schemes, many people from the world of education and business became aware that collaboration was necessary to prepare young people for working life, or at the very least to cushion the impact of unemployment on leaving school.

In the ensuing ten years a large number of schemes appeared: on the education side the emphasis was upon pre-vocational education, and on the employment side the emphasis was upon schemes for publicly subsidized initial skill training. The Industry Year 1986 campaign was launched by the government to lay a foundation for a positive change in the anti-industrial attitudes that were perceived to be a major social obstacle to the improved performance of UK industry. One offshoot of this was an attempt to map the organizations and initiatives centred on education–industry links that had come into existence. In 1987 over thirty such link organizations were identified as operating either centrally or nationally across the UK (see Appendix 14.1). These organizations spawned an even greater variety of initiatives, and offered resources directed at improving education–industry links.

This burgeoning activity led to waves of school pupils flooding into various forms of work experience, employer involvement in the curriculum and, to a lesser extent, secondment of practising teachers to industry and commerce. If anything, most initiatives were home-grown, within a national framework of guidelines and funding. The pattern of activities and involvement varied between individual schools, let alone between education authorities. Outside policy-making circles in government departments (education, employment and industry), few except the local education and careers services had an appreciation of the complete picture. In particular, personnel managers, with whom the responsibility for managing an organization's links with the local community frequently rests, were bewildered at the range of education–industry links, overcome by the demands upon them, and exasperated at the seeming lack of overall local co-ordination. The following case study illustrates the experiences of a London employer's links with a local education authority in the labour market conditions of the late 1980s and early 1990s.

Background to the case

The youth labour market in the Royal Borough of Kingston upon Thames

The Royal Borough of Kingston upon Thames is a small local authority in the Greater London region with a resident population of just over 130,000. Economic activity rates in the late 1980s were high, and unemployment rates were some way below the national average (albeit rising rapidly after 1990). Although manufacturing employment was undergoing a steady decline, service-sector employment was above the national average, and three industries – public administration, retail distribution and education – made up one-third of all employment, with the fastest growth most evident in business services, medical services and construction. Kingston's educational provision for sixteen-to-nineteen-year-olds consists of a number of school sixth forms and one large further education college. As yet there has been no move to a tertiary college-based system, and selection for grammar school entrance still takes place at the age of eleven.

Employers' expectations of future workforce requirements in the 1980s were optimistic, although recruitment difficulties were reported – especially for clerical and 'making and repair' occupations. It was reported that about half these shortages were for higher-level technician and professional skills, but that a sizeable number of vacancies were hard to fill for 'other reasons', including low pay, unsocial hours, inconvenient location or unpopular image. This situation was likely to be aggravated with a projected decline in the number of new entrants to the labour market.

On the other side, the pattern of destinations of sixteen-year-old school pupils appeared to be reinforcing the trend of declining entrants to the labour market. There was strong encouragement to stay on at school, as head teachers were anxious about the effects of falling school rolls upon class sizes and the viability of sixth forms – a situation that was complicated by the presence of a popular further education college.

Until Industry Year 1986 there was little in the form of education–industry links within the borough. Since then schools have developed a wide range of activities. So far there has been no borough-wide policy, but most initiatives have originated out of the Technical and Vocational Education Initiative (TVEI), which was begun as a pilot in the late 1980s, in which all maintained and special schools were involved.

Midland Bank

The Midland Bank is over 150 years old, and today is one of the world's leading financial groups, with branches, businesses and around 50,000 employees throughout the world. In the UK it has just under 2,000 branches. The Midland has diversified into other businesses by acquiring subsidiary companies – Forward Trust (an instalment finance company), Thomas Cook (the well known travel agency) and Samuel Montagu, the merchant bank, are all part of the Midland group.

As well as the effects of diversification, changes have also come about at Midland Bank as a result of the Financial Services Act, 1986. The net effect of the legislation was to 'liberalize' the whole financial services sector – the strict demarcations between bank, building society, merchant bank, insurance provider, estate agency, etc. were relaxed. In the case of clearing banks such as the Midland, it brought keen competition from building societies in the area of retail banking. Designing an attractive and competitive range of financial 'products', and an emphasis upon customer service, led to a rethink of staffing structures and, in particular, career opportunities. The style of banking changed – heavy oak panelling and sober business suits were replaced by a more open-plan layout and less formal dress.

Furthermore, there was an open acknowledgment that 'people mattered'. In the retail bank, Personnel was headed at the regional level by human resource directors to whom a number of area personnel managers would report. In the case of the southern region, six new areas were created in February 1990, one of which was the Surrey area (which incorporates the former South West London area on which this case study is based), covering a large wedge shape stretching from Walton to Wandsworth in London (and thus spanning green belt, suburbs and inner city).

The situation

Midland Bank's interest in work experience

During the 1980s recruitment of staff was a high priority for the Surrey area office personnel staff. Local labour market conditions meant that historically labour turnover was high in Surrey and the south-east, usually reaching 20–5 per cent. There was an additional problem caused by the geography of the area, in that staff could not be easily redeployed from one part to another. Recruitment was also affected by the image of the bank. Little had been done to promote the changes of style to prospective recruits, especially school-leavers. For many the image of the bank manager was the *Dad's Army* Captain Mainwaring type – an authoritarian, status-conscious figure presiding over a formal hierarchy of underlings employed in counting up banknotes and coins. This image was at considerable variance with the reality of work, where selling and interpersonal skills were of key importance. Banking was not seen as a glamorous career choice by many sixteen or eighteen-year-old school leavers, and in the Surrey area personnel staff were concerned that young people with talent were not applying.

In addition, the Midland's concern with its corporate image stretched beyond prospective recruits to a focus upon the wider community. In particular the bank was keen to promote itself as a 'caring institution' which had a duty to the community. It needed to be seen to 'give' as well as 'get'. For this reason, closer links with the education service would bring a pay-off in terms of a better network with schools and parents, which in turn could be a vehicle for attracting both potential recruits and the clients of the future.

One means of achieving this was seen to be work experience placements. During the mid-1980s, and in response to requests from the education service, the bank started to provide work experience placements for school pupils. Schools were invited to send sixteen-year-old school-leavers for a two-week work experience placement during which they were shown how the bank 'worked'. They were placed in an undemanding junior clerical position, observing and assisting in routine tasks as and when needed. At the end the manager or a designated member of staff would send a written assessment to the school of the pupil's performance during the placement.

The scheme had operated without any major problems, but in 1989 Surrey area personnel staff at Midland decided to review their arrangements for work experience placements and education–industry links. Branch managers were questioning the benefits of the programme, given the other demands on their time. Also, pressures from Head Office were starting to lead to a 'squeeze' on head-count. The impact upon the branches was felt in 1990, when many vacant posts were not filled. By the end of that year all the major clearing banks were operating a freeze on recruitment. Surrey area personnel staff had also estimated that the cost of two-week work experience placements was around £200 per pupil. In this context the relative worth of continuing with work experience placements was in question.

The work-related curriculum in Kingston

Although a measure of work experience was present in a number of the borough's secondary schools prior to 1985, the start of the Technical and Vocational Education Initiative pilot that year provided the impetus and central support to expand the programme greatly. By 1990 all the borough's secondary school students aged fourteen to sixteen had received at least one period of planned work experience. In 1989/90 1,360 students were involved, and 503 employers offered one or more placements. Placements occurred in every month of the year with the exception of January, August and September, with slightly over 70 per cent taking place in June and July.

The management and co-ordination of such large numbers of placements were greatly helped by the creation of a central support structure involving an advisory teacher responsible for work experience, plus a clerical assistant. Together they:

- Co-ordinated placement dates across the schools.

- Established and updated a detailed register of employers willing to offer placements.
- Formulated and published borough guidelines on work experience.
- Ensured that legal requirements were met (especially in the area of insurance).
- Developed and produced a pack of student and teacher materials to support the placements.

The net effect was that work experience became accepted as part of the entitlement of fourteen-to-sixteen-year-olds in all the borough's schools. It was seen as part of the mainstream curriculum rather than as a 'bolt-on' or peripheral activity. This meant that the advisory teacher's responsibility widened to include all aspects of the work-related curriculum, and liaison with subject teachers in schools. All the schools designated a teacher to be the work experience co-ordinator – a role usually combined with career education and guidance. In one case the role was seen as sufficiently important for the work experience co-ordinator to be included in meetings of the school's senior management team (heads of department and other curriculum initiatives), which greatly enhanced the integration of the work-related curriculum into the rest of the school's activities. In other schools there were moves to integrate work experience into programmes of Personal and Social Education – often called 'The World of Work'. These lasted for half a term, and the work experience placement often fell within this time.

Thus it can be said that the development of a programme of work experience placements was a key element in the establishment of the 'work-related curriculum'. The 'work-related curriculum' is taken by the borough to refer to all aspects of a school curriculum which deliberately relate to the world of work. This includes:

- A set of general aims concerning the preparation of students for adult and working life.
- Courses, programmes of study or aspects of personal and social education which are related to the world of work, such as courses accredited by vocational examination bodies like the Business and Technician Education Council (BTEC) or the Royal Society of Arts (RSA), aspects of GCSE courses like Business Studies, and the National Curriculum cross-curricular themes of Careers Education and Guidance, and Economic and Industrial Understanding.
- Specific work-related activities such as work experience, enterprise activities, insight into Industry Days, workplace visits, work shadowing and industry-linked projects.

Indeed, the expansion of the work-related curriculum for the fourteen-to-sixteen age group also provided the basis for building in further experience of work at the upper secondary level (sixteen to eighteen). At one end of the spectrum, there was a range of vocational and pre-vocational courses in which work experience was a formal requirement. This is especially the case at the college of further education. At the other end, there has been an attempt to 'enrich' the studies of students following two-year A level courses by using visiting speakers from industry, visits to workplaces and 'work shadowing' (usually lasting no more than one week).

Thus by 1991 the Royal Borough of Kingston upon Thames had reason to be pleased with its progress in the range and quality of the work-related curriculum. The regular flow of students into work experience placements, and the extent and variety of links with individual employers, were seen as grounds for considerable satisfaction. It was a singular achievement for the education service to be able to offer all this to students and yet persuade them of the value of staying on at school.

Activity brief

As area personnel manager of Midland Bank you wish to retain a programme of work experience placements at a time of increasing pressure upon resources.

1   What changes would you make to the existing arrangements for work experience at the bank? What would be your recommendations for the design and delivery of such a programme?
2   How would you persuade branch managers that such a programme 'added value' to their activities?
3   What would be your strategy for liaising with schools and for achieving effective collaboration?
4   What other aspects of education–industry links with schools could be considered?
5   Are there any issues which could be a source of problems in your dealings with the local education authority?

Recommended reading

BERKELEY, John, 'A better pay-off from work experience', *Personnel Management*, April 1988.

HOLMES, S., *et al.*, *Work Experience in the School Curriculum*, London, Project Trident and the Schools Council Curriculum Industry Project, 1983.

HUTSON, Helen, *Learning from Work Experience*, Longman Resources Unit, Longmans Vocational Preparation series, Harlow, Longman, 1983.

INSTITUTE OF PERSONNEL MANAGEMENT, *Improving Work Experience: a Statement of Principles*, London, IPM, 1987.

JAMIESON, Alan, *Teachers' and Organizers' Handbook on Work Experience*, second edition, Cambridge, CRAC, 1984.

MILLER, A. *et al.*, *Rethinking Work Experience*, Brighton, Falmer Press, 1991.

TRADES UNION CONGRESS, *Work Experience Guidelines: TUC Guidelines on Work Experience for School Pupils*, London, TUC, 1987.

WATTS, A. G., *Work Experience in Schools*, London, Heinemann, 1983.

WOOD, Sue, 'Work experience that works', *Personnel Management*, November 1986.

Appendix 14.1 Education–industry link organizations

ABCC	Association of British Chambers of Commerce
BA	British Association for the Advancement of Science
BIC	Business in the Community
BIM	British Institute of Management
BIS	Banking Information Service
CBI	Confederation of British Industry
CECS	Civil Engineering Careers Service
CRAC	Careers Research and Advisory Centre
CSCS	Centre for the Study of Comprehensive Schools
DE	Department of Employment
DES	Department of Education and Science
DTI	Department of Trade and Industry
EC	Engineering Council
ECIS	Engineering Careers Information Service
GSIP	Geography, Schools and Industry Project
IEE	Institution of Electrical Engineers
IMechE	Institution of Mechanical Engineers
INDEX	Industrial Experience
IoD	Institute of Directors
IS	Industrial Society (Industry Education Unit)
LEACS	Local Education Authority Careers Service
MSC	Manpower Services Commission
NEC	National Electronics Council
ORT	Organisation for Rehabilitation through Training
PT	Project Trident
RSA	Royal Society for the encouragement of Arts, Manufactures and Commerce
RSC	Royal Society of Chemistry
SATRO	Science and Technology Regional Organisation
SCIP	School Curriculum Industry Partnership
SCSST	Standing Conference on Schools, Science and Technology
SEO	Society of Education Officers
TUC	Trades Union Congress
UBI	Understanding British Industry
UI	Understanding Industry
YE	Young Enterprise

14

Acknowledgements

I should like to thank Hilary Barnett, Area Personnel Manager of Midland Bank, and Pat Maitland, TVEI Advisory Teacher for the Royal Borough of Kingston upon Thames, for their help in providing the information on which this case study is based.

Case 15

Career development and matrix management at Joiner Construction

Alexander Lord

Joiner Construction ('Joiner's') is the UK branch of a large US multinational corporation. Its head office is based in the Home Counties and employs 2,500 people at this site. It is an engineering construction contractor, dealing mainly with the oil, chemical, petrochemical, fertilizer, pharmaceutical and power industries in Europe and the developing world.

Since the oil recession in the mid-1980s it has seen a gradual decline in new business, but this has not affected Joiner's as seriously as many of its competitors (who have not diversified as much from their base in the oil industry). For instance, a typical installation contract lasts about three years, costs tens of millions of pounds and uses anything between 200,000 and 1,000,000 staff hours.

Background to the case

Task forces

Since the mid-1970s Joiner's has been using the dedicated task-force system for its major projects. Prior to this, work had been shared out among and conducted within the various contributing departments. In effect, each project manager was little more than a contract manager responsible for chasing progress in different parts of the company – a task requiring persistence and a thick skin!

During the oil boom Joiner's (like many other contractors) found that clients' needs could best be met by forming a full-time task force with a project manager in overall charge. In those days contracts usually had a substantial reimbursable component, so that contractors such as Joiner's could expect the client in question to bear the cost of any inefficiencies or extravagances.

Providing task forces which occupied at least one floor of the building was initially considered to be a selling point but soon became a standard feature of major projects throughout the engineering construction industry. Even today, when Joiner's is forced by the drop in the oil price to deal with much tighter profit margins and fewer reimbursables, its management must still provide (albeit somewhat grudgingly, owing to the cost) dedicated task forces.

Project managers themselves generally approve of the task-force system because it gives them direct access to the project team, a guaranteed minimum level of resources, a visible collection of subordinates (as many as 300, though accountable primarily to their function heads) and direct control over the running of the project. Any functionally based work reflects the constraints of time, cost and, above all, technical support and takes up approximately 10–15 per cent of the total project staff hours. These include rare and expensive specialists such as metallurgists who work part-time on a variety of projects.

Company matrix structure

The company structure (see Figure 15.1) consists of standard departments such as:

- *Engineering*: process, piping, mechanical, electrical, instrumentation, civil, architectural and project.
- *Operations*: project management, planning and programming, materials control and expediting, and inspection.
- *Finance*: estimating, cost control, project purchasing, contract administration and project accounting.
- *Construction*: site management, site inspection, safety and industrial relations.
- *Sales and marketing*: tenders and proposals, advertising and publicity.
- *Personnel*: recruitment, appraisal, administration, employee relations, training and development.

Each of these departments has a director or a general manager who reports to the chief executive, Mark Barnes. Mark is toying with the idea of expanding the existing Quality Assurance function, part of Engineering, although, in the absence of a clear rationale, he is concerned that current interest in the topic may just be a fad. When there are too few on-going task-force projects, the majority of functional staff reside in their normal departments, working on less profitable mini-projects, administration or general R&D – a strong indicator of lean times for the company and a costly overhead.

While they are working on the task force, usually spread across one or two floors of the building, functional staff report to their relevant 'lead discipline manager', who in turn reports to the project manager. For a given task force, the lead discipline managers from all the functions represented on the project form the 'core team', usually about six to fifteen people, which meets regularly and is chaired by the project manager. Although each functional line reports to the project manager during its contribution to the project (often two years or more) the functional lines are also expected to keep their departmental managers and director informed of their work load and progress. This dual reporting affects the lead discipline managers most directly, but any specialist knows that he is accountable to both project

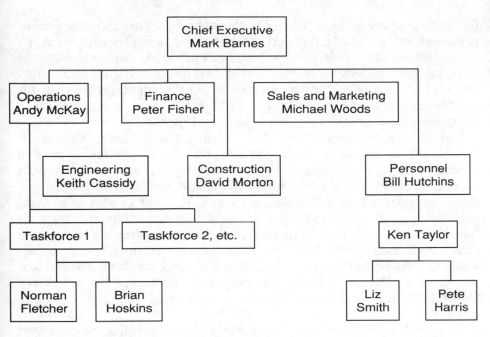

Figure 15.1 Joiner's organization chart

and functional management. In effect the company is operating a highly project-oriented matrix.

The personnel function

This department (see Figure 15.2) is managed by the personnel director, Bill Hutchins, a former accountant who moved into personnel in his late thirties, fourteen years ago. It is safe to say that Bill likes to run a 'tight ship', keeping the quality of company staff adequate but controlling the wage bill carefully. He has a reputation for tough talking and won a lot of prestige in his early days with the department when he sorted out (somewhat acrimoniously, some of those dismissed would say) an industrial dispute with contracted construction site staff. He gives his departmental team a lot of autonomy, but in recent years he has built up a reputation for missing the monthly senior management team meetings on the grounds that he is always 'too busy'.

Ken Taylor, personnel manager, a former civil engineer, has been in personnel since his late twenties and is now in his mid-forties. He believed, rather idealistically, earlier in his career that much could be done to develop engineers' team-building, commercial and managerial skills with their enthusiastic compliance. Latterly, he has come to realize more pragmatically that people from highly technical backgrounds will accept the intervention of such personal development only when clear, direct, quantifiable and preferably immediate benefits can be demonstrated.

At present, Ken works very closely with his two direct subordinates: Liz Smith, personnel officer for appraisal and training, a bright, enthusiastic twenty-seven-year-old graduate who has a reputation among older managers for 'ruffling a few feathers' when she thinks she is right; and Pete Harris, personnel officer for selection and administration, a highly competent but unimaginative thirty-four-year-old who has worked his way up through the company from a clerk's role. Along with two recent graduate engineering recruits, Liz is one of the few women in Joiner's more senior than the receptionists and the typing pool. They share three young personnel assistants who are receiving general personnel experience.

Having won the support and trust of line management, Ken prides himself on a reasonably high graduate recruitment policy, compared to competitors, and a well supported in-company and extra-company training scheme, albeit aimed primarily at new recruits and people who require specialist technical skills, such as CAD courses at a local technical college. Graduate induction is exclusively limited to the entrant's 'host' department for the remainder of the year, after an initial general introduction in the first fortnight. Ken is currently trying to persuade the operations director, Andy McKay, and the sales and marketing director, Michael Woods, that project proposal and bid teams can fruitfully include a human resource management facilitator in client negotiations.

Nevertheless, any attempt to interfere in normal line management functions such as staff appraisal is usually met with staunch resistance. All staff are appraised annually in informal *ad hoc* interviews exclusively with their direct line manager. There is no standard form for doing this and, if it is used at all, it is usually as a means of disciplining particularly poor, or rewarding particularly good, workers. In general, line managers see little direct benefit in the appraisal process and have scant respect for Personnel.

As Ken is all too aware, this attitude is in marked contrast with the US parent company's policy of pioneering innovative human resource management strategies, but devoting more resources to developing appraisal systems is a low priority when the training budget is being so tightly squeezed by the downturn in business in the industry.

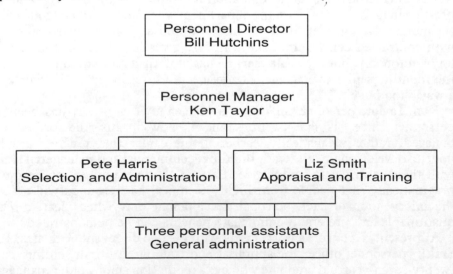

Figure 15.2 The personnel function at Joiner's

The situation: staffing and career development problems at Joiner's?

Norman Fletcher, a senior project manager

Norman Fletcher is a senior project manager, aged fifty-four, who has been with the company since his mid-twenties, having joined as a process design engineer. He is known and respected throughout the company as a loyal servant whose track record in managing projects has been extremely dependable. Norman is the sort of person who sincerely operates 'an open-door policy' but becomes extremely annoyed when he thinks his time is being wasted.

Although he is well established in his position and justly proud of his and the company's achievements, he is a bit wary of developments in the last decade. For instance, he has seen clients become increasingly powerful, interfering, as he sees it, in company procedures. Even though the move away from reimbursable contracts implies less direct involvement on the part of clients, their increased buying power means that, in practice, they can dictate terms while offering the incentive of repeat business. Clients are getting more involved today, even in turnkey jobs. As well as the usual milestones, they are insisting on intermediate check points – as many as 200 in a three-year contract. In contrast, during the early 1970s the company might have to see only the client's production manager. Since then clients have built up their own sizable teams of expert technicians.

Norman has also become somewhat disillusioned with developments in planning and control technology. He feels slightly pressured by clients into accepting particular methodologies and systems which he does not really understand. Unbeknown to Norman, his fear that the 'young computer and CAD cliques are becoming increasingly influential' is well founded, because Personnel has come to the same conclusion when selecting project managers for highly systematized contracts.

Staffing projects

As for many project managers, the start of a new project is always a stressful time for Norman because decisions made at this stage have far-reaching implications for the whole project life cycle. Probably the most important of these decisions are those concerning the recruitment of 'core' team members – no mean problem when, at any one time, the best people are likely to be tied up on existing projects. Worse still, there are likely to be fewer skilled people entering the work force in the next few years, a problem further exacerbated for engineering companies like Joiner's by the attraction to talented young graduates of consultancy and the financial services sector.

On his present project, designing modifications for an oil refinery in the Middle East which are now well into the design phase, recruitment was particularly problematic. In line with normal company practice, Norman Fletcher, Andy McKay, Brian Hoskins, the nominated chief engineer, and various planning and contracts people had drawn up a detailed project plan. It included general design specifications, special procedures to suit client needs, mostly minor modifications of existing Joiner's procedures, resource, time, staffing and cost estimates. These estimates were used to produce a planning and control network which the various contributing departments had to approve and then sign off.

Although this had all taken place without any major difficulties, problems arose when the departments nominated staff to meet their resource commitments. Since this contract was very definitely what Norman liked to call 'hard', i.e. it had a large lump-sum component, it was crucial that financially astute staff were selected. When offered two technically competent but older piping engineers by their section of the engineering department, Norman suspected almost immediately that they would not be suitable for his project because of their lack of financial awareness.

He explained his misgivings to Ken Taylor of Personnel, the department responsible for administering project staffing. While Ken was not unsympathetic, he pointed to a less prestigious project being conducted for a state oil corporation in the developing world in which it was common knowledge that less outstanding design staff were being used. In theory Norman knew he could demand that the piping engineers should be replaced because, as project manager, he had the power of veto. In practice, however, this prerogative could be exercised only if he could make a very strong case – which would hardly be possible in advance of any evidence of negligence. Ultimately, therefore, he persuaded Ken to do whatever he could, and they compromised on Norman receiving only one of the engineers in question.

Ironically, when the client inspected the c.v.s of the project team members the replacement piping engineer was rejected as being what the client project manager called 'a bit too wet behind the ears', so that the original candidate was reselected. Around the same time Norman had been forced to dispel an embarrassing rumour that his own position was under threat owing to client reservations about his ability to cope with the high-technology component of the project. Although the rumour was almost certainly groundless, Norman still resents the fact that members of his own company had been prepared to repeat it.

Procedures

Since Joiner's management have never been totally satisfied with the task-force system owing to its cost, they have not completely revised procedures from the days when work was conducted in separate departments. As already explained, this has caused problems with project managers' authority to recruit, but the area of greatest tension is that concerning overtime.

The company costing system is clearly biased towards departmental rather than project cost centres. This does not usually create too great a problem for medium to long-term human resource allocation, because departments agree on it during project planning. If, on the other hand, a new member of staff is required at short notice, or an existing project member needs to put in extra hours, departments are often reluctant to give authorization. The problem is exacerbated by different projects simultaneously chasing the same staff.

Departments rarely set out to be awkward, but they find it difficult to set priorities in a multi-project environment. It does not help matters when the operations director publicly remarks that departments are only there to service projects and provide technical back-up when it is absolutely necessary. Such attitudes have led to a project/function rivalry which recently forced Norman to spell out his position in an overtime dispute with the manager of the metallurgical engineering section, whose workers are especially well paid but regularly leave for better jobs.

Staff turnover

Like many other contractors in the engineering construction industry, Joiner's has found it extremely difficult in recent years to retain its most talented staff, particularly recent graduates. There has been a marked trend towards new employment patterns such as using the self-employed and recruiting temporary or part-time employees from agencies and consultancy companies. It is also common practice for contractors to reduce their overheads by hiring out superfluous staff to more prosperous companies, hoping to woo them back when business picks up.

Perhaps not surprisingly in this climate of change and uncertainty, morale is sometimes a problem, and occasionally people are sent back to their departments knowing that there is no job for them as a result of market forces. Another consequence of the oil recession and general increase in competition has been a move towards greater diversification. This means that traditional expertise which may have been developed in the oil or petrochemical industry is not necessarily that which is needed in new business areas such as power plants and food processing.

In a meeting with Andy McKay, Ken Taylor tried to spell out the problems:

> *Ken.* We just don't have the resources in personnel to cope with all our training demands. Our clients are getting tougher and tougher over vetting our staff and quality systems as a condition of working with us, or even our suppliers and our suppliers' suppliers in some cases. I know we're not actively involved in running projects but you're the people who feel it most when we lose business or can't hold on to bright young graduates because we don't offer them enough training.
>
> *Andy.* If we did that, we wouldn't have enough money left to do the thing we're here for – sell projects. How can we guarantee that a well trained graduate won't leave anyway? In any case, my project managers would be a lot more sympathetic

if they felt more involved. They have a very limited say in recruitment and they're always complaining to me that they'd take more interest in their staff if only their department heads consulted them more during appraisal. I know it's difficult trying to remember all the faces when you've got a couple of hundred people on your task force but it would still be nice to be asked occasionally.

Ken. That's just it! They expect so much from their first job but we so rarely deliver – some want to do more design work but find themselves handling administration and others have the opposite problem. I know for a fact that Engineering hate to promote a talented specialist out of his technical discipline, but they know that they wouldn't hold on to him if they didn't. Also, they're your main source of up-and-coming project managers. That said, we've got some guys who love the work, but we can't give them a pay rise without promoting them into more general management.

Andy. Of course, you're right, but what can we do about it? Project managers only review their half-dozen or so direct subordinates.

Ken [*shakes his head*]. The problem doesn't end there. Even if you finally make it to project management – like Norman – where do you go to next?

Andy. Well, they can't *all* become operations directors like me!

Activity brief

1 How would you ensure that the career development of functional staff is not neglected? How should responsibility for this task be divided between the project manager and various functional managers?
2 Consider what more could be done to improve career development for people at the start, in the middle and near the end of their career. In this particular case, what ought to be the role of the personnel function in the short, medium and long-term future?
3 Discuss the human resource management issues raised by working in such a matrix organization and suggest ways of overcoming similar problems in the future. For instance, how does the seconded task-force arrangement compare with employees remaining in their normal functional departments?

Recommended reading

ARMSTRONG, M., *Management Processes and Functions*, chapter 9, London, IPM, 1990, pp. 114–29.

DEPARTMENT OF TRADE AND INDUSTRY, *Getting to Grips with Quality*, Mid-Glamorgan, DTI, 1990 (a series of publications).

GUEST, D., 'Personnel and HRM: can you tell the difference?' *Personnel Management*, 21, January 1989.

HOPSON, B., 'Transition: understanding and managing personal change', in R. HOLDSWORTH (ed.), *Psychology for Careers Counselling*, Basingstoke, Macmillan/British Psychological Society, 1982.

LAWRENCE, P. R., *et al.*, 'The human side of the matrix', *Organizational Dynamics*, 6, 1977, pp. 43–61.

LEICESTER, C., 'The key role of the line manager in employee development', *Personnel Management*, 21, March 1989.

MAYO, A., *Managing Careers: Strategies for Organizations*, London, IPM, 1991.

MCGOLDRICK, A., and COOPER, C. L., *Early Retirement*, Aldershot, Gower, 1989.

TORRINGTON, D., and HALL, L., *Personnel Management: a New Approach*, chapter on manpower planning, Hemel Hempstead, Prentice-Hall, 1991.

TORRINGTON, D., and WEIGHTMAN, J., 'Middle management work', *Journal of General Management*, 13, 1987, pp. 74–89.

WEIGHTMAN, J., *Managing Human Resources*, chapter 4, London, IPM, 1990, pp. 48–57.

Note

Joiner Construction is a pseudonym for a company researched by the author which has been slightly fictionalized to retain anonymity.

Promotion and equal opportunity in a local authority college

Alan Peacock

This case is based on the author's experience when acting for a local authority at an industrial tribunal. It focuses on both direct and indirect discrimination and promotes consideration of policies, procedures and practices that could lead to allegations of discrimination on grounds of sex or marital status. Whilst the case provides proper consideration of the legal frameworks associated with discrimination at work, it links well with general aspects of human resource planning and development.

Background to the case: promotions and the new post in Economics

Kingsbury College of Technology employs some 200 academic staff and covers a wide range of subjects and courses at further education level. As a result of new course developments, the Business and Management Studies Department at the college was able to promote two lecturers in Business Studies and Management from grade 1 to grade 2. In addition to the promotions a newly established appointment of a grade 2 lecturer in Economics was also to be made within the college. This post was advertised in the *Times Educational Supplement*:

KINGSBURY COLLEGE OF TECHNOLOGY
DEPARTMENT OF BUSINESS AND MANAGEMENT STUDIES
Ref. L2 Econ./Bus. Mgt Lecturer Grade 2 in Economics

Applicants must be graduates in Economics with acceptable teaching experience able to offer both macro and micro-economics, preferably with some business or industrial experience. The department has a group of full-time staff engaged in the teaching of the subject which is headed by a Principal Lecturer.

The work will be mainly with Ordinary National Diploma and Certificate courses and a suitable applicant will be given the opportunity of working on advanced courses.

Members of staff are normally expected to live within a reasonable distance of the College. The Local Education Authority is prepared to offer assistance with removal expenses in approved cases.

Completed application forms must be returned to the Principal, Kingsbury College of Technology, Outer Road, Kingsbury, Hants, by 19th March.

The career path and number of staff in post were:

Grade	No. of staff in post
Head of department	1
Principal lecturer	1
Senior lecturer	2
Lecturer grade 2	6
Lecturer grade 1	12

The situation: the selection and promotion procedure

The candidates

Liz Padfield and two other lecturers, Brian Smith and Paul Banks, were eligible for these internal promotions and for the new appointment of grade 2 lecturer. They were informed accordingly and sent a form on which to apply for the new appointment of Grade 2 Lecturer in Economics. The three internal candidates were not required to fill in an application form in respect of the two promotions as it was intended that their applications for the new post could also be used for the purpose. A comparative summary of the qualifications and experience submitted by the three internal candidates on their application forms is shown in Table 16.1.

The interviews

The promotions and appointments panel consisted of the college principal, the vice-principal, the head of the Department of Business and Management Studies, a person working in the section concerned of a higher grade than the position to be filled, and the Personnel Officer, Gordon Brown. All members of the panel were male, all were married. Selection could be on the basis of a majority vote and each member of the panel had one vote in respect of each selection.

The panel sat on 14 May. They first considered the two internal promotions and interviewed the three internal candidates, starting at 10.00 a.m. Each candidate was seen for about twenty minutes. Mrs Padfield was the second of the three candidates to be interviewed. In the result, the two male candidates were chosen for promotion to Grade 2 Lecturer in Business Studies and Management.

Table 16.1 Qualifications of the three internal candidates, Kingsbury College

	Mrs Padfield	Mr Smith	Mr Banks
Degrees	B.A. Hons (third class) Economics	None	B.A. Hons (lower second) Economics
College/ university	Keele University	Kingston Polytechnic	Wolver-hampton Polytechnic
Main subjects	Economics	Business Studies	Economics
Other qualifications	None	HNC in Education, Diploma in Marketing	Postgraduate Diploma in Economic Statistics
Work experience	Lecturer at three schools and six colleges of further education (ten years)	Salesperson with three industrial organizations (six years)	Bank clerk at Barclays Bank (eight years)
Grade and present salary point	Lecturer grade 1, point 8	Lecturer grade 1, point 8	Lecturer grade 1, point 8
Years of service at Kingsbury	Three	Four	One
Age (years)	Forty-one	Thirty-four	Twenty-eight

This left Mrs Padfield to be considered by the panel for the newly established appointment of Grade 2 Lecturer in Economics. The external candidates for the appointment were interviewed after the selection for the internal promotions. Mrs Padfield did not appear before the panel again. They had already interviewed her for the promotion and did not wish to see her again, although they considered her for the appointment. Interviews with external candidates continued late into the evening of 14 May and an appointment was made. The principal decided to inform Mrs Padfield early the following morning that she had not been successful.

Early next day he telephoned to break the news. Mrs Padfield asked for clarification and was told that the main reason for her non-appointment to the promoted posts was that she was less dedicated to her career than the two male candidates. The telephone conversation ended abruptly when Mrs Padfield forcefully replaced the receiver, cutting short the principal's explanation. Having reflected on the matter for several hours, she asked to see Mr Brown, the personnel officer.

Interview with the personnel officer

Mrs Padfield first complained that she had not received any details of the requirements for the two internal promotions. She claimed that during the promotion interview she was asked more questions about her family than were the two male candidates. She was asked questions about her husband, his occupation, the location and nature of his work, her family responsibilities and her children's schooling. She said that these questions should not have been asked just because she was a woman or else the questions should have been asked of all the candidates. The two candidates for the internal promotions were both married and one of them had children. In her view the tenor and content of the questions during the interview and the occasionally flippant interviewing style indicated that the panel were not taking the interview seriously. Because she was a woman with children, assumptions about her actions and family commitments were given greater weight than her qualifications and experience. She said that her qualifications and experience were superior to those of the male candidates.

Mr Brown agreed that some questions at interview related to her marital status but not that they were discriminatory in nature. He suggested that Mrs Padfield should seek an interview with the principal. She agreed, and the interview was arranged for the following Monday, 18 May.

Interview with the principal

Mrs Padfield entered the principal's study apprehensive but determined to indicate her dissatisfaction with the way she had been treated. She opened the interview by referring back to the allegation that she was less dedicated to her career than the other two candidates. The principal replied that he believed that she had not been able to concentrate on her career as well as the two male candidates. He reaffirmed that Kingsbury College had a written policy stating that the organization was an Equal Opportunity employer. He also reminded her that two recent promotions in the college had been awarded to female candidates in competition with male candidates.

He indicated that he understood that Mr Padfield had just accepted another job offer some sixty miles from Kingsbury College. She had discussed this with her head of department, intimating that it would involve moving house. Mrs Padfield had used the college staff news sheet and notice board to advertise her house for sale. He enquired whether Mrs Padfield would be moving with her husband. This upset Mrs Padfield considerably, and she indicated that it was a tactless remark which made no difference to her ability to undertake her work at Kingsbury.

The principal suggested that Mrs Padfield had volunteered the information during the interview that she had a family of four children and that she had had to drop certain activities because of her family. She also indicated that all her children were now attending a local convent boarding school and that she would therefore have more time to devote to college requirements during term time. The panel accepted this as a point in favour of possible promotion.

He agreed he had suggested that she had not been able to concentrate on her career as much as a man. He had come to that conclusion by reference to her employment record. She had been employed by nine different educational establishments during the last sixteen years and been self-employed as a freelance writer of historical novels. The panel felt that the two other candidates for promotion had demonstrated more commitment to the college than Mrs Padfield. They attended the college more frequently during vacation periods and spent more time at the college during term time. In the panel's view all three candidates were suitably qualified academically.

Mrs Padfield said that although she did not attend an interview before the appointments panel when they were deciding the appointment of a grade 2 lecturer in Economics she had made no complaint whatsoever about that appointment. Nor did she complain that there had been any discrimination against her in selecting another candidate for that appointment. She was sure that discrimination had taken place in the promotion interview, and she would be seeking legal advice from her trade union.

Additional details

Mrs Padfield has been employed at the college for three years. She was appointed as a Lecturer Grade 1 in Business Studies. Grade 1 was the lowest grade. She worked a five-day week which comprised ten teaching sessions, each session being of three to four hours' duration. She has a third-class honours degree in Economics and Political Institutions obtained at Keele University. She also read Mathematics with Statistics and Moral and Political Philosophy at university as subsidiary subjects in her first and second year. She had qualified as a teacher as a result of her practical experience and was registered by the Department of Education and Science after a year's probation. In her practical experience Mrs Padfield had served three years at Kingsbury College of Technology and in addition had worked for four years in technical colleges on a part-time basis with a length of service totalling 1,000 hours.

Activity brief

1   In your role as a legal adviser to the trade union or management, prepare a case to present before an industrial tribunal that will either

promote or refute the allegation by Mrs Padfield that she was unlawfully discriminated against by her employers in the way that affected her access to equal opportunities of promotion to a grade 2 lecturer in Business Economics. In particular consider the allegation that she had been treated less favourably on the grounds of her sex than a man would have been treated and that she had been treated less favourably than an unmarried person.

2 What procedures and practices should Kingsbury College promote in order to justify the claim that it is an Equal Opportunity employer? Consider, in particular, ways in which the employer could promote equal opportunities in career development.

3 Assuming that you are the personnel officer, how would you persuade the principal that the college would benefit from the policies, procedures and practices suggested in question 2? Indicate both qualitative and quantitative criteria that could be persuasively used and link them to wider Organization Development strategies.

Recommended reading

KAKABADSE A., *et al.*, *Managing in Organisations*, London, Fontana, 1989.

MARTIN, P., and NICHOLLS, J., *Creating a Committed Workforce*, London, IPM, 1987.

MULLINS, L. J., *Management and Organisational Behaviour*, London, Pitman, 1989.

SCHEIN, E., *Career Dynamics: Matching Individual and Organisational Needs*, Reading, Mass., Addison Wesley, 1978.

SMITH, I. T., and WOOD, J. C., *Industrial Law*, London, Butterworth, 1989.

Case 17

International management succession and development at IDL

Terence Kenny

This case concerns the problems faced by International Distribution Ltd (IDL) in planning and implementing personnel policies in general and management succession and development policies in particular. It is a subsidiary of a UK-based multinational conglomerate, Kenyon plc. The case is written from the perspective of the subsidiary and focuses on the problems faced by its new personnel director.

Background to the case

The business

IDL is a freight forwarding company which organizes the movement of goods around the world by land, sea and air. It specializes in 'groupage', in which a containerload of goods is put together from different consignors, this being more profitable than a full load from one consignor. It has a big business in moving machinery, including Kenyon agricultural and packaging machinery, but will move practically anything, from a circus to an art exhibition. It does not move bulk cargoes like oil, ores, etc., nor does it move letters and small packets. The company has its own large warehousing facilities at ports and at airports as well as inland. It has many bonded warehouses and several highly automated distribution warehouses from which food manufacturers' goods are directed to supermarkets. In some countries there is a fleet of trucks for domestic and intra-European transport, and there are river barges in Switzerland and Germany. Logistics management has been developed and the company acts for some large manufacturers as their internal logistics department.

The company employs 5,000 people in a world-wide organization (see Figure 17.1) which, however, is predominantly made up of small units, except for the 1,800 strong German company. In 1990 it produced a pre-tax profit of £12.5 million, which is some 7 per cent of the total pre-tax profit of the Kenyon group. Its share of the total world market is not great, but it is a large organization by the standards of the industry.

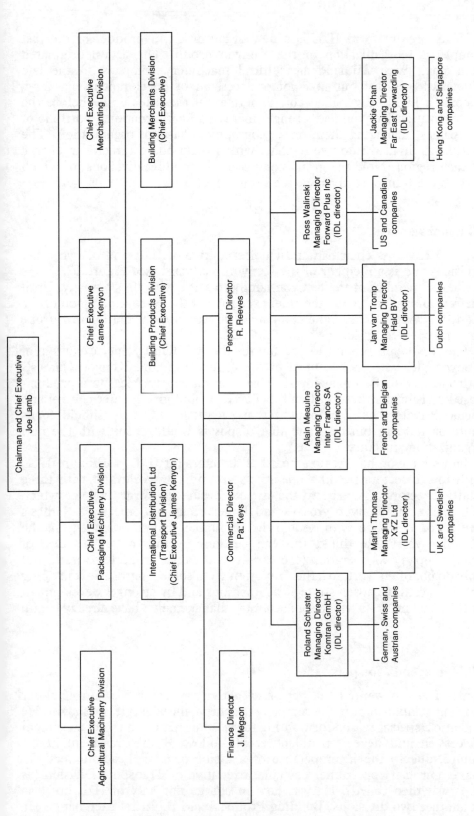

Figure 17.1 The organization structure of IDL post-1985

In its present form IDL is a new organization, a product of the just completed reorganization of the Kenyon group. The group originated as a small West Midland agricultural machinery company in the late nineteenth century but in a long succession of developments has now become a highly diversified conglomerate. In the last decade before the reorganization Kenyon had strongly increased its international portfolio of companies, managing them on a geographical basis of organization. The world was divided into five regions, with a main-board director in charge of each region. Now the group comprises six product divisions, of which IDL is the transport division (see Figure 17.1).

The management

James Kenyon is chairman and chief executive of IDL and of two other divisions and is a member of the Kenyon plc board (see Figure 17.1). He is the last member of the Kenyon family to serve with the company. Until the reorganization he was the chief executive of the European region of the Kenyon group. Most of the companies he was responsible for in Europe have reappeared under his control in IDL.

James Kenyon reports to Joe Lamb, the non-family chief executive of Kenyon plc, who took control of the group from Bill Kenyon (James's father) in 1976. Reorganizing the firm from a geographical to a product-based divisional structure, Lamb believed, would give greater control and focus. Privately he also thought that eventually the firm should focus more on its core business and that disposals would ensue with the new organization structure.

James Kenyon has set up a board of directors for IDL (see Figure 17.1) with four directors heading operations around the world and with three 'staff' directors. As a body the directors have to forge policies which will realize the Kenyon group's and James Kenyon's objectives. James's key stated objective is to double the profitability of the company in the next five years. He thinks this can be done by dint of a great deal of inter-company co-operation (the various companies around the world not only do not often work together but often go to some lengths to avoid doing so), by carefully chosen strategic acquisitions and by stronger development of the niche markets which some country managements have already begun to exploit.

Hidden agenda for personnel

James Kenyon wanted the personnel activity to assist his aim of closer working relationships in the company to achieve the synergies he sought. He had also a special reason for wanting to see some action in the management succession and development sphere. It followed embarrassment at his failure, due to the incompetence of a major firm of 'head hunters', to make a crucial appointment as chief executive of Transport Division (as IDL was then called). He was now in charge not only of IDL but also of another two divisions, Building Products and Builders' Merchants. He had wanted to have chief executives in all three divisions, reporting to him.

Now he had to take direct charge of IDL himself but hoped not to have to do so for longer than six months or a year.

Kenyon believed that management in the forwarding industry generally was not very good, and that the very justification for remaining in such a low-margin business was that he could develop better management than his competitors. Less clearly formulated was his aim of keeping the company as separate as possible from the 'interference' of the parent company and his hope of using the personnel director as a watchdog on the possibly too powerful 'barons', as he called his operational directors. He appointed Rachel Reeves as personnel director to IDL and another division, making her personally responsible to himself.

Jobs and careers

A great number of clerks deal with imports and exports, with a hierarchy from junior clerk to senior and thence to supervisor and manager. The import manager and the export manager then report to a branch manager. In the larger branches there may be a further sub-division into sea and air activity. There are frequently clerks and managers responsible for particular traffic lanes which may be of special importance to the branch or the company. A warehouse can be attached to the branch, or, if it is a large one, it may report directly, like the branch, to regional or national headquarters.

A key job in the company is that of the branch manager, who has full profit responsibility for the branch and has to develop business while keeping a very 'tight ship', margins being traditionally very small in this industry. A branch may have as few as five or six staff or as many as 300. Frequently branches are grouped under a more senior manager, either geographically (north, south, etc.) or functionally (air, sea, etc.) or by a mixture of categories. At company level within IDL the managing director typically has a finance manager, a commercial manager and an operations manager heading the branches and, for larger branches, a personnel manager as well. No particular policies dictated the development of these forms of organization before the start of the new division.

At the time of reorganization little attention was being paid to the question of careers. Branches were localized within their own country and often still bore the marks of the small family companies from which they had come. A career beyond that of branch manager was not very realistic for most, though, with increasing size, jobs at local company HQ level were beginning to appear. Taking over senior posts in other countries was uncommon, but promising young employees were sent to work in overseas forwarding companies. The idea was not so much to prepare them for management responsibilities as to prepare them better for dealing with the day-to-day work of international freight forwarding on return to their home office.

A typical career path might begin as a freight forwarding apprentice in Holland or Germany, a very thorough academic and practical training with experience in exports, imports and a variety of traffic lanes, with a move through the clerical grades to supervisor and manager of imports or exports and – a final move for most – to branch manager. Successful branch managers could move to the biggest branches; beyond that lay the possibility of a regional management job in charge of several branches, and beyond that again the job of operational director in charge of all branches. Finally there was the managing director job at the local company. The careers of specialist staff were not following any discernible pattern.

As Rachel Reeves was his personal appointment, and as Kenyon was committed to 'doing something about management', there was considerable impetus to a thorough review of personnel practices and policies with a view to ensuring that they made a positive contribution to company performance. Rachel Reeves's first major task after coming into post was thus to prepare a personnel strategy.

The situation: developing a personnel strategy

Business objectives

Rachel Reeves began by questioning more closely the business objectives as seen by James Kenyon. She noted that although the corporate objectives from above seemed to stress profitability they also stressed cash generation for the corporation. James Kenyon saw this latter objective as a constraint and had the informal objective of maximizing the net worth of the company. Reeves detected a feeling that the IDL division might well be a candidate for future disposal, and that James wanted to build up a strong organization which could be free-standing and which could well survive intact any future amputation from the Kenyon group. Reeves followed this discussion with talks with the other board members. She wanted to find out how they saw their business objectives and learn something of their own more personal objectives.

The immediate plan of campaign

Reeves wanted to know of any inputs or constraints from the Kenyon group personnel policy or practice which could affect a personnel strategy for IDL. However, a discussion with the head of personnel did nothing to clarify the issue. Reeves put it to Kenyon that she would start from the basis that IDL was a more or less self-contained system and that this system was about to undergo a fundamental change. Her immediate suggestion that an Organizational Development consultant should be appointed was brushed aside as unnecessary, even ridiculous. So Reeves said she would make her own diagnosis of the problems and would produce a personnel strategy to meet them, but would give priority to Kenyon's concern for some immediate action towards helping along integration in IDL and towards a management succession and development system. 'Just get around and get something going in the key areas,' James said.

Reeves planned a series of visits to senior managers around the organization. She saw a need for spending perhaps months to develop a wide-ranging personnel strategy for the division, but on the other hand she wanted to make an immediate impact on her boss and her colleagues with a view to 'establishing her credentials'. It was also necessary to identify very soon at least the broad outlines of a personnel strategy, since issues would be bound to arise at any time that would need decisions. These, she felt, should be taken within the framework of a strategy and not on an *ad hoc* basis, possibly quite at odds with what would later be settled policy. She decided to make study visits and to collect data as a sampling exercise. If the ideas found acceptance from both boss and colleagues, that should be verification enough that they were sound.

Reeves's findings on the present personnel situation

Salaries and bonuses

There was no common policy on salaries around the division. Each country saw itself as in a separate market for staff at all levels. Even within one country, two separate IDL companies might have quite different salary policies and practices. Ideas and practices about profit-sharing schemes and performance-related pay in all its forms varied very widely. The UK company had a fairly traditional salary grading structure, based on a relatively arbitrary ranking of jobs, while several other countries operated job evaluation-type schemes, though nowhere were there schemes on a reasonably comparable basis.

Whilst Reeves saw no early need for drastic action here, she did not feel the same way about bonuses. Bonuses for top company managements were in many cases realizing huge sums. In the case of the top team at Komtran, another IDL company based in Germany, bonuses were comfortably exceeding in value the already very adequate salaries. The bonus system (*Tantieme*) for the top team gave a pool of 5 per cent of the carefully defined Komtran profit to be shared between the Geschäftsführer (the three top managers) in the proportion of 40 per cent for the managing director and 30 per cent each for the other two. This formula formed part of the five-year fixed-term contracts of all three and had been devised when profits were running at no more than DM 4 million per annum. It was contractually necessary to begin discussions on the renewal of these contracts a year before the date of their expiry, and the due date for discussion was imminent. Reeves argued with Kenyon that now was the time to end this bonus scheme. It was too open-ended. The more Komtran earned, even with capital and assistance from outside itself, the sooner the bonuses would reach astronomical and totally indefensible levels. Reeves argued for a scheme based on the achievement of annually changed targets. This idea was fiercely resisted by Roland Schuster, the German managing director, and Kenyon compromised, leaving the *Tantieme* in force on the same general principles as before but with the 5 per cent bonus pool being replaced by a 3.5 per cent pool. The whole arrangement would be looked at again towards the end of the next five-year contract.

Although Kenyon had agreed with all Reeves said on what was wrong with the German scheme, and how very necessary it had become to change it, yet when it came to discussion with Schuster he backed away from confrontation, leaving Reeves to continue an increasingly bitter dialogue. She was now less confident of the backing of her boss, and it soon became clear that her relationship with Schuster had acquired a distinct 'edge'.

Recruitment and selection

Each country followed its own recruitment policies. Most relied on an intake at the apprentice level to provide not only the immediate operational needs but also, in time, the management of the company. Recruitment at a senior level was seen as exceptional, and even as a failure. The UK company found it difficult to recruit young people and seemed to rely on 'poaching' from other companies from time to time. No companies relied on any other selection method than the interview, except the Germans, who were strongly wedded to the use of graphology for the selection of all staff above supervisory level.

Pensions and other benefits

The different national arrangements concerning pensions, life and accident insurance, medical benefits, etc. were so complex that Reeves felt it was safer to leave consideration of them for a while. She noted that none of the companies seemed to have heard of the existence of multinational pooling of insured benefits.

Industrial relations

There was a very low level of unionization at IDL. There were a few T&GWU members at some UK branches, and rather more members in Germany of the union covering transport workers. Reeves learnt of no problems with unions at the local level and found no sign of any union organization or activity at international level. There were no works councils in the UK, though they existed in other countries, and in Sweden and in Germany there were employee representatives on the board. Few problems with any of these institutions were reported to Reeves. She made a point of trying to meet the employee representatives on the company boards. She was gratified to find a great deal of goodwill towards IDL. She was glad to hear from the German representatives that they felt their company was strengthened by its membership of the group, that they would like to see more integration within it, with all the opportunities to which it would give rise for employee development. They had not been aware that the objective of the IDL division was indeed to integrate more closely. Reeves determined to learn German and get herself on to a supervisory board.

Management succession

While Reeves would have liked to undertake a thorough human resources audit at the outset, she was handicapped by a lack of data. Classifications and grades differed between various companies, even though at first sight they might seem similar. Matters were not helped by the different hardware and software in use around the division. There was disagreement over which technology to develop, and progress to common systems was clearly going to be painfully slow. Kenyon demanded early action to find a plausible internal candidate for the IDL chief executive job and required some immediate impression of the succession situation.

Reeves calculated the number of retirements from the most senior posts during the next three years. Besides Kenyon himself, who was due for retirement at the age of sixty-two (he was currently approaching sixty), none was due to retire from an IDL board position. The managing directors of two medium-size companies were due to go in just over two years, as were three operational directors and two sales directors from large companies. Apparently, immediately below these levels there were significant numbers of important posts due to become vacant over the next few years. Although some companies had sketchy plans to meet some of the gaps which would open up, there was little systematic planning for succession. Beyond the needs of the individual companies there were a range of senior jobs that were likely to be created at IDL level of which the companies in IDL had as yet no cognizance.

Appraisal
Policies and practices regarding appraisal were as varied as everything else seemed to be in the division. In the UK the appraisal system was apparently strongly oriented to the discovery and nurture of future potential, but not a great deal resulted from the scheme in practice, owing to sloppy administration and cut-backs on training expenditure.

In France an appraisal scheme had been tacked on to an earlier DPO (Management by Objectives) scheme, a very top-down scheme which was not conspicuously helping succession and development there.

In Germany the scheme covered only junior and middle management levels. It was an 'open' scheme, including an element of self-assessment, and was seen as providing the means of maintaining and improving current performance. One mechanism was the regular and reliable follow-up on the recommendations for training and the experience which flowed from it. Comments on the potential of employees formed a minor part of the scheme and did not receive such close attention or action.

In the USA maintaining and improving current performance was claimed to be the major objective but was not obviously succeeding, largely, Reeves considered, because of its close link with the company salary system. No consistent patterns emerged from the appraisal activities of the remaining companies.

Development
What management development was being carried out was not very closely related to appraisal. There was generally a clear difference between training managers in business specialisms and training them for management as such. The need to follow up early training, where it existed, with instruction on, for example, the development of computer systems for tracking the whereabouts of goods in transit was well recognized. The knowledge and skills essential to most management jobs were not catered for quite so readily.

Experience was everywhere prized highly. In the branches and numerous small companies, managers frequently gained all-round management experience at a much earlier stage than they would have done in a larger organization. There was no very systematic planning in this, however.

Formal courses were used everywhere, sometimes following appraisal and not infrequently when someone persistently asked for one. James Kenyon had occasionally sent a very senior executive from his European division to a short course at a major American business school. Most companies used local courses for managers, and frequently provided finance courses for non-financial executives. Increasingly communication and people management short courses were being used. In the UK two executives were following a Henley distance learning management course.

Learning was also taking place, as Reeves noted, outside those activities recognized as providing the opportunity for it. One instance was an *ad hoc* problem-solving meeting Reeves attended, chaired by one IDL director, Ross Walinski, at which he brought the operational and sales teams together to thrash out difficulties for which each team was enthusiastically blaming the other. Everyone seemed to learn a good deal and Reeves noted several equally valuable opportunities for learning as she moved round the division.

She was discouraged to find from several companies that they had failed to learn much from courses organized and run by the Kenyon group staff. Most of those attending the courses were from the UK manufacturing companies, and the foreign members found the courses so 'UK and manufacturing-oriented' that they were 'lost'. None of the foreign companies would now consider sending staff to them. The American company had been able to participate in first-class training schemes under their former ownership but had done little since joining the Kenyon group.

Training
The standards and amount of training in general varied as much as everything else in the division. Some countries were by law and tradition more committed to it than others. In the UK young people were given practical encouragement to take up day release studies in forwarding, and short forwarding-related courses were used from time to time. At the other extreme the Komtran company had highly organized apprentice training under the German 'dual system' (a national commitment to the preparation of young people for the world of work involving carefully structured educational components and thorough training within the firm, with strong involvement of local chambers of commerce), and had a complete programme of training activities covering technical, commercial and personnel-type activities. An elaborate manual of the year's courses was produced and each company was required to send given percentages of their staff on the courses. Training in most companies fell somewhere between these two extremes. Reeves noted that nowhere was there any serious attempt at an evaluation of training.

Overview of the personnel situation
Reeves came to some general conclusions on the situation which faced her. As she observed, the management teams in IDL were no different from those of other predominantly small and medium-size companies in the industry. A further characteristic of the more successful managers, she discovered, was that they tended to be much more entrepreneurial and

much less bureaucratically-minded than the managers she had thought likely to be the bedrock of a dynamic and successful future IDL.

The extent of the lack of knowledge about one another on the part of companies within the division was a big surprise, and Reeves found the level of misunderstanding and even distrust disturbing. She could not but believe that James Kenyon's plan for closer integration was not going to be easy to bring about. While the lack of knowledge was most apparent at lower levels of the companies, misunderstanding and mistrust seemed to be as high or even higher among the most senior managers.

Rachel Reeves's personnel strategy report

Two months after her appointment the second board meeting of IDL was due to take place. James Kenyon had put 'Personnel Report' as item 4 on the agenda and had told Reeves that he wanted a brief mention of any urgent personnel issues that had arisen since the last board meeting. He also wanted some proposals on management succession and development. Reeves agreed to do this and to circulate suitable documentation in good time before the meeting.

On reflection she felt it would be wrong to address the succession and development situation outside a broader strategy. She decided to circulate a more wide-ranging document which would be short on detail but which would highlight major issues. Although Kenyon had asked for a sight of Reeves's paper before it went out, it was produced so late that there was no possibility of his seeing it before the meeting, since he was on holiday for the week before. While she regretted this, Reeves felt that the late circulation could work to her advantage. Strong critics on the board would not have time to concert opposition to her ideas and she would have an opportunity to get explanations of them across before they had perhaps already been 'written off'. Her lengthy report, entitled 'A personnel strategy for IDL', is summarized below.

Rachel Reeves's paper was duly circulated. This case ends where the board meeting begins. James Kenyon was annoyed that Reeves had circulated a wider-ranging paper than agreed, thrusting issues into the spotlight that he would have preferred not to address at this stage. Roland Schuster, the German managing director, had already told Reeves as the meeting was about to start that he was astounded that she had the cheek to be telling everyone what they should be doing before she had had time to get to know the company. No other board member overhearing this seemed to be rushing to her defence.

A PERSONNEL STRATEGY FOR IDL
EXECUTIVE SUMMARY AND RECOMMENDATIONS

1 Integration and culture

1.1 A single distinctive culture needs to be developed out of the different national and organizational cultures within IDL.

1.2 This should be modelled on the Kenyon parent company, but as an 'overlay' rather than a substitute for existing local cultures.

1.3 The culture should be disseminated by a communication programme and training events.

2 Human resource planning

2.1 Data need to be collected in a systematic fashion, and regular reports should be made to IDL head office.

2.2 The board needs to appoint a computer working party at director level, on which Personnel will be represented, to hasten the development of compatible computer systems and packages in the division.

3 Management succession

3.1 Charts showing possible successors to middle and senior management posts should be kept by each company in the division, and the Personnel Director should be responsible for top management succession planning.

3.2 Appraisal systems should be standardized across the division and should incorporate all management levels. The focus would be the maintenance and improvement of performance, although some attention should be paid to the identification of potential.

3.3 A Management Development Committee, chaired by the Managing Director and with the Personnel Director and two other directors as members, should be established to oversee:

3.3.1 Career development and planning for the top 100–200 'high flyers'.

3.3.2 The present and future structure of the organization.

3.3.3 Career planning for all senior managers.

3.3.4 The work of regional Management Development Committees to be set up below board level.

3.3.5 Expatriate career planning, with a view to reducing the length of overseas assignments, and where this is not possible to give greater attention to the management of long-term postings.

3.4 A new grading structure for management is urgently needed to facilitate succession planning and to assist the rationalization of salary and benefit structures (see 7.1 and 7.2)

3.5 An interim management grading structure based on the size of branches and companies with about fifteen grades and assimilating non-line manager posts is proposed (viz. managers responsible for a turnover of about £1 million would be placed on grade 2 and those responsible for around £8 million would be on grade 8).

4 Management development

4.1 Formal courses need to be supplemented by less formal experiential learning:

4.1.1 Maximum use should be made of working groups called together from different countries on either an *ad hoc* or a standing basis.

4.1.2 Multi-disciplinary 'Profit Improvement Teams' to be set up to act as internal consultants. The Managing Director would assign promising young managers to these for a period of twelve to eighteen months.

4.1.3 Job rotation could be introduced to maximize opportunities for international experience, especially via foreign assignments in circumstances where local consultants or temporary management help might have been employed.

4.2 The existing range of formal courses used by companies within the IDL division should be continued, with the following enhancement:

4.2.1 A two-week residential course for 'high-flying' managers on freight forwarding in the changing international context facing IDL.

4.2.2 A one-week outdoor training course bringing together younger managers from different nationalities and job levels. This should be monitored with a view to extending its availability to more senior groups.

4.2.3 The whole portfolio of management education courses from M.B.A.s to Management Centre Europe seminars would be kept under review by Personnel.

5 Training

5.1 Current practice should be adhered to for the present, but changes proposed for the mid-term include:

5.1.1 A review of the specific UK training situation.

5.1.2 A six-month to one-year programme of apprentice exchange between countries, consisting of both on and off-the-job training.

6 Recruitment

6.1 Common systems of international advertisement in each country should be established at divisional level for senior posts.

6.2 Efforts are needed to raise the general standard of recruits, and the Personnel Director of IDL should be involved in all appointments above grade 12.

7 Salaries

7.1 An interim grading structure needs to be defined pending a more thorough review based upon job evaluation.

7.2 Although the same structure would apply across all countries, salaries relating to the same grade might differ in each country in accordance with national salary norms.

7.3 All bonus payments for the most senior grades to require approval from the Managing Director. Bonus schemes based upon a stated percentage of company profit would no longer be acceptable.

8 Participation

8.1 It is recommended that the wide range of practice within the division should be rationalized by a process of 'levelling up'. Suggestions are invited as to how this could be best achieved.

17

This case raises issues not only of personnel strategies and policies of succession and development in an international context, but also of how a personnel manager can best succeed in gaining support and acceptance for them. The following questions should test your understanding of these issues.

1 How appropriate is Rachel Reeves's 'Personnel strategy for IDL' to the needs of the situation?
2 Comment on Rachel Reeves's approach to the development and presentation of her strategy, with particular reference to the perspectives of James Kenyon and Roland Schuster. How would you have set about the task?
3 How well do Rachel Reeves's proposals on management succession and development meet the needs of career management at IDL?
4 Discuss the relationship between organizational development and management development in the context of this case.
5 List the extra complexities which you believe are brought to the personnel problems on account of the international basis of IDL.

Recommended reading

BERRY, A., and MARSHALL, J. (eds.), 'International management and development', *Management Education and Development*, special issue, 17, 3, 1986.

DAVIS, S. M., *Managing and Organizing Multinational Corporations*, Oxford, Pergamon, 1979, pp. 177–192.

DESATNIK, R. L., and BENNETT, M. L., *Human Resource Management in the Multinational Company*, Aldershot, Gower, 1977.

DOWLING, P. J., and SCHULER, R. S., *International Dimensions of HRM*, Boston, Mass., PWS-Kent Publishing Company, 1990.

GARRATT, R., and STOPFORD, J., *Breaking down Barriers: Practice and Priorities for International Management Education*, Aldershot, Gower for ATM (now AMED), 1980.

GRATTON, L., *Heirs Apparent: Succession Strategies for the 1990s*, Oxford, Blackwell, 1990.

GRATTON, L., and SYRETT, M., 'Heirs apparent: succession strategies for the future', *Personnel Management*, January 1990.

HIGGINS, A., and BLAKELY, C., 'Preparing the groundwork to track the high-flyers', *Personnel Management*, February 1990.

HOGG, C., 'Human resource management and the international market place', *Manpower Policy and Practice*, 3, 4, 1988, pp. 25–34.

IDS/IPM, European Management Guides series: *Terms and Conditions of Employment*, 1991; *Recruitment*, 1990; *Industrial Relations*, 1991; *Pay and Benefits*, 1992; *Training and Development*, London, IPM, 1992.

MAYO, A., *Managing Careers: Strategies for Organizations*. London, IPM, 1991.

OTTERBECK, L., *The Management of Headquarters and Subsidiaries: Relationships in Multinational Corporations*, Aldershot, Gower, 1981.

SCHEIN, E., 'Culture as an environmental context for careers', *Journal of Occupational Behaviour*, 5, 1984, pp. 71–81.

SMILEY, T., 'A challenge to the human resource and organisational functions in international firms', *European Management Journal*, 7, 2, 1989, pp. 189–97.

WILLIAMS, R., 'What's new in career development?', *Personnel Management*, March 1984.

III
Employee Relations

Case 18

An experiment going sour at Pinta plc?

Tim Claydon

The following case concerns a decision to move away from collective bargaining as part of an attempt to structure employee relations along unitarist lines, in the belief that such a move can enhance efficiency and profitability while at the same time being acceptable to employees. The problems and tensions arising from this course of action are described below. The case also raises more general issues concerning the ability of firms to initiate and sustain managerially led forms of employee involvement as an alternative to unionized relationships at work.

The extent and significance of the challenge to collective bargaining which some have discerned during the last twelve years is a matter of considerable debate. Generally, however, it is agreed that its main manifestation has been an erosion of union power and influence through the reassertion of managerial power within the context of reformed bargaining structures, rather than an attack on collective bargaining *per se*. Nevertheless, withdrawals from collective bargaining, while unusual, have grown in incidence since the mid-1980s, with perhaps as many as 13 per cent of companies with over 500 employees having withdrawn collective bargaining rights from at least part of their work force (Gregg and Yates, 1991). In a number of these cases, such as the one described below, withdrawal from collective bargaining has not been synonymous with deunionization, nor has it deprived unions of all representative functions within the organization. Often the unions retain the right to represent individual members' grievances, and in a few cases remain able to represent members collectively through consultation or, even more rarely, negotiation over non-pay issues (Claydon, 1989).

The Pinta case is unusual in that the derecognition is of a manual workers' union, whereas most of the cases which have been investigated have affected white-collar unions. However, it shares common features with a number of other derecognitions of manual unions in process manufacturing, notably chemicals. Derecognition has been confined to a single plant, at least initially; it has been associated with moves towards harmonized pay and single 'staff' status, and with an increased emphasis on direct and indirect forms of communication with employees and on employee 'involvement' and 'commitment'. There is an important difference, however. In the case of the chemical companies derecognition occurred in existing plants which were already unionized. The Pinta experiment took place at a newly developed plant on a brownfield site with a hand-picked work force. All Pinta's other plants, in common with the rest of the industry, are highly unionized.

18

In association with union derecognition Pinta have tried to promote teamwork as part of the drive for increased flexibility and efficiency. In introducing the concept of teamwork at the new plant, management have attempted to move in the direction of 'employee involvement', something which has been widely advocated in personnel management circles for a number of years. Much is claimed for such moves as a way of increasing workers' commitment to management goals, helping to create a co-operative climate conducive to change, reinforcing the leadership role of line management and ultimately leading to more efficient output of better-quality products. However, it is much less clear *how* employee involvement results in improved performance or even whether it does at all. There has been little rigorous, systematic evaluation of employee involvement initiatives by independent researchers until very recently and the evidence it has produced has been contradictory (Beaumont, 1990). This could mean either that the benefits associated with employee involvement are illusory, or that much depends on the precise nature of involvement policies and their implementation. The Pinta case illustrates some of the issues in this debate.

Background to the case

Pinta plc

Pinta is a large dairy products firm. Much of its activity centres on the milk trade, being the bottling of milk for doorstep delivery and, more recently, packaging milk in cartons, known as NRCs (non-returnable containers), for sale to large supermarket chains. The dairy industry has experienced growing market pressures over the last ten years or so. Sales of bottled milk, mainly for doorstep delivery, where profit margins are high at around 17p per unit, have been falling by 6–8 per cent per year. NRC sales have grown, but competition among producers for contracts to supply the large supermarket chains which dominate this market has forced profit margins down to about 2p per unit. These developments have led to widespread closures and rationalization of bottling plants and to pressures to reduce costs in NRC plants. At the same time, producers have been forced to pay greater attention to quality of the product and reliability of delivery in order to obtain and retain supermarket contracts.

The brownfield site

Pinta's own rationalization took the form of the closure of two bottling plants and the redevelopment of one of the sites as a highly automated NRC plant, commencing operation in 1987. In planning the new development the project team looked at Pinta's own experience of developments in new technology and the experience of other UK companies operating new technology on greenfield sites. This in turn led to working arrangements and

industrial relations at the new plant emerging as a key issue. It was decic
that the operation of the plant provided an opportunity to move away fro
established practices elsewhere within the firm and the industry, since t
fact that the plant was new and that a new work force would be hir
allowed it to be treated as a 'greenfield' rather than a 'brownfield' site.

Pay bargaining

Pay and conditions for weekly paid employees at Pinta were traditionally
determined by collective bargaining, mainly with the TGWU, which is the
dominant union in the industry. Minimum basic rates for the industry were
set by a Joint National Negotiating Committee, set up in 1974. A number
of large firms withdrew from the national agreement from the late 1970s,
but Pinta continue to operate it in all their plants, except the one discussed
here. The agreement leaves considerable scope for plant-level bargaining
to build upon basic rates. Local bargaining between plant managers and
sophisticated shop stewards' committees was already highly developed by
1974 and has remained significant since.

The union's bargaining strategy reflected the nature of the product: its
perishability and the need to maintain daily supplies for doorstep delivery.
This had always meant that workers on a particular shift had to 'finish
the job', and overtime working was an accepted feature of the industry.
Thus shop stewards' committees sought to establish entitlement to regular
overtime working at premium rates. High levels of overtime and rest-day
working permitted high earnings over and above relatively modest basic
weekly pay. Relations with management were perceived by both sides as
good. However, when planning the operation of the new NRC plant, newly
appointed senior managers at Pinta felt that industrial relations stability in
the bottling plants had been bought at a high price in terms of efficiency
and profits. There was a strong feeling that the ideas associated with
'human resource management' offered an alternative to traditional collective
bargaining, which would result in more effective working. This appraisal
played a significant role in the development of management's vision of the
employment relationship in the new plant.

The situation

Developing team working

Management's vision was also influenced by the nature of the wholesale
milk market, the technology of the new plant and changes in organizational
structure within Pinta. The pressure to reduce costs, while maintaining and
improving the quality of the product and its delivery, stemming from the
market power of the multiple retailers as purchasers, was seen to require
a high degree of commitment and flexibility of hours, in order to ensure
efficient production and limit the cost of overtime payments. The operation

of automated process plant, incorporating quality control at each stage of production, required individuals who were able to accept relatively high levels of responsibility and were capable of performing routine maintenance jobs, as well as operating equipment. These features in turn suggested that status distinctions within the plant should be minimized and a 'team spirit' developed. This in turn led to a decision to go for a flat management structure, something that was further encouraged by wider moves to decentralize decision-making within Pinta plc.

The consequent arrangements for managing the new plant and the terms and conditions offered to manual employees differ markedly from the norm within other Pinta plants and the industry generally. A senior management team consisting of site manager, operations manager, personnel manager and three departmental managers determines policy and general standards at the plant. Within each department there are a number of 'team leaders' who are responsible for the supervision of operators, carrying out team briefings and dealing with day-to-day employee relations issues, including discipline up to the stage of appeal and the first stage of grievance procedure. However, in an attempt to implement the spirit of teamwork, policy on discipline is that, although formal procedures exist, disciplinary standards should be based on common agreement and understanding, with minimal recourse to formality. This highlights the role of team leaders in developing and sustaining desired behaviour among manual employees. This structure means a relatively high supervisor to operative ratio, with, on average, one team leader for every ten operatives.

The team concept is, however, a loose one. Work itself is not organized on a team basis. Rather, teamwork is seen as an 'attitude', to be fostered by a combination of rigorous selection among applicants for jobs, communication via team briefings and harmonization of most elements of pay and conditions, except holiday entitlement. The role of team briefings, held weekly, is to inform employees of plant performance, market developments and to deal with problem issues raised by operatives.

The closure of the old plant and the dismissal of all employees gave management a free hand in staffing the new operation. In selecting workers who would give the commitment sought by management, in terms of willingness to accept flexibility of hours and high levels of responsibility, use was made of sophisticated selection methods, including psychometric testing, and preference was given to young people without family or other outside commitments. Special attention was given to the recruitment and selection of team leaders, who were typically young graduates in their mid-twenties. All new employees were inducted into the management philosophy as well as being trained in the technical aspects of the plant's operation. Team leaders were also sent on an Outward Bound-style leadership course. In the early days at the plant it was often said that to be an employee there 'you had to be able to walk on water'.

Pay harmonization and a move away from collective bargaining

The harmonization of conditions of employment involved fitting operatives into Pinta's salaried staff structure. Salaries are paid monthly by direct transfer. The salary policy is central to the way in which the plant is managed, as it attempts to ensure maximum flexibility of hours while minimizing the costs of overtime. The salary package is set at a level which incorporates an allowance for hours flexibility plus a supplement for each job in respect of the amount of unsocial hours' working, e.g. weekends, late and early shifts. No separate overtime payments are provided for.

These changes have also involved a break with established industrial relations practice. Pay harmonization has played a crucial role in the drive for greater flexibility of working, not only by obviating the need for paid overtime but also by taking manual employees at the plant out of collective bargaining, since salaried staff at Pinta are not covered by collective agreements. Management felt that collective bargaining was incompatible with the team commitment which they wished to foster. Initially, senior management favoured an entirely non-union operation at the new plant; this view was encouraged by product market developments, in particular, the dependence of NRC plants on contracts with large multiple retailers. This dependence was seen as making the plant vulnerable in collective bargaining because of the need to maintain production and the inability to pass higher wage costs on to the customer. At the same time, the fact that the plant was completely new encouraged the company to start from scratch with a new approach.

Union derecognition

This plan was, however, frustrated by the threat of industrial action throughout Pinta's other plants. Instead, an agreement was reached with the TGWU whereby the union was given eighteen months to establish a membership, plus the right to represent individual members within the grievance and disciplinary procedure and to be consulted over pay reviews. This agreement was clearly seen by the union as holding out the promise of full recognition once membership had been built up. By the end of 1989, when the agreement terminated, a 'substantial' membership was claimed, around 50 per cent. However, management remained adamant that it should not have collective bargaining rights. In response to union protests management claimed that it had never agreed to the union having anything more than the right to represent individual members in grievance and disciplinary procedures and to informal consultation whereby the union 'makes its views known' to management on pay. Since then the union has continued to perform these roles.

The changes in operation

The operation of the new plant has, however, been problematic. Capacity working has not been reached, and the plant has only just become marginally profitable. To a great extent these problems are rooted in relations with the work force, raising doubts about how well the teamwork concept has worked. Difficulties in retaining and recruiting staff are one reason for below-capacity working, and management are also concerned at what is seen as lack of discipline, particularly in respect of timekeeping.

18

Recruitment problems have also meant that the initially rigorous selection procedures applied to applicants for jobs have had to be relaxed.

At the beginning of 1990 management called in external consultants to analyse the problems at the plant. A number of factors were identified. Team briefings worked well in general but many employees had become cynical, feeling that the system was too 'top-down', with little in the way of response to problems raised by the work force. Employees saw briefings as consisting of the management message followed by a 'gripe session' which led to little in the way of practical outcomes. At the same time, while the management message was seen as providing good information on general issues facing the plant, employees felt that they had little idea of what was happening at the level of their own performance, how they were doing on a day-to-day basis.

Discipline problems were analysed as being related to the difficulty which team leaders experienced in managing their relations with subordinates. 'Team spirit' had tended to be interpreted in such a way as to lead to 'chummy relationships', which made the exercise of authority difficult. Many workers felt positively about the discretion they were allowed in their roles, yet team leaders and senior management frequently interpreted it as slack discipline and were anxious to reinforce disciplinary standards. In this connection the TGWU argued that team leaders' lack of experience in managing people, together with the ambiguity of their role in terms of its identification with both operatives and management – 'being the union as well as the management' – placed them under considerable stress. This was seen as leading to incidents involving arbitrary and authoritarian action by team leaders. At the same time it was observed that there were no real teams, team leaders having shifting responsibilities among different groups of workers. It was also pointed out that turnover among senior management had been high, five site managers having been appointed since 1987.

The TGWU's argument is that earnings and long hours are the main cause of grievance, which has led to both high turnover and rising union membership. Although salaries at the plant are substantially higher than the national minimum basic rate for the industry, earnings are low compared with those in other plants owned by Pinta because no separate overtime payments are made. One comparison was of a fork-lift truck driver's earnings of around £14,000 at the NRC plant compared with £18,000 at a nearby bottling plant. Additionally, employees are aggrieved at the extent of hours flexibility, since fourteen to fifteen-hour shifts are not uncommon.

These grievances have led to heightened union activity at the plant. In response to complaints about excessively long hours management introduced 'lieu time', whereby additional hours worked above 45¼ per week could be accrued and taken as additional rest days. However, so much lieu time accrued that it could not be honoured. As a result management entered into discussions with the TGWU to buy out outstanding lieu time. Since then the union has been pressing for overtime payments for rest-day and 'excessive hours' working. At first the company position was that there should be no premium payment for overtime and that rest-day working should be paid for at the standard salary rate, i.e. excluding the salary supplement from the calculation. Subsequently the company has agreed to the principle of premium payments for 'excessive hours' but only after

45¼ hours have been worked. It also wants to calculate extra hours on a cumulative basis, offsetting them against weeks when fewer than thirty-nine have been worked. This is unacceptable to the TGWU, which has continued to press for the equivalent of time-and-a-half for rest-day working and for overtime to be calculated on a daily basis. In the course of this campaign the union claims to have raised membership to 80 per cent and to have three shop stewards in post, and is pressing for formal bargaining rights. So far management have remained insistent that all discussions with the TGWU have had the status of informal consultation and that the union has no bargaining status at the plant.

Activity brief

1 Evaluate Pinta management's approach to the issue of union recognition at the new plant from 1987 onwards. What factors have determined the current role of the TGWU?
2 Analyse the difficulties associated with the teamwork concept at the plant. How would you seek to improve its operation in practice?
3 Consider the options open to management in response to the TGWU's request for bargaining rights and their possible outcomes. Make recommendations as to a course of action based upon your analysis.

Recommended reading

BEAUMONT, P. B., *Change in Industrial Relations: the Organization and its Environment*, London, Routledge, 1990.

CLAYDON, T., 'Union derecognition in Britain in the 1980s', *British Journal of Industrial Relations*, 27, 2, 1989.

GREGG, P., and YATES, A., 'Changes in wage setting arrangements and trade union presence in the 1980s', *British Journal of Industrial Relations*, 29, 3, September 1991, pp. 361–76.

MARCHINGTON, M., 'Employee participation', in B. TOWERS (ed.), *A Handbook of Industrial Relations Practice*, London, Kogan Page, 1989.

TOWERS, B., 'Trends and developments in industrial relations. Derecognising trade unions: implications and consequences', *Industrial Relations Journal*, 13, 3, 1988.

Case 19

Union recognition in polytechnics and colleges

David Farnham

This case study examines an employer strategy aimed at introducing a private-sector model of union recognition into a restructured public service, the English polytechnics and colleges, where national-level collective bargaining had previously been firmly entrenched. When the'new' polytechnics were created after a government White Paper in 1966, they remained or were placed under the control of local education authorities (LEAs). The LEAs assumed responsibility, until the Education Reform Act, 1988, for financial matters and the employment of staff, but not control of courses.

The situation described here arose from the consequences of the Education Reform Act, 1988, which took some 24,000 full-time and 8,500 part-time higher education teachers out of local government employment and into the Polytechnic and Colleges Funding Council (PCFC) sector. Also affected were 17,000 full-time administrative staff and 4,000 manual workers. The PCFC sector consists of over eighty 'higher education corporations', thirty-two of which are now polytechnics, funded primarily by grants from the Department of Education and Science. The higher education corporations became the new budget holders and legal employers of teachers and other staff on 1 April 1989. One of the first tasks facing the PCFC employers was to seek a new recognition and bargaining procedure with the trade unions in a sector with a long tradition of union recognition, high union density and national collective agreements for all groups of staff.

Background to the case

The development of collective bargaining

Union recognition for polytechnic and college teachers in England and Wales has a long history. Unions representing academic staff in what was originally called 'technical education' were first recognized by the education authorities for collective bargaining purposes in the Burnham Technical Committee in 1920. The main union representing 'technical teachers', the Association of Teachers in Technical Institutions (ATTI), was formed in 1904 and had been lobbying for improvements in its members' pay and conditions, such as hours, holidays and pensions, for many years. The purpose of the Burnham Technical Committee was to determine the salaries of all teachers, from classroom staff to college principals, in technical colleges and 'junior technical schools' through national collective bargaining.

One of the provisions of the Education Act, 1944, was to standardize teachers' pay through national salary scales. Pay and the salary structure, in what was now described as 'further education', continued to be determined by national bargaining in the reconstituted Burnham Further Education Committee (BFEC), or 'Burnham Committee'. Establishments of further education, where local education authorities were the legal employers, covered a wide range of institutions in terms of size and functions, including institutions of 'advanced further education', such as the large colleges of advanced technology and regional colleges of technology, teaching from national diploma to postgraduate levels; and 'non-advanced further education' institutions providing technical, craft and commercial studies in smaller local colleges.

Union recognition and negotiation arrangements

Arrangements for union recognition and negotiating machinery tended to follow the various attempts aimed at restructuring advanced further education during the 1970s and 1980s. This is reflected in a bewildering proliferation of related committees, often referred to in abbreviated form. (Appendix 19.1 lists the various abbreviations used in the case.) In 1965 the Remuneration of Teachers Act, 1965, gave statutory authority to the national negotiating machinery and to the salary agreements, staffing establishments and course gradings created in the Burnham Committee. In 1975 further education and teacher education were brought under common regulations and the Burnham Committee merged with the Pelham Committee, which negotiated salaries for teachers in the colleges of education. By then, some of the former colleges of advanced technology had become universities, while thirty of the regional colleges of technology had been given polytechnic status from the late 1960s but remained under LEA administrative control. By the late 1970s the BFEC covered 76,000 teachers in further education, including 14,000 polytechnic teachers.

The major teacher union recognized nationally for salary and related negotiations in the BFEC was the National Association of Teachers in Further and Higher Education (NATFHE). The Association had been formed in 1976 by a merger between ATTI and the Association of Teachers in Colleges and Departments of Education. It claimed to represent about 85 per cent of the full-time teachers covered by the further education regulations and, as shown in Table 19.1, with twelve out of sixteen seats on the teachers' panel of Burnham, NATFHE was the dominant union. The management panel consisted of eight representatives from the Association of County Councils (ACC), six from the Association of Metropolitan Authorities (AMA), one from the Welsh Joint Education

Committee and two from the Department of Education and Science. The chair was an independent person nominated by the Secretary of State.

Table 19.1 Membership of the Burnham Further Education Committee, 1980

Management panel		Teachers' panel	
Association of County Councils	8	NATFHE	12
Association of Metropolitan Authorities	6	Association of Principals of Colleges	2
Welsh Joint Committee	1	National Society of Art Education	1
Department of Education and Science	2	Association of Agricultural Education Staff	1

Independent chair nominated by Department of Education and Science.
Plus non-voting observers.

Note. APT was granted a seat on Burnham in 1981.

Another teacher union, the Association of Polytechnic Teachers (APT), was not recognized by the employers and remained unrepresented on the BFEC until 1981; it had 2,500 members in the new polytechnics, compared with NATFHE's 11,000. APT was formed, as a breakaway body from ATTI, in May 1973. Its main purpose was to establish separate pay-negotiating machinery for polytechnic teachers, outside Burnham. APT derived its impetus from dissatisfaction among polytechnic teachers with their salaries and their more limited career prospects in comparison with those of university teachers. What distinguished APT from NATFHE was its view that pay relativities between polytechnic and other further education teachers in the Burnham structure were unfair. This arose, it was argued, because of the greater weight given by NATFHE to the demands of its majority membership in non-advanced further education than to those of its polytechnic members. If the polytechnic experiment was to succeed, APT asserted, polytechnic teachers were a special case deserving separate salary negotiations and pay scales appropriate to their skills, qualifications and status. Their professional interests, APT claimed, were different from those of other teachers in further education. This position contrasted with that of NATFHE, and previously the ATTI, which wanted a unified post-school educational system, with common salary scales. Other factors separating the two unions were NATFHE's affiliation to the Trades Union Congress, its militant leadership and its support of left-wing policies.

The Burnham Committee agreed salaries for all academic staff, including college principals, heads of department, teachers and researchers. It also determined the grading of courses into level of difficulty and the associated staffing establishments required. Its decisions were subject to the approval of the Secretary of State and were authorized by statutory instruments. The 'Burnham Report' was normally issued annually by the Department of Education and Science but, where it was not, an amending order was made. If there was a failure to agree within the Burnham Committee, the issues could be referred to independent arbitration, normally with the agreement of both sides. In practice arbitration was rarely used, since the Secretary of State could veto the decisions of the arbitrators by securing a majority vote in Parliament on the grounds of the national financial interest.

The separation of pay and conditions of service

It was one of the features of English further education that teachers' pay and other conditions of service were determined separately. Salaries and staffing establishments were settled under statute, in the Burnham Committee, while conditions of service were determined by voluntary negotiations between the local authority employers and the unions nationally. Until 1974 representatives of the teacher unions and the local authorities drew up model agreements for consideration by individual LEAs, covering:

- Sick pay.
- Redundancy procedures.
- Conditions of tenure.
- Maternity leave.
- Consultation and negotiation.
- Collective disputes.
- Facilities for union officials.

After local government reorganization in 1974 a new body was formed by ACC and AMA for dealing with education matters, consisting of twelve representatives from each institution. It was called the Council of Local Education Authorities (CLEA) and it assumed the employer role in negotiating conditions of service for further education teachers with the unions on the BFEC. One of the most far-reaching agreements was reached in 1975 covering the length and distribution of the academic year, teaching loads, contact hours and extra payments. In 1979 the National Joint Council for Further Education Teachers in England and Wales (NJCFET) was established. Its membership mirrored that of Burnham, consisting of representatives from CLEA and the teachers' panel, and excluded APT representation. Its purpose was to deal with conditions of service. One of its first tasks was to codify the agreements made between the LEAs and teacher unions over the years. In 1981 the NJCFET published this codified document, which became known as 'the Silver Book'.

By this time CLEA and the recognized unions believed that the continued separation of bargaining on pay and conditions was unsatisfactory. By 1985 the first steps had been taken by the two sides to amend the NJCFET's constitution to allow it to consider remuneration matters. Although the 1965 Act precluded the NJCFET from determining pay, the amendment reflected the growing maturity of the NJCFET, which became the forum for discussing all issues of pay and conditions of service in the bargaining rounds of 1985, 1986 and 1987. By now APT had secured a seat on the Burnham Committee, on the decision of the Secretary of State in December 1981, though the other teacher unions – led by NATFHE – had refused to co-operate with APT in Burnham. They had also resisted attempts by APT to obtain a seat on the NJCFET.

The repeal of the Remuneration of Teachers Act, 1965, by the Teachers'

Pay and Conditions Act, 1987, was a watershed in industrial relations in further education. The 1987 Act enabled the LEA employers and the teacher unions on the former Burnham Committee to establish their own free-standing national collective bargaining machinery, outside any statutory provision. The reconstituted National Joint Council for Lecturers in Further Education in England and Wales (NJCLFE), which had an independent, non-voting chair, was able to negotiate on all terms and conditions and provided for arbitration, with the consent of both parties, where negotiations had broken down. As shown in Table 19.2, APT was included in membership, but only by governmental imposition and without the agreement of the other member organizations.

Table 19.2 Membership of the NJCLFE, England and Wales, 1987

Employers' representatives		Lecturers' representatives	
Association of County Councils	8	NATFHE	12
Association of Metropolitan Authorities	6	Association of Principals of Colleges	2
Welsh Joint Education Committee	1	National Society of Art and Design Education	1
		Association of Polytechnic Teachers	1
		Association of Agricultural Educational Staffs	1

Independent chair nominated by the Department of Education and Science.
Plus non-voting observers.

With the repeal of the Remuneration of Teachers Act, 1965, and the uncertain legal standing of the Burnham Report, which had last been published in 1983, the NJCLFE intended to incorporate it, and the Silver Book, into the NJC machinery and to create a single document for easy use. The links between national, LEA and local joint machinery are shown in Figure 19.1. Like the previous council before it, the NJCLFE had an important role in guiding local bargaining, since many authorities already had parallel local agreements. They did this by establishing local committees replicating the NJC, with national arrangements helping to resolve local disputes. However, the presence of APT nationally was not

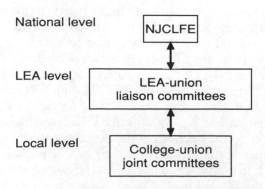

Figure 19.1 National, LEA and local joint machinery prior to incorporation

190

seen by the employers as imposing any obligation on individual LEAs to recognize APT locally, though some did.

The situation

The Education Reform Act, 1988

The NJCLFE, however, was short-lived as far as polytechnic and other higher education teachers were concerned as a result of the Education Reform Act, 1988, which received the royal assent on 29 July 1988. The consequences were:

- The removal of advanced further education from local authority administrative control, and its separation from non-advanced further education, on 1 April 1989.
- The funding of higher education corporations through the Polytechnic and Colleges Funding Council (PCFC).
- The replacement of the LEAs as the employing authorities for advanced further education and their replacement by the governing bodies of the higher education corporations.
- The need for a fundamental restructuring of the industrial relations machinery for higher education.

The PCFC employers' responses

After the Education Reform Bill had been published in November 1987, the Committee of Directors of Polytechnics and the Standing Conference of Principals of Colleges and Institutes of Higher Education set up a task group to examine the industrial relations implications of PCFC incorporation. By March 1988 the committee's Industrial Relations Task Group had rejected the idea of buying industrial relations expertise in from the universities or local authorities. It recommended either establishing its own secretariat or using external services. The leader of the task group was also on record as saying that the PCFC sector would need a national collective bargaining framework to set pay and conditions of service but that there would need to be provision for flexibility locally.

It was decided to create a national employers' association, open to all employers in the sector, which would provide the focus for negotiations on pay and conditions with the unions for all staff in PCFC institutions. The first meeting of what is now called the Polytechnic and Colleges Employers' Forum (PCEF) took place in early June 1988. Over 150 representatives of the future PCFC institutions endorsed the recommendation for creating an employers' negotiating body and established a shadow negotiating committee. The aims of the committee were:

- To establish a coherent national negotiating framework, reflecting the needs of PCFC institutions.

- To decentralize many of the existing national agreements so as to provide institutions with more local flexibility.
- To negotiate nationally those issues affecting the sector as a whole.
- To provide, through an industrial relations unit, professional advice and support to PCFC institutions.

The PCEF was established as a company limited by guarantee on 23 September 1988 and it was added to the list of employers' associations maintained by the certification officer. A chief executive was appointed and secretarial assistance provided. One of its first tasks was to implement its policy on national trade union recognition. The PCEF's strategy was determined by employment legislation, the Education Reform Act, 1988, and a set of guidelines established at a meeting of the PCEF on 20 December 1988. The December meeting proposed inviting six unions, out of the twenty-seven in the sector, to sign a single national recognition and procedure agreement replacing three separate local authority NJC agreements covering teachers, administrative and manual staff. The six unions invited to participate in negotiations were NATFHE, the National and Local Government Officers' Association (NALGO), the National Union of Public Employees, the General Municipal and Boilermakers' Union, the Transport and General Workers' Union and APT. Union density for teachers tended to be higher in the colleges than in the polytechnics but NATFHE, with at least 61 per cent overall, was the largest union. NALGO had 58 per cent among administrative staff and NUPE 43 per cent among manual staff.

In January 1989 the chief executive of the PCEF met senior officers of the six unions for preliminary discussions, explaining the employers' position. By this time the PCEF had rejected union proposals, tabled earlier, for an NJC-type recognition agreement. The employers' response was to table their own draft Recognition and Procedure Agreement on 6 February 1989, based on private-sector practices, for discussion with the unions. They also wrote a letter urging the unions to sign the agreement as soon as possible. The employers' aim was to establish a national bargaining arena, called the Polytechnic and Colleges' National Negotiating Committee (PCNNC), with a view to completing negotiations by March 1989, in time for the first round of pay bargaining with the teachers' unions. But the employers added that there would be no national negotiations with any of the unions until the national recognition and negotiating machinery was in force.

The 6 February first draft agreement (see Appendix 19.2) prepared by the PCEF contained a mixture of items, but written within it were a number of employer objectives:

- To create national negotiating machinery containing a small number of unions.
- To ensure the new machinery could only make recommendations, so guaranteeing the supremacy of governing bodies.
- To ensure the creation of the PCNNC, covering all staff.
- To bring TUC and non-TUC unions together.
- To create Common Interest Group panels for lecturers, administrative and manual staff respectively.

- To break links between national and local recognition.
- To create streamlined machinery, reflecting private-sector arrangements.
- To emphasize local management functions.
- To emphasize the business aspects of administering PCFC institutions.
- To reject compulsory arbitration.
- To limit the agreement to twenty-four months initially.
- To provide a mechanism assisting local interpretations of national PCNNC recommendations.
- To reject *status quo* clauses.
- To deny negotiating rights to key senior staff.
- To harmonize certain conditions of employment.

Activity brief

1 What were the likely grounds for the recognized teacher unions resisting the recognition of APT on the BFEC between 1973 and 1980 and on the NJCFET from 1979 to 1987?
2 For what possible reasons did the employers (PCEF) reject union proposals for NJC-type recognition and negotiating procedures for the sector after 1 April 1989?
3 Comment on and analyse the employers' industrial relations objectives incorporated in the first draft agreement. (See points above and objectives (i) to (vii) in Appendix 19.2.)
4 Why did the employers wish to exclude 'senior key staff' from the new collective bargaining arrangements? What are some of the industrial relations consequences of this?
5 What is the significance of the statement in the draft agreement reproduced in Appendix 19.2 that 'The PCNNC can however make national recommendations which will be given due regard by the [PCFC] institutions' Boards of Governors'?
6 Redraft the proposed national Recognition and Procedure Agreement in a form likely to have been mutually acceptable to the PCEF and the signatory unions after negotiations had taken place between them.
7 With the national Recognition and Procedure Agreement settled, what advice would you give to individual PCFC employers on negotiating recognition procedures with the trade unions locally?

Recommended reading

COMMISSION ON INDUSTRIAL RELATIONS, *Trade Union Recognition: the CIR Experience*, London, HMSO, 1974.

FARNHAM, D., 'How apt is APT?', *Higher Education Review*, 7, 1, 1975, pp. 39–52.

FARNHAM, D., 'The politics of Burnham representation', *Higher Education Review*, 14, 3, 1981, pp. 65–8.

FARNHAM, D., 'Staffing in higher education: the emerging agenda', *Higher Education Review*, 18, 1, 1985, pp. 43–60.

FARNHAM, D., 'Employee relations in the PCFC sector: what happens after vesting day?' *Higher Education Review*, 21, 1, 1988, pp. 27–52.

FARNHAM, D., 'From model employer to private sector model: the PCFC sector', *Higher Education Review*, 23, 2, 1991, pp. 7–32.

INSTITUTE OF PERSONNEL MANAGEMENT, *Trade Union Recognition*, London, IPM, 1977.

LOCKE, M., *et al.* (eds.), *College Administration: a Handbook*, London, Longman, 1988.

Appendix 19.1 Abbreviations used in the case

ACC	Association of County Councils
AMA	Association of Metropolitan Authorities
APT	Association of Polytechnic Teachers
ATTI	Association of Teachers in Technical Institutions
BFEC	Burnham Further Education Committee
CLEA	Council of Local Education Authorities
LEA	Local education authority
NALGO	National and Local Government Officers' Association
NATFHE	National Association of Teachers in Further and Higher Education
NJC(s)	National Joint Council(s)
NJCFET	National Joint Council for Further Education Teachers in England and Wales
NJCLFE	National Joint Council for Lecturers in Further Education in England and Wales
PCEF	Polytechnics and Colleges Employers' Forum
PCFC	Polytechnics and Colleges Funding Council
PCNNC	Polytechnics and Colleges National Negotiating Committee

Appendix 19.2 The draft agreement

The text of the draft agreement, dated 6 February, submitted by the PCEF for consideration by the unions, reads as follows:

Foreword

Under the Education Reform Act all Polytechnic and Colleges Funding Council (PCFC) institutions become legal employers of their own staff. The Act gives institutions' Boards of Governors the power 'to enter into contracts . . . for the employment of teachers and other staff'.

The PCFC institutions recognize the importance of good employee relations. The institutions have created the Polytechnics and Colleges Employers' Forum (PCEF) to regulate, at national level only, the relationships between the institutions and the signatory unions to this agreement.

This Recognition and Procedure Agreement and the Polytechnics and Colleges' National Negotiating Committee structure set out in full in this document governs the relationship between the PCEF and the Unions. Institutions belonging to the PCEF will wish to have regard to recommendations made under this Agreement when determining the pay and conditions of service of their own staff.

1 Introduction

The purpose of this Agreement is to establish a national framework between the PCEF and the Unions regarding pay and conditions recommendations relating to staff employed in all institutions listed as within the PCFC except where those staff are paid on rates determined by conditions of a research council, grant, government department or similar such body.

2 General principles

(a) *Objectives*

(i)   The PCEF and the Unions agree that it is in the interests of the PCFC institutions and all their employees that the institutions' business should function effectively to the benefit of both the institutions and the employees and that this is a common objective.

(ii)   The PCEF and the Unions accept that nothing in this Agreement is intended to replace detract from or weaken the direct and positive relationships which exist between individual employees and their employers.

(iii)   The PCEF and the Unions recognize the right of institution managers to organize, appraise and reward staff according to the contribution they make to the work of the institution.

(iv)   The PCEF and the Unions recognize the need to match staff effort according to institutional needs and programmes including the provision for evening work, weekend work and work during vacations.

(iv)   The PCEF and the Unions jointly seek the elimination of unnecessary differences between teaching and support staff (one major difference will continue, namely two superannuation schemes).

(vi)   The PCEF and the Unions jointly recognize the need for the creation of a proper contract for teaching staff within which they can be recognized for the full range of their professional duties.

(vii)   The PCEF and the Unions jointly recognize the need for the provision of strong and effective administrative organizations including proper recognition of senior support staff and the establishment of career structures.

(b) *Recognition*

(i)   The PCEF recognizes the signatory Unions as the sole bargaining agents.

(ii)   The Unions recognize that it is the right and responsibility of the institutions to manage their affairs.

(iii)   The Unions recognize that whilst the Agreement confers national bargaining rights, it makes no recommendations and has no implications for local recognition.

(c) *Membership*

(i)   At all times employees who are members of the Unions will work alongside and will co-operate with those employees of institutions who are non-members.

(ii)   The signatory Unions recognize that TUC affiliated Unions will at all times attend meetings with non-TUC affiliated signatory Unions.

3   Negotiating procedures

The existence of this procedure in no way detracts from an employee's right of access to institution line management or the institution's right to communicate with its employees or the Unions' right to communicate with their members.

(a) *Introduction*

(i)   The PCEF and the Unions agree that in order to maintain good constructive relationships any problems should be discussed without undue delay and be resolved at the earliest stage through constructive collective bargaining.

(ii)   To this end there will be the minimum of delay in arranging meetings between the PCEF and the Unions.

(iii)   Requests for meetings of the Polytechnic and Colleges' National Negotiating Committee (PCNNC) or any of its subsidiary common interest group committees may be initiated by the Unions or the PCEF.

(b) *National framework negotiations*

(i)   National framework negotiations will take place between representatives of the PCEF and full-time National Officers of the Unions with a view to reaching joint recommendations on subjects listed in Appendix 2.

(ii)   Representatives of the PCEF and full-time National Officers of the Unions will join together for meetings in the PCNNC having due regard to a limited number of representatives being present in order to effect efficient and speedy resolution of mutually agreed agenda items.

(iii)   The PCNNC may establish common interest group sub-committees by mutual agreement. These sub-committees will report to the PCNNC.

(c) *Procedure for dealing with unresolved issues*. In the unlikely event of the PCNNC failing to resolve an issue within its defined remit the Union and the PCEF shall consider the matter jointly and may, if mutually agreed to do so, refer it to conciliation, arbitration or other forms of assistance.

(d) *Disputes*. It is mutually agreed that the aim of the negotiating procedure outlined above is to avoid disputes until all stages of the procedure have been exhausted and all other means of reaching a settlement have been explored.

(i)   If circumstances arise in which the procedures outlined above have been exhausted and industrial action is being proposed, only those employees involved in the particular dispute will have the right to determine whether or not they will commence such action. In the event of action being proposed there will be adherence to current legislation and related codes of conduct.

(ii)   In the event of industrial action from whatever cause, there will be a need to ensure the safety and security of institutions' property and plant personnel. Both the Unions and the PCEF will agree in each situation how this shall be done.

(iii)   This Agreement is independent and separate from any other agreements between trades unions and PCFC sector institutions in respect of other groups of employees. Employees who are members of the signatory Unions will not therefore be involved in any action arising from disputes concerning any such other groups or actions not connected with the PCFC institutions.

4   Variation, duration and termination of this agreement

Variations or changes to the Agreement can only be made by mutual agreement between the Union side and the PCEF side of the PCNNC.

Either the collective Unions or the PCEF may terminate this Agreement by giving six months' notice in writing.

The Agreement will exist from 1 March 1989 to 1 March 1991 unless terminated during that period.

There will be a meeting of the PCNNC at least six months before 1 January 1991 to examine the prospects of renewing and/or revising this Agreement.

Appendix 2 stated that 'The Board of Governors of each PCFC institution has the right and responsibility to determine the pay and conditions of service of its own staff. The PCNNC can however make national recommendations which will be given due regard by the institutions' Boards of Governors.' It also outlined the topics which the PCNNC would deal with nationally and items which would be 'entirely for local implementation'.

Case 20

Decentralized collective bargaining at the Century Company

Jane Weightman and Will Blandamer

This case concerns a large company, the Century Company, and its move towards decentralized collective bargaining. This move cannot be seen in isolation, as it is part of a more general trend towards the decentralization of pay bargaining in industry as a whole. For many years the trend was for all personnel and administrative issues to be dealt with centrally in the organization, and collective bargaining therefore often took place at a national level. More recently there has been an increasing trend to devolve these activities down to plant, branch or site level. Research (Weightman *et al.*, 1991) indicates that there are five main reasons why this change has taken place in many organizations.

- A change in corporate strategy towards local profit centres, and the associated move towards greater autonomy for business unit managers, bring with them a desire for local pay settlements. Control over collective bargaining must go with responsibility for labour costs. Another reason for decentralization is to maintain head office control and co-ordination, so that in effect the organization can have the 'best of both worlds' by providing scope for local managers to do their own negotiating at the same time as sharply limiting that scope. In 1988, survey results suggested, 'only 17 per cent of establishments reported that there was no higher level policy or guidelines, or prior consultation' (IDS, 1989).
- The growth of profit-related pay schemes has the effect of making national bargaining arrangements increasingly remote and therefore irrelevant. This is especially true when a culture of profit-centred management is being cultivated.
- Decentralization makes it easier for pay settlements to be linked with concessions from unions at plant level on changes in local working practices, such as flexibility agreements.
- The introduction of legislation emphasizing local union democracy prompted inter-plant comparisons. Union strength was considered weak and therefore unable to resist such developments.
- Increased regional variations in earnings also stretched the relevance of national negotiations.

There are major implications from the decentralization of collective bargaining for the personnel function at both plant and head office level.

Background to the case: the Century Company

This company is a large British private-sector corporation. It is notable for the diversity of operations it is involved in. It has, for example, a large number of retail outlets, food manufacturing plants, financial services, opticians, farms, forestry concerns and even a large (and successful) undertaking business. The Century Company prides itself in having a strong set of socially responsible values and principles. These are expressed in perhaps two ways. First, the nature of the organization is very pluralistic. There is a continuing commitment to the recognition of trade unions. Seventeen different trade unions are recognized, although USDAW represents between 66 per cent and 75 per cent of the work force. Secondly, the company feels obliged to keep non-profitable shops open in remote areas for the sake of the local community. A simplified organization chart is given in Figure 20.1. Each division has its own personnel and finance staff at head office. Individual plants report to the appropriate division and have their own personnel and finance staff.

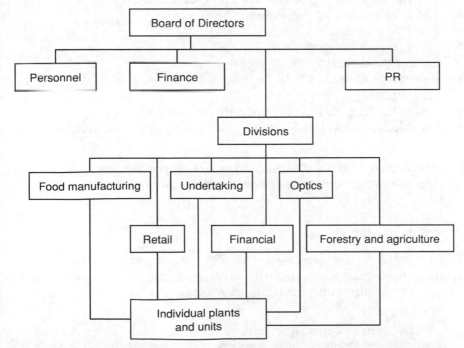

Figure 20.1 Organization chart of the Century Company. Each division has its own personnel and finance staff at head office. Individual plants report to the appropriate division and have their own personnel and finance officers

The situation

A new agenda: a move to decentralized collective bargaining

Decentralized bargaining required local managers for the first time to be responsible for the setting of pay rates. This meant plant managers and local personnel managers negotiating pay rates and related issues with trade unions at a local level. Previously, negotiations had taken place at a national level, with the agreements produced covering all employees throughout the country. This was seen to be increasingly inflexible and inappropriate in the 1980s. The company decided to devolve responsibility for bargaining to each site.

In order to do this the site management had to know what factors were relevant in setting pay and conditions appropriate to the local labour market. Various managers in the organization came up with the following list of factors important in determining the management's position in the local pay round.

- The local labour market going rate.
- Ease of recruitment.
- The national negotiated rate for group or industry.
- The average company going rate.
- The rate of inflation.
- The financial position of site.
- Labour productivity.
- Judgement of what would be acceptable to the group-level personnel department.
- Understanding of the local trade union position.
- Knowledge of local trade union officials and their particular concerns.

It can be seen that very local factors are important, but there is also considerable reference to the national and group-level factors.

Implementing the change

This organization has been decentralizing its pay and bargaining arrangements over the past ten years, with greater success in some places than in others. The group industrial relations manager claims:

> It has taken seven to eight years to break out from the plethora of national agreements to local negotiation. We had a hell of a muddle of rises on the anniversary of an individual's recruitment. We wanted to break away from recruitment problems and different sick pay arrangements. We had an anomaly if we wanted one.

The importance of each unit being in some sense a successful organization was emphasized as crucial to the implementation of local bargaining. One corporate manager's view was that the success of devolving national arrangements depended on the success of the business unit. The experience of three divisions bears this out. The optics division was not successful financially, owing to national changes and poor market climate, and here the devolvement of collective bargaining has not been a success. On the other hand, the undertaking business division (a market leader) and a factory producing tea (part of the food manufacturing division and a brand leader) were both highly successful in devolving the collective bargaining. To ensure the success of devolved collective bargaining, this corporate manager believed, the firm needed to sell the message of business success to employees and their representatives and to develop clarity and commitment to business needs among management. In addition, the units would have to be clearly identifiable and successful businesses. Confidence in the firm and its success needed to be built up in employees if they were to have confidence in local negotiation structures. This would require a lead time of two years at least for the changes.

With hindsight, the divisions' comments on how to achieve local negotiations were:

> Go quietly . . . have local structures in place . . . don't try to do everything at once . . . pick up priority employees first . . . note how the priorities in bargaining change, because the organization as a whole is changing and the business unit is also changing . . . the process of decentralization is never finished. [Corporate manager]

> If you are decentralizing, don't go half and half; only see trade unions at the place of the issue, not at headquarters. [Corporate manager]

The new arrangements in practice

The decentralization of collective bargaining involves the development of new roles for both the site-level and the head office personnel function. The head office staff need to start thinking of the factory manager as a client. The head office needs a clear role in order to meet the needs of this client. However, corporate-level personnel managers often prefer hands-on involvement, and the problem is that to devolve negotiations is effectively to do themselves out of a job. The result is that they often interfere in the 'nitty-gritty' of negotiations. Plant-level personnel staff often feel that it would be more useful if they concentrated on being internal consultants. Clearly, however, there are political issues about where power lies in a decentralized organization, particularly where it is not seen as a good career move to be at unit level. The major political issue is the extent of control exerted over the site level by the head office.

An example of head office being seen to interfere is in the use of a mandate system. In the Century Company a form is sent to the units five months before the beginning of each pay round, asking about their proposals. The form is returned for approval at divisional and group level. The units dislike this; changes are made to the proposals, often, in the unit manager's view, using out-of-date information. Those at unit level would prefer head office to offer expertise rather than imposing this type of control. Local management have to discuss with head office what they wish to do, to try and justify their decision and get the decision authorized. In considering the proposal, head office will look at:

- Paybill and profit.
- Labour turnover.
- Absenteeism.
- Last year's prediction.
- The number of people involved.
- The anticipated claim.
- The effect on the rest of the organization.

For example, corporate personnel are particularly concerned about the possible knock-on effects through the rest of the organization. One example here is the repercussion on other units of one unit reducing hours.

Not all the organization is involved in the devolution of collective bargaining. Administrative, technical, professional and managerial staff pay rates are retained centrally, because in their case it is a national market and the company wishes to maintain geographical mobility for these groups of staff.

One site's experience was that in 1986 they changed over to local bargaining after persuading managers at the Harlow site that it was necessary. They had three craft trade unions, two production unions (Bakers and USDAW), one clerical and one management trade union. The management had no idea how to adapt to the new system, so the group industrial relations manager brought the unions together and gave a presentation to everyone. In retrospect the management at this site felt they had seriously underestimated the time it would take to implement local bargaining. They thought it would take eighteen to twenty-four months: it actually took four and a half years! There was a 'cooling off' period for a year in the middle of the change when it had all gone wrong and relations had soured. The personnel manager left and negotiations over holidays and sick pay had to be put to one side.

The final outcome of this arrangement was claimed to be:

- Labour turnover halved.
- Absenteeism reduced from 10 per cent to 5 per cent.
- Savings on training costs because of reduced turnover.
- Savings on selection costs.

Activity brief

1 What are the advantages of decentralized bargaining?
2 What are the disadvantages of decentralized bargaining?

3 How does decentralized bargaining affect the culture of the organization? How do you keep a sense of being one organization?
4 Why might national negotiations over pay be inappropriate for the Century Company?
5 Which of the list of factors identified by managers in determining the firm's position in the local pay round would you consider the most important? You could try and rank these factors in order of importance.
6 How should the Century Company define success in the implementation of decentralized collective bargaining?
7 Why do you think head office staff at the Century Company found it difficult to give up the 'nitty-gritty' of negotiations?
8 What alternative forms of control could head office have exerted on site-level negotiations at the Century Company?
9 What training and resources are required for the plant-level personnel function at the Century Company?

Recommended reading

INCOMES DATA SERVICES, Report, February 1989.
KINNIE, N., 'The decentralization of industrial relations? Recent research considered', *Personnel Review*, 19, 3, 1990.
PICKARD, J., 'Engineering tools-up for local bargaining', *Personnel Management*, March 1990.
PURCELL, J., 'How to manage decentralized bargaining', *Personnel Management*, May 1989.
WEIGHTMAN, J., et al., 'Pay Structures and Negotiating Arrangements', unpublished paper, North West Regional Health Authority, UMIST, Manchester, 1991.

The power of the ballot box: balloting and collective bargaining at Engineering Company

Huw Morris, Patricia Fosh, Roderick Martin, Paul Smith and Roger Undy

Engineering Company is a large multi-divisional engineering concern based in the UK. In the last three months of 1988 and first month of 1989, management and manual grade unions at the company's four Rutnam plants were involved in pay talks which eventually led to an industrial action ballot and three weeks' overtime ban. This case study describes the background to events at Engineering Company and the use of ballots. The aim is to demonstrate the importance of balloting during negotiations and to outline the issues with which managers and union representatives have to contend when ballots are used.

Background to the case

The general corporate and economic background

Engineering Company's principal business is the design, manufacture, sale and support of engineering products for commercial customers. At the time of the dispute the parent company was organized into five divisions, consisting of three product divisions supported by two functional divisions. In the UK the group as a whole employed 40,400 at twelve manufacturing sites. The business was generally rated as very successful and had risen rapidly to become the world's third largest operator in the markets it served. In 1988 profits generated by the company had increased in each of the three preceding years and, although sales had declined that year, they had grown during the previous four years. On the eve of the dispute the company's order books were full for the next two years.

Engineering Company has not always been a successful business. In the early and mid-1980s it underwent a period of cut-backs, with many staff losses. In 1985 the company employed 42,700 personnel, but by 1988 the figure had been reduced by 5.5 per cent. These reductions in staffing levels were achieved with few difficulties through voluntary redundancy and early retirement, and by 1988, according to the managing director, the rationalization programme was complete. Accompanying these reductions in staffing there had been improvements in productivity achieved through the adoption of new technology and changes in working practices.

In 1988 senior management focused their attention on reorienting the company towards a business strategy of expansion in its traditional product markets and diversification into related areas, usually through joint ventures. These developments in the strategic focus of the company were prompted by mounting research and development costs, increased competition from abroad and the threat of a hostile take-over bid.

At the beginning of Engineering Company's 1988/89 pay negotiations the wider UK economy was beginning to experience problems. Of chief concern to financial commentators was the large balance-of-trade deficit and the rising level of price and wage inflation. The rate of pay inflation was officially recorded as 9.4 per cent in January 1989, almost 2 per cent above the retail price index of 7.5 per cent. To combat these symptoms of economic 'overheating', interest rates had been raised to 13 per cent by the end of 1988. On the plus side, the level of unemployment had been declining for eighteen months, and exchange rates were relatively stable and favourable to UK companies like Engineering Company, which earned the bulk of its income from exports.

Management organization

At Engineering Company the employment relationship is regulated by a wealth of written agreements accumulated over the past thirty years, and in the areas where discretion is allowed both sides describe their approach as 'pragmatic'. The general relationship of mutual trust between management and union negotiators has remained intact throughout the 1980s despite changes in the law and the national economy. Although economic and legal changes may have swung the balance of power nationally behind employers, at Engineering Company plant managers were generally reluctant or unprepared to take advantage of the fact. Indeed, the only major change in the conduct of industrial relations during the 1980s was management's removal of the post-entry closed shop agreement in response to the Employment Acts, 1980 and 1982. Union leaders and members at the plant accepted the change as inevitable and did not oppose it.

Though the general relationship between union representatives and managers was friendly, there had been a few minor and sporadic disputes at the Rutnam plants which normally took the form of spontaneous unofficial walk-outs by manual-grade employees. The last such incident, in 1986, was prompted by the award of an extra day's holiday to employees at the Slipham factory in the north-east. Interestingly, in response to these stoppages, managers at the company made no attempt to use the law against the unions. In the words of the works employee relations manager, 'I have every confidence in the unions' ability to organize their own affairs. They appear to do it very well, and I'm happy to let them get on with it. I'd rather not go looking for problems.'

Recent management-led employee relations initiatives have concentrated on strengthening and extending the range of employee participation schemes at the Rutnam plants. Joint consultation committees have operated at the plant since World War II, quality circles were established in the mid-1970s, and during the 1980s the use of team briefings, videos and staff bulletins was extended. However, more radical attempts to alter the employment package through the negotiated introduction of performance-related pay for staff grades failed in 1987/1988.

Trade union organization

At the end of 1988 five trade unions represented manual-grade employees at the four Engineering Company plants at the Rutnam site. These five unions were divided into eight sections of membership. (See Table 21.1 and Appendix 21.1 for a list of abbreviations.) The structure of joint union representation at the site was highly formalized but nevertheless effective (see Figure 21.1). AEU members dominated this representational system through strength of numbers and the deference of other groups to their skilled status. Consequently the most senior workplace union representatives, the works convenor and deputy convenor, were AEU members by custom and practice, while the local AEU full-time official took the lead in offering advice to workplace representatives.

The workplace representatives at Engineering Company were provided with 'facility time' and administrative resources far in excess of those required by statute and the ACAS code of practice. The company provided the works committee with secretarial support, offices and equipment,

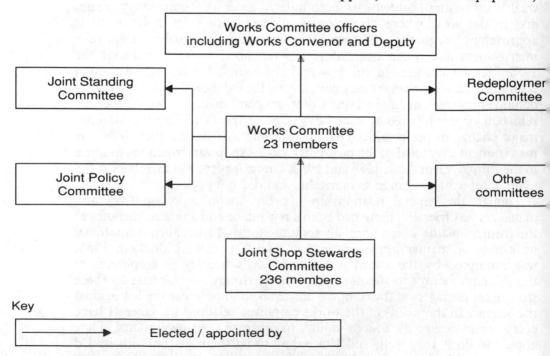

Figure 21.1 The joint union committee structure at the Rutnam plants of Engineering Company

and as a result of this highly developed bureaucracy the sophisticated workplace organization was insulated from national developments in the union movement. For example, the merger of TASS and ASTMS to form MSF in 1987 had not altered local union organization at the time of the 1988/9 pay negotiations. If there was any friction between union groups at the Engineering site it existed between newer members of the joint shop stewards' committee (JSSC), on one side, and the works committee and management on the other. The joint shop stewards' committee provided a forum for 236 shop stewards to discuss and agree a position on work-related issues and trade union matters.

Table 21.1. Union membership at Engineering Company

Union	Membership
AEU	
Engineering	3,720
Foundry	174
TGWU	828
GMB	129
EETPU	285
MSF (TASS)	
Metal mechanics	547
Sheet-metal workers	316
Pattern makers	51

Source. Union Records.

The negotiating framework

The company's bargaining constituencies did not mirror the formal divisional structure of the business; pay rates were set separately for the staff and manual employees through negotiations with their respective union representatives at each of Engineering Company's twelve geographical locations. The four Rutnam plants made up one of these twelve sites.

At the Rutnam site management drew up their offers and proposals for negotiation on the basis of an annual survey of local employers' rates of pay and conditions. Information from this study formed the basis of consultations with the board of directors of the parent company over an appropriate annual pay budget and other objectives for the negotiations at the Rutnam plants. Local managers needed the prior approval of the board of directors if they wished to exceed this centrally determined mandate during negotiations.

In 1988 employees at Engineering Company's Rutnam sites were paid a basic shift rate calculated on the basis of a job evaluation system. There was no payment by results or similar merit pay for manual employees, although there remained the vestiges of an individual productivity bonus scheme which dated back to 1975. The use of this bonus had degenerated in the 1980s to the point where it was used only as an attendance and good behaviour payment.

21

Before the 1988/9 pay negotiations it was the company's policy to pay within the upper quartile of local rates and to offer better conditions of employment than other firms in the vicinity. At the time of the dispute the basic weekly pay for labourers and technical trades at opposite ends of the eleven-grade, skill-based manual employees' pay scales was £105.81 and £157.11 respectively. Each grade on the manual employees' scales had four incremental steps (each worth 2.7 per cent of the base rate), awarded annually. In addition employees were able to supplement their income through overtime working, which was running at an average of over eight hours per week per manual employee at the time of the study.

In line with the general climate of good industrial relations, the four plants at the Rutnam site had a history of smoothly run, uncomplicated pay negotiations, but in the eighteen months preceding the 1988/9 pay talks difficulties had arisen, fuelled by increasing employee wage expectations. For example, the previous set of manual grades' pay negotiations in 1987/8 had dragged on for six months, when it went to an 'external conference'. This is the penultimate stage in the agreed EEF/CSEU collective bargaining procedure. It usually involves an 'off-site' meeting of senior company site managers, supported by an EEF officer, and union representatives backed by their respective union full-time officers. The final stage in the procedure is the formal registration of a 'failure to agree'. As a result there was a narrow vote against industrial action by the trade unions, and the final settlement of a 4 per cent increase in basic pay was agreed upon. Six months later, in response to rising inflation, staff grades were offered a 6 per cent pay increase which they overwhelmingly accepted by a margin of four to one, in a reference-back ballot (a vote on the acceptability of an offer which does not ask whether members are prepared to take industrial action).

The situation

The pay negotiations

The works committee at Rutnam (principally the deputy convenor) began preparations for negotiation of the 1988/9 pay settlement by drawing up a timetable for the talks. This was done before any meetings with management, and was produced with the aim of ensuring that the unions maintained an advantage throughout the negotiations. Union leaders hoped that by planning beforehand for the possibility of a reference-back or industrial action ballot they would be able to prevent the pay talks from dragging on for six months as they had in previous years. The plan set out the dates of scheduled meetings and a timetable for a ballot if a 'failure to agree' was recorded. At each stage in the balloting process alternative courses of action were mapped out in response to possible moves by management. The ensuing events which occurred in the pay talks were as follows:

Unions prepare timetable and strategy for pay talks.

18 October. At the regular JSSC meeting the works committee agree to present management with non-negotiable 8.5 per cent pay claim. Management respond with 5 per cent pay offer.

26 October. JSSC formally reject offer: works committee request 'external conference'.

9 December. At the external conference management fail to improve offer sufficiently. Unions prepare for ballot.

20 December. Ballot results announced.

The negotiating process formally began on 18 October 1988 at the regular monthly meeting of the JSSC. The meeting had been called to consider and formulate a pay claim for 1988/9. At this meeting many stewards urged the union negotiators to press for a substantial pay increase, and the figure of 20 per cent was bandied about by some. During the debate about the claim, members of the works committee, who would be involved in negotiating the agreement, pressed for moderation but had little success in reducing the stewards' expectations. By the end of the meeting the committee had agreed to present a claim for an 8.5 per cent increase on basic rates. This claim would be 'non-negotiable' and the works committee was mandated not to accept a lower offer. In addition the unions sought consolidation of the 10 per cent individual productivity bonus, i.e. removing productivity bonus and adding the 10 per cent to basic pay. This second element of the claim had been a union objective since 1981, and the convenor privately set considerable store on achieving it. After the meeting a copy of the claim was sent to the works employee relations manager.

The works employee relations manager (representing the management side) responded to the claim with an offer of 5 per cent, the limit of the pay budget, and refused to consolidate the productivity bonus. The union negotiators described the offer as 'derisory' and it was formally rejected at a meeting of the JSSC on 26 October 1988. At this meeting the stewards reaffirmed their support for the original claim and pressed their negotiators to adhere strictly to the previously formulated negotiating strategy. Following the meeting, the works convenor stepped up pressure on behalf of the unions by writing to the works employee relations manager. The letter stated that unless a response to the unions' claim was received before 22 November 1988 the negotiating committee would press for an 'external conference'. The conference was held on 9 December 1988. Despite lengthy talks and an offer by management of a further 1 per cent, failure to agree was recorded. The non-negotiable nature of the union's claim had proved a sticking point, as the union representatives were unable to offer any areas of compromise. After the meeting the unions began preparations for a ballot on industrial action short of a strike. (An example of the standard paper used in the ballot is shown in Figure 21.2.)

Members of four of the plant's five trade unions took part in the workplace ballot (GMB, TGWU, AEU and MSF). EETPU members and those temporarily absent from work registered their votes by postal ballot. Members eligible to take part in the workplace vote were issued with a standard ballot paper by their respective senior shop stewards. For security reasons the ballot papers were numbered and printed on coloured paper. In addition, when the voting papers were handed out each steward recorded a tick against the member's name on a list of all members at the Rutnam plants.

Members placed their completed voting papers in the ballot box, and these were later counted in the locked union office by the convenor, the deputy convenor and the administrative secretary to the works committee. The administrative secretary was employed by the works committee to do the unions' office work and, as such, was a member of the white-collar union APEX. These three tellers/scrutineers were judged by the union representatives to be sufficiently independent to count the vote fairly. As with previous pre-industrial action ballot counts, representatives of management were invited to observe but declined. However, throughout the negotiations and subsequent dispute, management made several attempts to inform employees direct about the progress of pay negotiations through line managers and the company newspaper.

The results of the workplace ballot were announced on a union-by-union basis on 20 December 1988 (see Table 21.2). The union representatives had decided to announce their results individually and not as an overall figure, as a result of the AEU representative's reading of the Trade Union Act, 1984, and Employment Act, 1988. MSF representatives argued strongly against

---

AMALGAMATED ENGINEERING UNION

ENGINEERING & FOUNDRY MEMBERS

Engineering Co.

Are you prepared to take part in action short of a strike in support of your wage claim?
(Details of the Company's offer are available.)

YES	
NO	

Please answer by putting an X in the appropriate box
Please place this ballot paper in the box provided

Your vote is completely secret

If you take part in a strike or other industrial action, you may be in breach of your contract of employment　　　　　　　　　**No. 1234**

Figure 21.2 Example of a standard ballot paper

this interpretation but were overruled. Subsequently, in the words of the works employee relations manager:

> The strength of feeling as expressed by the ballot results caught both sides (works committee and management) by surprise. Normally, the negotiations are stage-managed for the shopfloor workers, but these results meant we were living on a knife edge. Both sets of negotiators wanted an agreement.

Table 21.2   The pre-industrial action ballot results

Union	No. of spoilt papers	Yes	No
AEU	3	2,897	612
MSF	1	749	189
TGWU	2	526	206
GMB	–	68	36
EETPU		143	40
Total vote		4,383	1,083
Percentage		80	20

Turnout: 84%.

Source. Union circular to members, 20 December 1988.

Engineering Company's directors were particularly keen to reach an agreement quickly, as one of the company's other divisions was at that time in the thirteenth week of an overtime ban which had been called without a ballot or exhaustion of the procedural agreement. At head office the directors hoped that, if an agreement was reached at the Rutnam plants, it would 'snowball' and lead to settlements at the other factories. Meanwhile the union negotiators were eager to get an acceptable agreement to placate the members. In short, both sides faced difficult decisions.

Activity brief

Questions to be discussed in groups

1   (a) What were the unions' intentions in conducting the industrial action ballot in this situation?

    (b) Do you think their approach could have been improved?

2   (a) What objectives did management seek during the dispute?

(b) What strategy did they pursue during the dispute?

(c) How could management have pursued their objectives more effectively?

3 How might the Code of Practice on Industrial Action Ballots (1991) have altered the conduct of this ballot? If you feel unable to arrive at a judgement as to whether approved procedure was followed, try to specify the nature of any further information you would require.

Role-taking

4 You have been asked, as adviser to the management negotiators at Engineering Company, to suggest an appropriate course of action in response to the unions' ballot results. What guidance would you offer?

5 From the perspective of the convenor and deputy convenor draw up plans to cover possible future developments.

Essay

6 Discuss the assertion of Hanson and Mather (1988) that the balloting process lends a spurious legitimacy to industrial action.

Recommended reading

Essential reading is starred.

DEPARTMENT OF EMPLOYMENT, *Statutory Code of Practice: Trade Union Ballots on Industrial Action*, London, Department of Employment, 1991.★

DEPARTMENT OF EMPLOYMENT, *Industrial Action and the Law: a Guide for Employers, their Customers and Suppliers and Others*, London, Department of Employment, PL870 (Rev. 1), 1990.

DEPARTMENT OF EMPLOYMENT, *Industrial Action and the Law (Employees' Version)*, London, Department of Employment, PL869 (Rev. 1), 1990.

FARNHAM, D., and PIMLOTT, J., *Understanding Industrial Relations*, fourth edition, London, Cassell, 1990, chapters 6 and 10.

FATCHETT, D., 'Ballots, picketing and strikes', in B. TOWERS (ed.), *A Handbook of Industrial Relations Practice*, London, Kogan Page, 1989, chapter 14.

HANSON, C., and MATHER, G., *Striking out Strikes*, London, Institute of Economic Affairs, 1988.

LEWIS, D., *Essentials of Employment Law*, London, IPM, 1990, chapter 20.

WILKINSON, T., *Workplace Balloting*, London, IPM, 1988.

Copies of all the Department of Employment publications are available free of charge from ISCO5, Dept IB, The Paddock, Frizinghall, Bradford BD9 4HG.

Appendix 21.1 List of abbreviations

ACAS   Advisory Conciliation and Arbitration Service
AEU   Amalgamated Engineering Union
APEX   Association of Professional, Executive, Clerical and Computer Staff
ASTMS   Association of Scientific, Technical and Managerial Staffs
CSEU   Confederation of Shipbuilding and Engineering Unions
EEF   Engineering Employers' Federation
EETPU   Electrical, Electronic, Telecommunication and Plumbing Union
GMB   General Municipal Boilermakers' Union
JSSC   Joint Shop Stewards' Committee
MSF   Manufacturing, Science and Finance
TASS   Technical, Administrative and Supervisory Staffs
TGWU   Transport and General Workers' Union

Acknowledgement

This case is based on an empirical research project conducted at the Management School, Imperial College, London, and funded by the ESRC (1987–9).

Case 22

Managing a dispute in the public sector: Branch 11

Ian McLoughlin and Ian Beardwell

The management of industrial conflict has always been an important issue in the handling of the collective employment relationship in Britain. Apart from the well publicized disputes that receive extensive media coverage there exists a widespread pattern of often unknown and little reported conflict that is connected with the management of the workplace. These disputes are frequently over specific issues rather than the 'great debates' that catch the public eye, but they nevertheless represent complex problems which present management with difficult choices in order to resolve them.

This case is concerned with the management of such a small dispute in a civil service organization. While emphasis is necessarily placed on the particular circumstances of the public sector, the case demonstrates that strategy and tactics in conflict handling expose problems and issues which are common to management regardless of the sector of the economy in which they operate. At the same time, the dispute is indicative of the rising level of industrial conflict that has emerged in the public sector in the last few years as industrial relations have become increasingly 'politicized', not least as a result of the policies of successive governments.

Background to the case

Throughout the 1980s industrial relations in the public sector became a heightened issue and during the decade came to involve, among others, such diverse groups as water workers, teachers, health workers and miners. Within the civil service the 1981 pay dispute marked a watershed in industrial action but, perhaps more significantly, many groups within the government service subsequently took part in various forms of official and unofficial action in pursuit of sectional claims: this was particularly true in areas such as social security and taxation.

214

Pay bargaining in the civil service is still predominantly carried out on a centralized basis; this means that many sectional disputes tend to be not about the actual earnings of civil servants *per se* but about the context of their work, e.g. working conditions and work environment, and extra or supplementary duties.

In this arena the government has sought to introduce various changes. Some of these are on the macro-level and have involved the setting up of agencies to run government functions, divorced from day-to-day political control but still answerable to Parliament via the relevant Secretary of State. In such circumstances, an important issue for management is the extent to which managerial issues can be contained within the agency and not be pulled towards the political arena and political direction.

At a micro-level, a wide range of matters within agencies are now dealt with by the local management without reference up to more senior officials, as was the custom and practice in the more traditional civil service departments of the past. One benefit has been that those involved in particular problems may be able to resolve them more readily; a drawback is that those decisions may be more openly disputed or local management may be viewed as operating 'managerially' rather than 'administratively' to achieve certain goals.

The situation

The introduction of the YTS into the civil service

The case involves a dispute in an agency which has its headquarters outside London, in a northern city. The agency has both headquarters staff and field staff, organized into five operating divisions, each of which operates on a nation-wide basis. The case concerns a dispute in the largest of the five divisions, which has some 1,800 headquarters staff and 5,000 field staff. Within the headquarters staff of this division are twenty-five smaller departments or branches. At the core of the dispute is the desire by the government to introduce the Youth Training Scheme (YTS) into the civil service. The YTS is a high-profile scheme designed to bridge the gap between education and full-time work by providing vocationally relevant training for unemployed teenagers. It is viewed by the government as a major plank in its labour-market strategy for training. A major embarrassment for the government is that, since the scheme's inception, it has not been able to introduce YTS into civil service departments because of opposition from the Civil and Public Services' Association (CPSA), one of the major unions.

To date, the senior management of the agency have played this issue quietly, and the Secretaries of State who have had overall responsibility have not applied pressure. However, there is now a feeling that something must be done to remove the politically sensitive point that the government, in exhorting other employers to participate in the scheme, cannot introduce it into its own direct employment.

The CPSA is the largest civil service union and represents clerical grades up to the first-line supervisory management. The CPSA has a history of being highly politicized. Throughout the 1980s the two main factions which battled for power were the broad left (an alliance of various soft and hard-left groups) and the Militant Tendency (a hard-left activist group), which has secured considerable success in seeking to gain control of key offices within the union. This political fragmentation has given rise to the popular description of the CPSA by other unions as 'the Beirut of the union movement'. An important factor for the case is that elections are due in three months' time to the national executive committee. There have been sporadic CPSA strikes throughout both headquarters and the field network as candidates have flexed their electoral muscles.

The dispute also affects a second union known as the Society of Civil and Public Servants (SCPS), which represents the main management grades. Work at headquarters is 'grade-rich', that is, there is a bigger proportion of highly graded posts there than in the field organization. In consequence the SCPS is numerically the largest union based at headquarters. The union is less overtly political and is not perceived as exhibiting anywhere near the same degree of factionalism as the CPSA. Indeed, the SCPS is still a very centrally run union which has less experience of the localized lay activism of the CPSA.

The point has now been reached where the senior management of the agency have decided to introduce YTS. Doing so will achieve the goal of avoiding direct political intervention on the one hand and on the other of serving to indicate that local management are willing to tackle issues that have hitherto been allowed to run on.

Management's approach has been very low-key: to date, YTS trainees have been introduced on an office-by-office basis in one region of the field network, and the process has been successful in all but one location. At this office the CPSA successfully called a strike, which lasted for the four months of the YTS placement. During the dispute the CPSA paid strike pay of 80 per cent of net salary.

At divisional headquarters a CPSA ballot of members in all twenty-five branches has resulted in an overall vote against industrial action over the introduction of YTS individuals into headquarters work. As trainees were introduced the CPSA repeated the ballot but on a branch-by-branch basis. The first ten branches replicated the vote against industrial action. However, the eleventh branch (Branch 11) into which a YTS appointee was to be placed voted fifteen to twelve in favour of strike action. The CPSA representative at this branch was the broad-left candidate in the forthcoming national executive committee elections.

As a consequence of management's declared intention of introducing a YTS trainee into Branch 11 for three months, and the branch's vote for industrial action, a strike has been called by the CPSA. This is to take effect from the Friday immediately prior to the YTS appointee's arrival on Monday morning.

The progress of the strike

What follows is a week-by-week diary of events relating to the strike. The information is based on notes recorded by one of the key managers involved in the dispute, management documents and correspondence, and trade union bulletins and other documentation.

Week 0 events

Friday: the strike begins with twenty-one of the twenty-seven staff in Branch 11 at headquarters going on strike. Two other staff are absent, one is on sick leave and another on maternity leave.

That evening a crisis meeting is convened by senior managers in the agency. One manager takes notes of this meeting, recording the main issues raised and points of view put forward. The following is extracted from his notebook scribblings:

> Disquiet is expressed at the prospect of a lengthy strike at HQ over the high-profile issue of YTS.
>
> The management of the dispute should be limited to the senior managers present and not be allowed to pass to the Secretary of State, which would invite a more 'political' approach. It is agreed to hold a senior management meeting every Monday evening throughout the duration of the dispute to assess the previous week's events and plan action for the forthcoming week.
>
> What would be the position of SCPS? Would they back CPSA – most other staff in the branch, including first-line supervisors, are SCPS members – and would the dispute spread to other HQ branches?
>
> There must be no concessions by Agency management which would prejudice their ability to introduce YTS elsewhere in the Agency.
>
> How is the work undertaken by the strikers in Branch 11 to be carried out in their absence? The work cannot be done by other branches and, although some backlog can be allowed to build up, the strike will probably start to bite in about two weeks.
>
> The possibility of using 'casuals' (temporary staff) to cover for the strikers is considered. In fact two casuals already employed in the branch are amongst those on strike. Of these two individuals, one has only three days of their term of employment left when a full-time staff member is due to return from sick leave, whilst the other's term of employment is due to end in four weeks time when another full-timer returns from maternity leave.

Two proposals for action emerge from the meeting:

- An 'open forum' is to be called for the following Monday to allow senior management to brief the staff at headquarters on the YTS scheme. To accompany this a 'Message to all head office staff' is also to be prepared and distributed (see Appendix 22.1).
- A stiffly worded letter is to be sent to the strikers coupled with an invitation to attend the information meeting.

217

Week 1 events

YTS trainee starts work at Branch 11.

Monday. No strikers attend the open forum but 250 other head-quarters staff do, including twenty-five CPSA activists from other head-quarters branches. The meeting is summarized by one senior manager as a 'bloody disaster', a view endorsed by most of his colleagues. Senior management give an ineffective presentation and are heckled by the audience.

The strikers start an 'information line' outside headquarters between 8.00 and 10.00 each morning to hand out leaflets to explain the CPSA position on YTS to other headquarters employees. This is augmented by daily strike bulletins. The strikers then do voluntary work at a local centre for the unemployed. It has the important effect of binding the strikers together and increasing their solidarity.

Ballots over the introduction of YTS trainees in two other headquarters branches take place. Both branches vote against strike action.

One further member of Branch 11, regarded by management as a strong supporter of Militant, joins the strike. (The member had previously been absent from work.)

The manager of Branch 11 writes to all the strikers, inviting them to contact their immediate supervisors to discuss matters. The intention is to avoid the alienation of first-line mangers from their staff, with whom they are generally on first-name terms and have good relations. During the strike at the field office striking staff had quickly become alienated from their supervisors.

As a result, a meeting takes place on Friday evening between the supervisors and some of the strikers. The supervisors report to senior managers that:

- Although staff are loyal to other employees, they do regard CPSA as having a good point on the YTS issue.
- Strikers are apparently shocked to hear that the YTS trainee would be in the branch for three months and do not relish the prospect of being out for that long.
- The supervisors, most of whom are SCPS members, do not like being used as 'pig in the middle' by senior management.

SCPS advises its members not to 'actively participate in the YTS dispute'.

Week 2 events

Monday. The senior management meeting is held, at which the following decisions are made:

- The commitment not to end the strike by compromising management's prerogative to introduce YTS is reaffirmed.
- A decision is reached that casuals will be used to cope with any work left undone owing to the strike. However, they will not be deployed

immediately, as that might provoke the supervisors who are members of SCPS and who would be responsible for them.

- A decision is taken to explore the possibility of disciplinary action against individual strikers for breach of their contracts of employment. Legal advice from Agency solicitors is to be sought.
- For this week a decision is made to sit tight and 'hold the fort'.

Senior management learn that the CPSA is financially hard pressed and that the commitment to pay 80 per cent of net salary is expensive.

Senior managers discuss the fact that this is the week in which they are due to implement an already announced reorganization of Branch 11. One section is due to be moved to another branch, which will involve ten of the strikers, including the broad-left leader, being moved. A key question is: should the reorganization go ahead?

The work in the branch begins to pile up. Supervisors start to do some of the work.

The CPSA strike bulletins issued by the daily information line become more militant and overtly anti-government (see Appendix 22.2).

The CPSA call a 'Jobs for youth' rally in the city to support the strikers and march on headquarters. About 200 supporters attend, but only around ten of the non-striking headquarters staff are present.

Week 3 events

Monday. The senior management meeting is held, at which a decision is made that the planned reorganization should go ahead next week, week 4 of the dispute, as not to do so would present a small victory to the CPSA. Moreover the reorganization would split the strikers into two separate branches when a return to work occurred, thus undermining the potential for future collective action by those involved.

Advice is received from solicitors (and noted at the senior managers' meeting) that because civil servants have no contracts of employment there are 'probably not' grounds for disciplinary action for breach of contract. (See W. Wedderburn, *The Worker and the Law*, second edition, Harmondsworth, Penguin, 1986, pp. 135–6.)

Senior management bring forward deadlines on work not being done, to encourage supervisors in the branch to see the need for management to introduce casuals.

Strikers write to the director of the agency, inviting him to meet them on neutral territory to discuss the dispute. The media have been invited and no starting points for negotiation are offered by the strikers.

At a social function for a former senior manager of the agency, senior management are informed by the SCPS full-time national officer that the union will not become involved in the dispute 'at any cost . . . no matter what management does'.

Strikes start to break out in the field network over a variety of issues. Most are short, but one 'indefinite' strike involving 120 staff begins.

22

Activity brief

1   Evaluate management's conduct of the dispute to date. What different decisions, if any, would you have taken and why?
2   Should management accept the invitation to the director, issued by the CPSA in week 3, to meet on neutral territory to discuss the dispute?

Appendix 22.1 Management message to all head office staff

YTS is transforming training opportunities and the job prospects of a whole generation of young people. Throughout the country companies and organizations of all sorts are currently providing nearly half a million opportunities.

After years of patient negotiation and preparation with the trade unions the Agency is now at last running YTS. The scheme is high-quality, no threat to jobs, offers the same allowances for trainees as other YTS schemes, and gives more young people in the city than there are immediate jobs for, the chance of high-quality training.

Although we started YTS last year, CPSA members in Branch 11 have gone on strike as a trainee starts practical training. It is unfair to the young woman concerned and extremely foolish to strike against a programme which helps young people so successfully and which provides thousands of jobs.

When strikes take place management will take whatever steps are necessary to maintain services to the public and our customers. If you want to know more come to the open forum for all staff.

Director

Appendix 22.2 CPSA strike bulletin

THE STRIKE IS SOLID

The 22 strikers at headquarters remain adamant in their opposition to the imposition by a dictatorial management of YTS. Management say the scheme is 'high-quality'; we say it is RUBBISH and a threat to all our jobs!

YTS AND THE PUBLIC SECTOR

The introduction of YTS into the public sector on a large scale comes at a time when jobs are being cut and the Government is planning yet another tax bonanza for the rich while more and more young people start their working lives on a pittance. We are fighting to defend our jobs and the right of young people to be paid a decent living wage.

PORTRAIT OF A STRIKER

'I am a 45-year-old Mum with two children. I am registered disabled. I have tried for over nine years to obtain a full-time job. In September the Agency gave me the chance I'd been waiting for all those years. Some people say that by being on strike I am repaying by biting the hand that helped me but I see things differently. I came out on strike to protest at the way management are paying trainees a pittance and not giving young people the chance of a job at the end of their YTS training, not granting them full employee status and providing poor-quality training. Come on, give these youngsters a chance!'

For further information contact Strike Headquarters.

Case 23

Improving employee involvement: the Royal Borough of Kingston upon Thames

Brian Willey

This case describes the way in which one organization, a local authority, has begun to reform its employee relations to enable line managers to respond effectively to change. The reforms, particularly in consultation and communications mechanisms, reflect the aims set out in the IPM/IPA code of practice. These aims are designed to:

- Generate the commitment of all employees to the success of the organization.
- Improve service delivery to customers and clients.
- Help the organization adjust to changes in technology and working practices.
- Improve employee satisfaction.

Background to the case

The Royal Borough of Kingston upon Thames is the smallest outer London local authority. It was established in 1965 under local government reorganization. Until 1986 it was run by majority Conservative councils. Then, for eighteen months, it was controlled by a Liberal/Social Democrat minority group, with occasional Labour Party support. Since 1987 Conservative political control has been very finely balanced, relying often on the casting vote of the incumbent mayor.

The staff

The authority has a staff of some 6,000, employed in nine directorates and the chief executive's department (see Figure 23.1). The largest of the directorates are Education, Contract Services and Social Services. These account for two-thirds of employees and half the managers. In organizational terms there are two important features about the deployment of the borough's work force: (1) over a third of employees and (2) over half of managers spend some proportion of their working day away from their work base. Two-thirds of employees and 40 per cent of managers generally work away from the Guildhall complex which is in the centre of Kingston. Other characteristics of the borough's work force are:

- *Length of service.* A sizable minority of employees (46 per cent) have relatively short service; by contrast, 42 per cent of managers have over eleven years' service.
- *Age.* Sixty-two per cent of employees are between thirty-six and fifty-nine years, as are 83 per cent of managers.
- *Gender.* Seventy per cent of employees and 37 per cent of managers are female.
- *Ethnic origin.* Ninety-five per cent of employees are white and only one directorate has non-white managers.
- *Employment status.* Sixty per cent of employees are full-time permanent employees; a significant minority (one-third) are part-time permanent.
- The majority of employees are *non-manual* workers.

Union representation

It is calculated that about half the work force are unionized. The principal recognized unions are NALGO and NUPE. Three other non-teaching unions also have small groups of members. The authority adopts the policy of encouraging union membership. It has never agreed on any closed shop arrangements. The main unions could be described as 'moderate', pragmatic and reactive. They aim to promote constructive solutions to issues. But they are not proactive, nor do they adopt strategic approaches to employee relations issues. Although all five unions co-operate with each other as appropriate, differences of sectional interest often still divide them and inhibit any more permanent and regular multi-union collaboration.

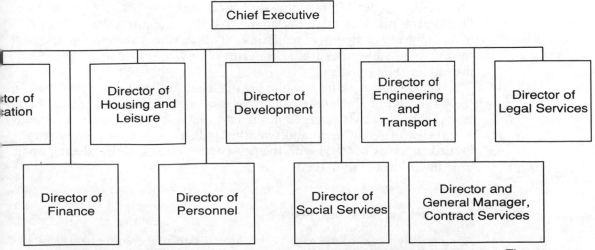

Figure 23.1 The directorate structure of the Royal Borough of Kingston upon Thames

Management structure

The directorates are usually headed by a directorate management team, comprising the director and assistant directors responsible for particular functions. Other managers are normally graded hierarchically as principal officers, senior officers and supervisors (Figure 23.1). There is considerable diversity between the directorates in terms of organizational structure, operational practice, the educational and professional experience of managers and employees, and their cultures and management styles.

A corporate management initiative

In 1988 an initiative was taken by a newly created chief executive (an internal appointment) to develop a more coherent corporate management structure. This initiative arose from earlier reports produced by two firms of management consultants and the external auditors. The authority accepted the criticisms as justified. A report to the council's Policy and Resources Committee (March 1988) said, 'In essence, too much energy and time is spent on detailed administration. There is not enough strategic thinking. Members and Senior Officers are grudging delegators and modest strategists.'

Organizationally it led to the creation of a corporate management team, designed to involve directors in discussions on strategic authority-wide policy developments. The aims and objectives of the new corporate structure are framed, in large part, in the context of a political will to provide 'cost-effective services and greater choice for clients and customers' and a need to establish 'for each key area of service measurable yardsticks by which to judge performance in service delivery'.

The achievement of these aims and objectives has been heavily conditioned by two significant factors. First of all, for most of the 1980s through legislation and administrative action, central government has promoted considerable reappraisal of local authority activity and finance. One central plank in this programme has been the introduction, in 1988, of 'compulsory competitive tendering'. This statutory measure is designed to shift local authorities from being direct service providers to becoming, instead, enabling bodies.

A second factor, affecting the borough and other local authorities in the south-east of England particularly, has been the scale of the skill and labour shortages that emerged in the late 1980s. They have given impetus to a review of recruitment and retention policies to deal not only with the immediate crisis but also with the prospective effects of the 'demographic time bomb' in the mid-1990s.

Personnel Services' initiatives

Against this background, then, the directorate of personnel services has been formulating, often in consultation with managers and unions, a range of longer-term policy initiatives. They include, for example: recruitment and retention; human resource planning; the implementation of an equal opportunities policy that can achieve bipartisan political commitment; and a review of managerial responsibility for communications and consultation with employees throughout the directorates, as a means of improving organizational effectiveness and enhancing employees' morale.

The situation

The new corporate management team and senior staff in the personnel services function were particularly concerned to review the nature of line management responsibilities for employee relations matters in the non-teaching sections of the authority, and, in particular, to appraise the formal machinery and informal arrangements for communication, consultation and negotiation.

Industrial relations machinery

This machinery had been established, in its present form, in the mid-1970s (see Figure 23.2). It comprises two separate negotiating and consultative bodies: the Staff Local Joint Committee for unions representing non-teaching white-collar workers and the Local Joint Works Committee for manual worker unions.

Additionally, the formal machinery comprises departmental consultative groups. The terms of reference of the groups were described, in 1976, as 'to provide an exchange of views and information on problems of concern to both management and employees'. The issues covered included working conditions, organization and reorganization matters, environmental conditions, health, safety and welfare. Five directorates have two consultative groups, organized usually on a separate 'officers' and 'manual' basis. Although many employee representatives are and have been union members, constitutionally they are not required to be so.

Informal arrangements

In the fifteen or more years since its establishment this formal machinery has been supplemented by various *ad hoc* arrangements, some of which have become semi-formalized. At borough level, monthly meetings are held between the personnel services directorate and NALGO and, separately, with the manual worker unions. These are consultation and information meetings on working conditions. At individual directorate level, *ad hoc* informally convened meetings of employees are used, on a departmental or sectional basis, to inform about and discuss changing aspects of employee relations (see Figure 23.2).

The view was increasingly developing among senior managers, personnel services staff and union representatives that the operation of the department consultative group machinery in particular was defective. Furthermore, some line managers were felt to be uncertain about the contribution they should make in sustaining effective communication and consultation links with their employees. It was seen as appropriate, therefore, in the light of the other changes being embarked upon by the borough, that this aspect of employee relations should be evaluated in a structured way.

An employee relations survey

The corporate management team then, on the recommendation of the director of personnel services, in 1989 commissioned an outside employee relations consultant to undertake a survey of specific aspects of employee relations. It was felt that this would lend the recommendations both objectivity and credibility. The brief was:

- To analyse existing communication and consultation arrangements.
- To identify the views of managers and employees.
- To identify the nature of the support necessary to assist effective communication and consultation arrangements.
- To make recommendations.

The organization of the survey was to be supervised by a joint management/union working party of nine people, which was to advise. (This employee relations survey would not consider the consultative arrangements

	White-collar / officers	Manual
Union-based (negotiation and consultation)	Staff Local Joint Committee (for non-teaching white-collar workers' unions)	Local Joint Works Committee (for manual workers' unions)
	Various *ad-hoc* semi-formal and informal meetings	
Employee-based (information and consultation)	Departmental Consultative Group (officers)	Departmental Consultative Group (manual)
	(Combined in some directorates)	

Figure 23.2 Mechanisms of consultation at the Royal Borough of Kingston upon Thames

with schoolteachers. These were to be subject to separate discussions within the directorate of education.)

After an initial small-scale pilot survey, it was confirmed that two separate, but related, questionnaires would be used, one for employees and one for managers (i.e. supervisory grades and above). All non-teaching employees were to be surveyed, either following a direct face-to-face briefing or through the internal post. In the event there was a 55 per cent response rate.

The diversity of directorates – in terms of traditions, values and cultures – was apparent. The role of the particular director concerned could often be influential in determining management style, the degree of commitment to employee communication and consultation and the extent to which line managers saw themselves as integrated into an effective management communication network. These personalized employee relations styles and approaches were subject to very limited constraints from the 'corporate' centre of the local authority. However, the emerging corporate approach, adopted by the new chief executive, strongly implied the need to move to greater consistency of approach and the acknowledgment of agreed principles for handling directorate-level employee relations. Overall, the need is for the borough to balance the operational flexibility essential to directorates with some more coherent corporate action.

Three sets of findings emerged from the survey. Although there were some differences in emphasis on particular points between directorates, the conclusions were generally applicable across the authority.

Information channels

The first set of findings in the survey confirmed the importance of line managers to employees within the channels of information. Almost half of all employees identified managers and supervisors both as their main source of information on what was happening in the borough and as the persons who answered queries, in the first instance, about pay and conditions. However, defects were evident in the flow of information from management in terms of speed, frequency and apparent blockages in the communication channel. Certainly any systematic briefing was generally absent. Employees were asked whether meetings or briefings had been held by their managers on a range of issues, for example departmental budgeting and cost information, pay and conditions, levels of service to the public, quality of work, borough policies. Over two-thirds of employees either could not respond to the question or said that such meetings or briefings never took place. Overall, only 39 per cent of employees reported that the channels of information from their management were 'very' or 'fairly' good.

In addition to management as the main source of information, a quarter of employees mentioned the 'grape vine' as their key source. Borough publications emerged as a strong secondary source throughout all directorates. Notice boards were an insignificant source of information.

For managers themselves there was particular concern about information flow. Less than a fifth rated inter-directorate communication as good. The inadequacy of information sent between directorates was the most significant problem mentioned by a sizable majority (85 per cent) of managers. However, an important exception related to information on pay and conditions. Less than a third experienced a problem in this respect.

As far as communication within directorates was concerned, two-thirds of managers rated theirs as 'very' or 'fairly' good. Also, there was high readership of the appropriate council committee minutes. However, the flow of information to managers about the discussions of the corporate management team was still limited.

Consultation arrangements

The second set of findings related to the departmental consultative groups. These were conceived of as the centrepiece of the authority's employee relations policy 'to bring together management and staff in consultation with the object, as a matter of mutual concern, of maintaining an effective service'. However, their record, to date, has been described by both managers and unions as very patchy. This verdict was confirmed by the survey, which revealed the system making very little perceived contribution to the management of change. Some change, whether operational or limited directly to employee relations issues, was reported to have taken place in the past two years by the overwhelming majority of employees. The most frequently mentioned changes were new equipment and new methods of working. When employees were asked to indicate the way this kind of change was made, half reported the decision as managerially determined with no consultation and one-third could not reply. By contrast, half the managers reported some form of discussion prior to decision-making – a view significantly at variance with that of employees.

When asked to indicate the communication and consultation methods by which the changes were handled, half the employees could not say. Only 5 per cent mentioned their departmental consultative group. A quarter mentioned some other face-to-face arrangement, e.g. a departmental or sectional meeting. Managers, likewise, reported consultative groups as playing a limited role in this process of change.

The defectiveness of the formal system is reflected in two other ways:

- *Limited knowledge about the communication arrangements*. So, for example, only 17 per cent of employees and 36 per cent of managers said that they had had the consultation arrangements explained to them.
- *Limited feedback from departmental consultative group meetings*. Eighty per cent of employees and 51 per cent of managers never attended briefings concerning feedback from consultative groups. Few read the group minutes.

The overall assessment of the departmental consultative group system was overwhelmingly negative. Few employees or managers were satisfied with the amount of consultation that took place between themselves and their representatives. Less than a fifth of managers and of employees reported their consultative group as an effective means of communication and consultation for keeping them fully informed on changes in the borough.

As already mentioned (see the section on industrial relations machinery and Figure 23.2) the departmental consultative groups are supplemented by two authority-wide negotiating and consultative bodies, the Staff Local Joint Committee and the Local Joint Works Committee, reflecting the traditional non-manual worker and manual worker dichotomy of employee relations. As employee relations policies are developing within the borough there is evidence of greater common interest and increasing harmonization. The management side of these committees is supportive of a move to some form of single-table arrangement. The trade unions, whilst accepting it in principle, are reluctant to progress rapidly to such a change.

The overwhelming majority of employees (89 per cent) did not know about the work of the committees, despite their key role in dealing with collective grievances and claims for improved conditions of service. Managers were only slightly better informed – with about a fifth reading the minutes of the committees regularly. Of all managerial grades, there was a marked tendency for assistant directors to be much better informed than other managers.

Back-up for consultation and communication
The third and final set of findings revealed limited back-up for existing consultative and communication arrangements and an absence of any regular monitoring and review.

Many managers acknowledged their employee relations responsibilities; two-thirds reported that consultation about workplace changes was one of these responsibilities. Half also said that they were responsible for communicating information on terms and conditions. Yet, despite this, less than a third had been provided with adequate training in communication and consultation skills. Furthermore, as described earlier, the character and quantity of the information available could have been improved.

As regards monitoring and review of the consultation and communications arrangements, there was little evidence of either having taken place. Just over a third of managers, and only 15 per cent of employees, had, in the previous two years, been involved in any review of arrangements for communicating information to employees.

Activity brief

You are an employee relations consultant and have been provided with the information set out in the case. You have been asked by the director of personnel to produce a set of recommendations to improve employee involvement (mechanisms and procedures) at Kingston borough council. In formulating your recommendations you should consider the relevance of (a) the IPM/IPA Code of Practice on Employee Involvement, (b) any knowledge and experience you may have of communication and consultation arrangements in other organizations, in the private, public or voluntary sectors.

23

Recommended reading

INDUSTRIAL PARTICIPATION ASSOCIATION and INSTITUTE OF PERSONNEL MANAGEMENT, *Employee Involvement and Participation*, Code of Practice, London, IPA and IPM, 1989.

KESSLER, Ian, 'Workplace industrial relations in local government', *Employee Relations*, 13, 2, 1991.

MARCHINGTON, M., 'The four faces of employee consultation', *Personnel Management*, May 1988.

MARCHINGTON, M., 'Employee participation', in Brian TOWERS, (ed.), *A Handbook of Industrial Relations Practice*, London, Kogan Page, 1989.

MARCHINGTON, M., 'Joint consultation in practice', in Keith SISSON (ed.), *Personnel Management in Britain*, Oxford, Blackwell, 1989.

MARGINSON, P., and SISSON, K., 'Single table talk', *Personnel Management*, May 1990.

TOWNLEY, B., 'Employee communication programmes', in Keith SISSON (ed.), *Personnel Management in Britain*, Oxford, Blackwell, 1989.

Case 24

Grievance and discipline in a district general hospital

Marjorie Corbridge

The Wellbeloved District General Hospital is the main general hospital in the Wellshire District Health Authority. It is situated in a mid-sized town in the south of England and provides health care for approximately 200,000 people. It has a total of 560 beds, providing all the general beds in the district plus a regional speciality burns unit. The hospital employs over 3,500 staff covering all staff groups; there is also an Accident and Emergency department providing twenty-four-hour cover.

The hospital, like others in the National Health Service in the late 1980s, has been under tight financial constraint. There have also been considerable changes in the management of the hospital and in the control of budgets. Since the implementation of the 'Griffiths Report' 1983 with the introduction of general managers, and the 1989 White Paper *Working for Patients*, there has been increased emphasis on cost planning. In the past the budget has been held centrally and the line manager has not really had to take account of the financial implications of operational decisions.

This case concerns an incident relating to the portering staff within the General Services department. In the past year the budget for this department has been devolved to the general services manager, and the head porter has been made increasingly aware of the cost implications of the decisions he is making. The case draws together issues for decision-making over staffing.

Background to the case

The General Services department

The General Services department provides a range of general services to the hospital, including portering services, telephone exchange and security services. The hospital porters provide a twenty-four-hour general portering service to the hospital worked on four shifts designed to give optimum cover. The shifts are:

Morning	06.00–14.00
Afternoon	14.00–22.00
Day	08.00–17.00
Night	22.00–06.00

There are a total of thirty-five porters who perform general portering duties: delivering meals to wards, taking patients for x-rays, etc. Also, there are six chargehand porters who in addition to general duties also undertake some supervisory duties such as work allocation. The porters report to a head porter, who in turn reports to the general services manager (see Figure 24.1).

Key participants

The head porter, Harry Poole, has worked at the hospital for fifteen years, and has been head porter for six years. He is responsible for the day-to-day running of the department, the organization of duty rosters and the management of the staff.

The general services manager, Gill Smith, has worked at the hospital for just over a year, and prior to that was an officer in the WRNS. Her duties include the planning of the work of the portering department.

Tony Millar has been a porter at the hospital full-time for the last six years. He is an active member of the reserve army and spends as much time as he can pursuing this interest.

Paul Ogden is the personnel officer. He is responsible for providing personnel advice and support to all the managers of ancillary and administrative workers in the hospital. This includes the general services manager and the head porter.

Sheila Simmons is a clerical officer in the medical records department and also a shop steward in the Hospital Workers' Union. She is responsible for providing members of the union in the General Services department with advice and support.

Union agreements

The hospital is unionized and Tony Millar is a member of the Hospital Workers' Union. The union has several local agreements with the hospital,

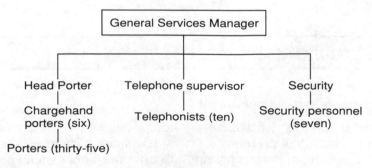

Figure 24.1 The General Services department at Wellbeloved District General

one of them concerning the numbers who are allowed time off (e.g. annual leave, sick leave, etc.) at any one time. The agreement states that 'no more than six porters should be allowed time off at any one time'. This number is seen as the optimum level to provide the required service with the minimum overtime costs. There is also an informal agreement with the union that no member of staff should be allowed to work a double shift (i.e. stay on duty for the shift immediately following the one he/she has just finished).

The union also has national agreements with the National Health Service, one of which concerns service with the reserve forces. This agreement states, 'Members of staff should be granted time off, with pay, for reserve forces duties. Such time off should be granted subject to the needs of the service.'

The situation

On Friday 2 June Tony Millar asked to see Harry Poole, the head porter, and explained that he had just received details of a weekend camp for the reserve army on Saturday and Sunday 10 and 11 June. He was due to work on those days, and asked for time off to attend the camp. The head porter explained that he would need to check rosters for that weekend and let him know. Later in the day Harry Poole saw Tony Millar and told him that he had looked at the work schedules for 10–11 June: there were already seven porters on leave that weekend (either annual leave or sick) and that he would not be able to give him the paid time off. (In fact requests for annual leave from three other porters had already been refused for that same weekend.) It was the first time in the six years Tony Millar had worked for the hospital that he had been refused leave to attend camp. He asked to see Gill Smith and requested her to allow him the necessary time off. She checked on the situation but returned to tell him that it was not possible.

The grievance

Tony Millar expressed his dissatisfaction and went to see his shop steward. After speaking to her he returned to his manager and told her that he wished to raise a formal grievance. The grievance alleged that he was being victimized by Harry Poole and that Harry Poole did not have the authority to refuse the request for time off, as the national agreement required management to grant time off for reserve duties. He again requested time off on 10–11 June. He attached a photocopy of a letter from the Minister of Defence, addressed to employers, urging them to support staff who were members of the reserve forces in the work they did.

Together with the personnel officer, Gill Smith arranged to meet Tony Millar and his union representative on the following Monday, 5 June, to hear the formal grievance. The grievance was heard, the issues were discussed and the request for time off was again refused. A further three stages of the grievance procedure were heard during the week, culminating in a meeting with the district general manager. (See Appendix 24.1 for copy of the hospital's grievance procedure.) All the requests were refused and Tony Millar was informed that he was required to work on the weekend in question.

The alleged disciplinary situation

On the Saturday morning, 10 June, at 07.30 (half an hour before Tony Millar was due on duty for his day duty) the chargehand porter on duty received a telephone call from Tony Millar's wife saying that he was sick and unable to attend work that day. The chargehand porter had no alternative but to telephone off-duty staff to arrange for someone to work overtime to keep the service operational. Later in the day he received a further telephone call saying that Tony Millar was still sick and would not be at work the following day. Further cover was arranged for the Sunday. Tony Millar was not due to work on the Monday and he reported for duty as planned on the Tuesday.

Activity brief

Imagine that you are the personnel officer, Paul Ogden, responsible for advising and supporting the management of the department.

Grievance

1   What advice would you give the general services manager, Gill Smith, in preparing for the first grievance hearing?
2   What facts do you think ought to provide the focus of the meeting?
3   Prepare a briefing paper which Gill Smith could use in conducting the hearing.
4   In groups of four – the general services manager, Gill Smith, with the personnel officer, Paul Ogden, and Tony Millar with the shop steward, Sheila Simmons – prepare for and role-play the grievance hearing.
5   Prepare a report of the hearing and the rationale of the decision you reach for briefing the next line of management.

Disciplinary

6   Taking into account the organization's disciplinary procedure, outlined in Appendix 24.2, what action would you advise the general services manager, Gill Smith, to take when Tony Millar returns to work?
7   What investigations would you undertake?
8   On discovering that Tony Millar attended the reserve army weekend camp what action would you take?

9　Prepare a briefing paper for Gill Smith outlining the issues to be covered in a disciplinary hearing.

10　In groups of four – the general services manager, Gill Smith, with the personnel officer, Paul Ogden, and Tony Millar with the shop steward, Sheila Simmons – prepare for and role-play the disciplinary hearing.

11　Write a letter to Tony Millar reporting the disciplinary hearing and what disciplinary action, if any, management will take.

Recommended reading

ADVISORY CONCILIATION AND ARBITRATION SERVICE (ACAS), *Discipline at Work*, London, HMSO, 1989.

SALAMON, Michael, *Industrial Relations: Theory and Practice*, Hemel Hempstead, Prentice Hall, 1987, chapters 21–2.

THOMPSON, A. W. J., and MURRAY, V. V., *Grievance Procedures*, Aldershot, Saxon House, 1976.

TORRINGTON, D., *Employee Resourcing*, London, IPM, 1991, chapter 17.

TORRINGTON, D., and HALL, L., *Personnel Management: a New Approach*, Hemel Hempstead, Prentice Hall, 1991, chapter 30.

Appendix 24.1 Wellbeloved District General Hospital grievance procedure

Definition

A grievance exists when an individual feels that (s)he has cause for complaint regarding:

- Duties.
- Conditions of employment.
- Working conditions.
- Working procedures.

This procedure is intended as a safety valve, for use by an individual when all other means have failed. It is not intended to be a means of criticism or complaint against an individual employee or another group of staff.

Need

A procedure for resolving grievances is necessary to:

- Satisfy staff that they have been fairly treated.

- Ensure speedy resolution.
- Encourage good staff/manager relations.
- Ensure uniform practice.
- Ensure that managers and staff know what to do.

Procedure

The procedure envisages a maximum of four stages in the resolving of grievances culminating in the District General Manager. These stages will relate directly to the management structure of the aggrieved individual's position in the organisation. At each stage it is the manager's responsibility to inform the employee of her/his right to be accompanied if (s)he wishes by a work colleague or her/his representative.

Stage 1. The aggrieved raises the grievance with her/his Head of Department, who should initiate the completion of the 'Grievance Form'. If there is no resolution of the grievance nor agreement on action to be taken *within two clear working days* the manager must advise the next level of management and pass on the 'Grievance Form', which should be signed by both the manager and the aggrieved.

Stage 2. The manager at this level should resolve the grievance with the aggrieved or agree on a course of action to be taken. If this is not possible *within five working days* from the raising of the grievance this manager must advise the next level of management and pass on the 'Grievance Form', which should be signed by this manager and the aggrieved.

Stage 3. The manager at this level should resolve the grievance with the aggrieved or agree on a course of action to be taken. If this is not possible *within eight working days* from the raising of the grievance this manager must advise the next level of management and pass on the 'Grievance Form', which should be signed by this manager and the aggrieved.

Stage 4. The manager at this level should resolve the grievance with the aggrieved or agree on a course of action to be taken. If this is not possible *within thirteen working days* from the raising of the grievance this manager must advise the aggrieved person and her/his representative in writing of the procedure for taking the grievance further.

The Personnel Department

The Personnel Department is responsible for advising all parties on the handling of staff grievances and may be directly involved at all stages.

The department should be responsible for monitoring the effectiveness of grievance procedures.

Appendix 24.2 Wellbeloved District General Hospital disciplinary procedure

1. Purpose and scope

This procedure is designed to help and encourage all employees to achieve and maintain standards of conduct, attendance and job performance. The hospital rules (a copy of which is displayed in the office) and this procedure apply to all employees. The aim is to ensure consistent and fair treatment for all.

2. Principles

(a) No disciplinary action will be taken against an employee until the case has been fully investigated.

(b) At every stage in the procedure the employee will be advised of the nature of the complaint against him or her and will be given the opportunity to state his or her case before any decision is made.

(c) At all stages the employee will have the right to be accompanied by a shop steward, employee representative or work colleague during the disciplinary interview.

(d) No employee will be dismissed for a first breach of discipline except in the case of gross misconduct, when the penalty will be dismissal without notice or payment in lieu of notice.

(e) An employee will have the right to appeal against any disciplinary penalty imposed.

(f) The procedure may be implemented at any stage if the employee's alleged misconduct warrants such action.

3. The procedure

Minor faults will be dealt with informally but where the matter is more serious the following procedure will be used:

Stage 1. Oral warning. If conduct or performance does not meet acceptable standards the employee will normally be given a formal ORAL WARNING. He or she will be advised of the reason for the warning, that it is the first stage of the disciplinary procedure and of his or her right of appeal. A brief note of the oral warning will be kept but it will be spent after . . . months, subject to satisfactory conduct and performance.

Stage 2. Written warning. If the offence is a serious one, or if a further offence occurs, a WRITTEN WARNING will be given to the employee by the supervisor. This will give details of the complaint, the improvement required and the time scale. It will warn that action under Stage 3 will be considered if there is no satisfactory improvement and will advise of the right of appeal. A copy of this written warning will be kept by

the supervisor but it will be disregarded for disciplinary purposes after
. . . months subject to satisfactory conduct and performance.

Stage 3. Final written warning or disciplinary suspension. If there is still
a failure to improve, or conduct or performance is still unsatisfactory,
or if the misconduct is sufficiently serious to warrant only one written
warning but insufficiently serious to justify dismissal (in effect both first
and final written warning), a FINAL WRITTEN WARNING will normally be
given to the employee. This will give details of the complaint, will warn
that dismissal will result if there is no satisfactory improvement and
will advise of the right of appeal. A copy of this final written warning
will be kept by the supervisor but it will be spent after . . . months
(in exceptional cases the period may be longer) subject to satisfactory
conduct and performance.

Alternatively, consideration will be given to imposing a penalty of
a disciplinary suspension without pay for up to a maximum of five
working days.

Stage 4. Dismissal. If conduct or performance is still unsatisfactory and
the employee still fails to reach the prescribed standards, DISMISSAL
will normally result. Only the appropriate senior manager can take
the decision to dismiss. The employee will be provided, as soon as
reasonably practicable, with written reasons for dismissal, the date on
which employment will terminate and the right of appeal.

4.   Gross misconduct

The following list provides examples of offences which are normally
regarded as gross misconduct:

- Theft, fraud, deliberate falsification of records.
- Fighting, assault on another person.
- Deliberate damage to hospital property.
- Serious incapability through alcohol or being under the influence
  of illegal drugs.
- Serious negligence which causes unacceptable loss, damage or
  injury.
- Serious act of insubordination.

If you are accused of an act of gross misconduct, you may be suspended
from work on full pay, normally for no more than five working days,
while the hospital authorities investigate the alleged offence. If, on
completion of the investigation and the full disciplinary procedure, the
hospital authority is satisfied that gross misconduct has occurred, the
result will normally be summary dismissal without notice or payment
in lieu of notice.

5.   Appeals

An employee who wishes to appeal against a disciplinary decision
should inform ———— within two working days. The senior manager
will hear all appeals and his/her decision is final. At the appeal any disciplinary penalty imposed will be reviewed but it cannot be increased.

Based on ACAS (1989).

Case 25

Sexual harassment at Public Relations Ltd

Diana Winstanley

Sexual harassment at work can be defined as repeated and unwanted sexual comments or physical contact that are found to be objectionable or offensive by the recipients and cause them discomfort in doing their job. It can be an intimidating or frightening experience, yet many people are reluctant to take action for fear of further embarrassment or through sheer lack of knowledge of any sources of help. One useful role that the personnel manager can adopt is in devising policies and procedures to deal with such incidents, but also in inculcating a culture to prevent them from happening in the first place. This case concerns a small company where the circumstances surrounding the issue were such that there were no easy or quick solutions.

Background to the case

The legal position in sexual harassment cases

In law there is no specific measure to make sexual harassment illegal, but there are provisions under the Sex Discrimination Act, 1975, which can be utilized.

There are cases in which it has been successfully claimed that sexual harassment may result in a victim being 'treated less favourably than a man would have been treated . . . on the grounds of her sex' (s. 1 (1) (a)). Further, where this has resulted in a resignation it has in some cases been claimed to be 'a detriment contrary to s. 6 (2) (b)' of the Act where sexual harassment constitutes the fundamental breach of contract by the employer required for a claim of constructive dismissal (see Western Excavating (EEC) Ltd v. Sharp, 1977). As a result some claimants have received compensation for sex discrimination and for unfair dismissal.

Furthermore the case of Wigan Borough Council v. Davies EAT demonstrates that it is the employer's duty to ensure that employees are not harassed by colleagues. Finally, the Sex Discrimination Act does not require the two-year qualification period as does the Employment Protection and Consolidation Act.

The company

Public Relations Ltd (PRL) is a small but fast-moving public relations, marketing and publishing company based in fashionable Kensington, with a subsidiary office in some converted stables at the home of the founder in Surrey. The firm has been built up largely through the hard work and personal charisma of its founder.

Its founder and director of public relations is Gerry Henley, who runs the business as a family concern, with tight control over each account, adopting a paternalistic style of leadership. He commutes between the two offices in his Bentley, keeping an eye on each of his staff. He fervently hopes that one day his only son, James, will run the business in his stead. To this end he has sent James to work for an American friend and colleague, who runs a much larger public relations firm, with which PRL has some links.

PRL employs approximately twenty staff, although the number fluctuates considerably. Many of them work as self-employed consultants, hiring their services to the firm on a part-time basis. Most of the staff are female, with the exception of Mr Henley himself, his son, and some consultants who help with art work and printing on a contract basis.

Although not having a clearly defined personnel function, there is a personnel and administrative officer, Anita Daly, who is based in the office in Surrey and sees to the day-to-day administration of the firm. She is involved in salary administration and a number of personnel duties, as well as having some responsibility for one PRL client. Anita has been with the firm almost since its inception a number of years ago and has become Gerry's right-hand woman.

The work of the offices consists of a number of PR accounts, largely servicing the pharmaceutical, veterinary and computer industries. The work is distributed on an account basis, with junior and senior account executives taking on a number of clients. The types of activities the account executives will commonly be involved with are the writing of press releases and brochures, organizing conferences, exhibitions, product launches, press briefings, publicity events, building up contacts and liaising with the press. As well as public relations, the firm publishes a number of journals and acts as an information and research service for a number of consortia.

The situation: a number of incidents

Suzie Clayton, aged twenty-two, had come to the London office of the firm a few months previously as a temp working for a secretarial agency. Her secretarial and administrative skills were good, and she demonstrated a calm and professional manner. She was also fun-loving and had willingly helped in a number of promotions with which PRL were involved, at a time when it was a case of 'all hands on deck'. At one, the launch of a new veterinary book, she had dressed up as a furry animal and circulated among journalists with bottles of champagne. This had led Gerry to offer her a permanent position as a trainee junior account executive, assisting other account executives on some of the larger accounts. Most staff working at the firm have been recruited through informal channels and contacts, some being the sons and daughters of Gerry's clients, friends and patrons.

One day, however, as she was clearing up some of the debris from a press briefing for journalists at the London office, to which Anita Daly had been seconded to help for the day, Suzie broke down in tears. She complained to Anita of Gerry Henley's behaviour towards her. When Anita asked her to explain what she meant she said that he had been leering at her and making suggestive remarks. He frequently asked her to come into his office, where he had a number of 'glamour' pictures of scantily clad women adorning the walls. Many of these were promotional calendars and advertising features for clients and their products. Recently he had detained her after work for quite trivial reasons. When she was out with him in the Bentley on company business he had often tried to pat her leg and had confided in intimate detail how his marriage was not what it used to be. She had been getting very upset and frightened, especially when she was left alone with him after work and everyone else had gone home.

Suzie was also feeling a crisis of confidence, as he had been suggesting to her that she should make more effort to get on with clients socially, implying that it might help business if she were more 'flirtatious' and 'friendly' with them. He said that clients would prefer her to dress with more 'flash' and 'style'. The previous day he had told her that she really was not up to being a good public relations executive. He thought it unlikely that she could get another PR job anywhere else, and she ought to be grateful to him for having recruited her.

Suzie is in a dilemma and is thinking of handing in her resignation, as she cannot face coming to work any longer. On the other hand, she realizes that this has been the luckiest break she has had in her career. She knows that, lacking qualifications and experience, and in the face of cut-backs in the industry, she would find it very difficult to get other work in public relations.

Anita Daly herself had faced a similar dilemma several months before. She had found Mr Henley's behaviour towards her to be embarrassing on occasions, but each incident had been too trivial and ambiguous for her to make any 'concrete' complaint – he stood that bit too close to her or put his arm round her shoulder when leaning over to discuss some work. Once, she had plucked up courage to ask him to desist, but he had laughed at her saying she was imagining it, which made her feel rather foolish and led her to question her own judgement.

At the end of one particularly bad day when Mr Henley's attentions had been the 'last straw', she had handed in her notice claiming the work was too stressful and gone home in tears,. It was only after much persuasion from Mr Henley (who had been genuinely upset), that she agreed to return. Since then she found the situation had improved.

Other women had also experienced similar incidents, however, most had been able to laugh them off or felt confident enough of their position to tell him to stop in no uncertain terms.

Activity brief

Taking on the role of Anita Daly, the personnel and administration officer, answer the following questions.

1　Do you think the behaviour of Gerry Henley towards Suzie Clayton constitutes sexual harassment?
2　What would you advise Suzie Clayton to do?
3　What action would you take (a) to help Suzie Clayton, (b) to prevent the situation arising again?
4　Should Suzie hand in her resignation and claim constructive and unfair dismissal at an industrial tribunal? (a) What factors would be taken into account? (b) What would be the likely result?

Recommended reading

DAVIDSON, M. J., and EARNSHAW, J., 'Policies and attitudes towards sexual harassment in UK organisations', *Personnel Review*, 19, 3, 1990, pp. 23–7.

EQUAL OPPORTUNITIES COMMISSION, *Towards Equality: a Casebook of Decisions on Sex Discrimination and Equal Pay, 1976–88*, Manchester, EOC, 1989.

LABOUR RESEARCH DEPARTMENT, 'Sexual harassment at work', *Bargaining Report*, December 1987.

RUBENSTEIN, M., 'Devising a sexual harassment policy', *Personnel Management*, February 1991, pp. 34–7.

STRAW, J., *Equal Opportunities: the Way Ahead*, London, IPM. 1989.

The Equal Opportunities Commission and various trade unions provide helpful publications and pamphlets. The European Commission have also produced a 'Recommendation and Draft Code on Dignity for Men and Women at Work'. Readers should refer to their own company's procedures in these areas.

IV
Integrated Human
Resource Management

Case 26

Human resource strategy in Hutton Borough Council

Hedley Malloch

This case concerns a Labour council in the north of England which, faced with social deprivation, high unemployment and restrictive government legislation, has attempted to develop a human resource strategy which is complementary to its organizational strategy of community building and service provision. The case outlines issues in the council's key human resource policies and employment policies and attempts to illuminate the relationship between strategy and human resource practice. Finally the case presents an alternative approach to human resource management from that generally espoused by 'flexible firm' writers and those advocating a segmentation of the work force into a core and a periphery.

Background to the case

The town of Hutton

Hutton Borough Council is a large metropolitan-type area situated in northern England, home to some quarter of a million people. The local industries are based on commodity chemicals, metal manufacture, construction, shipbuilding and heavy engineering. There is a small Anglo-Asian and Afro-Caribbean community.

Hutton grew rapidly during the nineteenth century and, despite many improvements over the last quarter of a century, it still has the air of a frontier town. Historically, few attempts have been made to regulate the pollution which emanates from local industry. Much of the housing stock is drab, low-cost Victorian terrace housing laid out in a depressing grid pattern. The town's basic industries were severely depressed during the 1980s and local unemployment soared to over 20 per cent, making it one of the worst affected areas on the UK mainland. In some areas the unemployment rate was in excess of 70 per cent. Many factories and offices closed during this time and the town has not been particularly successful in attracting new industry.

Hutton is a deprived area as measured by a range of social indicators.

Whilst average earnings are surprisingly high, average income per household is low. A high proportion of wage-earners work well away from Hutton on contract-type work, giving the local economy some of the characteristics of a 'remittance economy' and causing some observers to liken Hutton to Eire or southern Italy. Health data indicate that in some parts of the town life expectancy rates and general levels of health are amongst the lowest in the UK.

Hutton Borough Council

The council has over eighty elected members, seventy-one of them Labour, the remainder Liberal Democrats and Conservatives. The town has been under Labour control since the First World War. However, some important changes took place in the composition and character of the Labour Party during the 1980s. The 'old guard' of the party were predominantly over forty-five, white, male and drawn from the craft unions which were so heavily represented in Hutton's basic industries. Over the decade they were replaced by younger party members who were much better educated, employed in professional white-collar work and represented by unions such as NALGO and MSF. They were also much more heterogeneous in terms of age, sex and ethnic background. Their group objective was to improve services and conditions in Hutton. They were committed to improving conditions in the local community, in part by the provision of a wider and better range of services. They had been elected under the banner of 'Build the community' and thought that the pledge was incompatible with marginalizing sections of the work force. One officer commented:

> The council feels that as part of its policies it should do something about what's happening outside. It's done all in its power to provide support for special employment schemes; and I think it feels that it should manage its affairs internally in such a way as they are compatible with what it's trying to do outside. So it doesn't see its role to lessen the number of employees internally to make the situation worse outside. I think those policies are compatible with each other. And it does move the way that we operate, and the attitudes that we have to manpower in the authority.

The situation: Hutton Borough Council's human resource policies

The human resource policies the borough has followed have been many and varied, but this case study concentrates on policies toward:

- Contracting.
- Harmonization and equal opportunities.

- Open recruitment.
- Close supervision of officers.
- Flexible working time.
- Redeployment of staff.

Contracting

The Local Government Planning and Land Act, 1980, forced the council to put engineering and building work out to tender. At the same time the government abolished the Fair Wages Resolution, thereby removing the need for potential contractors to observe local government rates of pay and conditions. These legal provisions were intensified by the Local Government Act, 1986: this extended compulsory competitive tendering to refuse collection, street cleaning, catering, estate and vehicle maintenance services. If the work was not put out to tender, or if a council was considered not to have acted fairly in the tendering process, the Department of the Environment could instruct it not to award the contract to its own in-house direct labour organization. These legal incentives added to the Department of the Environment's encouragement to Councils to test the cost-effectiveness of their services in the market place, and reinforced the norms, performance reviews and guidelines published by the Audit Commission. The commission was established in 1972 to ensure that councils conformed to their financial obligations as laid down by law. Such legal and administrative encouragement of greater cost-effectiveness came against a background of reductions in rate support grants and rising expectations among the local community about the level of service that should be provided.

An important objective for the borough council was employment and good terms and conditions of employment for its employees. The council's policy was summed up by its chief executive:

> The council's committed to do all it can to create more jobs, more services, and to improve the earnings of the low-paid against the back-cloth of expenditure cuts. Consequently they regard value-for-money exercises as being in conflict with their basic philosophy. The council is not willing to select options which would be seen to be to the detriment of low-paid employees; they do have a certain sympathy with, as they see it, the plight of manual workers; and they certainly won't encourage officers to undertake assignments which appear to chase the lower-paid.

Contracting was dealt with by a strategy known as 'tactical tendering'. This involved the managers complying with the letter of the law but tendering the work in such a way that contractors would find it a very unattractive proposition. Tenders could be overspecified; for example, managers could ask contractors for a grass-cutting contract price based on twenty cuts per season, the in-house tender price being based on thirteen cuts, a figure that was known to be adequate. Work could be bundled up in lots which were too big for any potential contractor to handle, or too small to be profitable. Timing was used: work would be offered for tender only at the last moment, leaving any contractor who was interested little chance of submitting a bid. Geography played a part: work would be offered in packages which involved contractors having to contemplate servicing split sites miles apart. The redundancy costs of the client's work force were added to all contractors' prices. Finally, contractors were advised that all contracts would be rigorously monitored and the slightest case of non-compliance would be met with instant termination of the contract.

Between 1980 and 1986, not one contract was awarded to an outside contractor, apart from a limited range of work where they had always been used.

Harmonization and equal opportunities

The council embarked on an ambitious programme to harmonize conditions of employment and to introduce equal opportunities. It permeated many aspects of human resource management strategy. Pay, training and staffing all fell under its influence. There was a policy of harmonizing conditions and area allowances for manual workers. The object was to facilitate a policy of redeployment, but elected members were also anxious to offer manual employees pay stability as a first step towards a unified remuneration structure covering all employees.

Equal Opportunity policies were a distinctive feature of the harmonization policies. Many managers define the problem of equal opportunities in terms of tokenism. They are interested in appearing to comply with the more obvious features of the legislation governing discrimination, especially those aimed at race and sex. This was not the case in Hutton. Here there were comprehensive Equal Opportunity policies. There were clear statements of objectives; resources and responsibility were allocated to implementation; the policies were communicated and monitored; staff were trained in their meaning and management. The policies were broad in scope, covering not only sex and race but also disability. There was realization that the route to equality lay in harmonizing all aspects of conditions of employment. Discrimination depended upon the existence of differentiated conditions of employment. In this sense equality of opportunity was inseparable from harmonization of terms and conditions of employment. All aspects of the council's human resource management system were checked for discriminatory practices. For example, disciplinary procedures for different grades of staff were harmonized to ensure that there was no potential for discriminatory treatment.

Open recruitment

The council implemented an open recruitment policy. It made a conscious effort to decasualize recruitment. Prior to the policy's introduction recruitment had been by 'word of mouth' and internal vacancy boards. These methods were abandoned, as they were believed to be incompatible with Equal Opportunity policies, to burden the unemployed with unnecessary costs, and to lay the council open to charges of, literally, 'jobs for the boys'. Instead job shops were created in local community centres and careers offices. They were located on large housing estates, thus saving unemployed people the cost of transport. All vacancies were advertised in job shops and the local free press. Finally, there were public displays of all job applicant waiting lists, so potential employees could check their position in the queue for employment.

Close supervision of officers

Unemployment released many councillors from full-time work. They began to take a closer interest in their elected duties than had previously been possible. They moved into the council offices and began attending conferences and courses on specialist aspects of management in local government. Supervision was not only closer, it also changed in nature. The basis of supervision shifted from naive enquiry to informed questioning. One senior officer remarked:

> A lot of the councillors are around more; some of them have more time to spare. The quality is different, too. Some of them are professionally qualified in the functions and the activities the council carry out and they show greater interest. They ask more pertinent questions and get more involved in the day-to-day running of the departments. The more you're exposed to elected members, the more you have to run with them. When I first came into local government, contact with elected members was only in committees and confined to the team of Chief Officers. But now if they want to contact you they know you're in here. They know your phone number. It's different now.

Flexible working time

The council had made many efforts to restructure patterns of attendance. Part-time work had increased substantially and new shift and rostering systems had been implemented, as part of the competitive tendering process, to match demand more closely to supply. Ancillary, catering, kiosk activities and some types of professional staff were the focus of these efforts. The use of temporary contracts had increased. The council used them to fund new projects which had relatively short time horizons, such as nursery education and publicly funded training activities. The council was not legally required to supply nursery education, and it was the market which was most immediately vulnerable to the key determinant of educational demand, that is, short-term variations in the birth rate. Publicly funded training project staff all operated on short-term contracts.

Redeployment of staff

The council needed to build up new services and products on static or declining labour budgets. The management services officer commented:

> Sixty per cent plus of our expenditure is manpower: if the council wants to pursue new policy initiatives, and it hasn't got the money to

finance the manpower, it can only do so by making the manual work force more able to be transferred. We'll do that by making sure that there aren't any contractual limits to the way in which we can move people around.

The council used redeployment to develop the concept of a service and to 'get close to the customer'. For example, housing department staff were redeployed from a central office in the town hall to area offices in residential areas specifically to make staff accessible to the local community. The area offices were linked with the engineering department and the housing department by an on-line networked system of personal computers. Tenants could pay rents and arrange housing repairs on the spot – they did not have to leave the estate, write or make telephone calls.

Thus new technology and redeployment of staff were used to bind the customer close to the producer in ways which could not be imitated. The council's competitive position was thereby improved in ways which a housing action trust could not reproduce. This was one concrete example of technology being used to improve a service, by binding the producers and the consumers of the service more closely together. Attendant changes in the pattern of work organization were addressed through redeployment. Attempts were made to redeploy refuse collectors from their usual jobs on to a range of environmental projects, such as graffiti removal.

Redeployment was also important in the education department. The principal administrative officer of the department commented:

> The major problem has been redeploying staff as a result of falling rolls. We've redeployed people whose jobs have actually gone as part of our policy of closing smaller schools; and we've redeployed people whose hours have been cut back, up to the hours that they used to work. We've spent a great deal of time doing that.

Redeployment was caused by falling school rolls, the ensuing programme of school 'rationalization' and the need to build up new services for new markets, such as nursery education and publicly funded training courses in the technical colleges. Old, small schools were closed, the pupils relocated into newer, larger, more economic ones. Teachers and ancillary staff followed them. Whilst demand was falling, the composition of demand was changing.

Activity brief

1 What are the underlying reasons that account for the human resource strategies and policies followed by Hutton Borough Council?
2 Assess the human resource management policies of the council. Do you think they are the correct and most appropriate ones to use?
3 What problems has the council had in implementing its HRM policies?

4   How would you account for the importance attributed to redeployment
     at Hutton Borough Council?

Recommended reading

ATKINSON, J., 'Manpower strategies and the flexible firm', *Personnel Management*, August 1984, pp. 28–31.

ATKINSON, J., *Flexibility, Uncertainty and Manpower Management*, Institute of Manpower Studies report 89, Brighton, IMS, 1985.

ATKINSON, J., and MEAGER, N., *Changing Working Patterns: how companies achieve flexibility to match new needs*, London, National Economic Development Office, 1986.

BREWSTER, C., and CONNOCK, S., *Industrial Relations: Cost-effective Strategies*, London, Hutchinson, 1985.

PORTER, M. E., 'How information technology gives you competitive advantage', *Harvard Business Review*, July–August 1985.

SHAEFF, M., 'NHS ancillary services and competitive tendering', *Industrial Relations Journal*, 19, 2, 1988, pp. 93–105.

Case 27

Human resource planning at Engindorf plc

Paul Sparrow

Human resource planning and management

Human resource planning (HRP) is a complicated topic. Its breadth often demands that practitioners have an understanding of complex human resource issues, nuances of data, and complex relationships between policies and practices. Attention needs to be focused both on conducting an HRP process and on implementing the results by creating a human resource strategy. Although these two topics are intrinsically linked, they often form separate activities within organizations.

Manpower planning versus human resource planning

In the early 1960s businesses were operating in relatively stable conditions. High levels of growth, and skill shifts as a result of new technology, were leading to national skill shortages in a number of key occupations. As a result, manpower planning became an important activity, first at a national level, then, later, within large organizations. This led to the traditional conceptualization of manpower planning as a linear process that used the past as a guide in planning the future. The aim was to ensure that organizations had the right number of people in the right place at the right time.

Human resource planning is not manpower planning. There is some overlap between the two, but HRP is a broader and more inclusive process. HRP is less gender-specific in connotation. In manpower planning the manager is most concerned with the numerical aspects of forecasting, matching supply with demand, and controlling the 'flow' of people through the organization. HRP still requires these activities but has an additional focus on the motivation of people (Bramham, 1989). In the early 1980s some of the limitations of traditional manpower planning became apparent. The business environment became highly volatile. The prevalence of business failures, high unemployment, mergers, downsizing and reorganizations invalidated tightly defined manpower plans. Cowling and Walters (1990) concluded that 'in the chill economic winds of the early 1980s manpower planning caught something of a cold'. Despite such disturbances, and the failure of planning techniques, it became increasingly clear that some form of planning for human resources was never more necessary (Walker, 1990). External pressures, such as demographic and skill shortages, coupled with the realization within organizations that competitive advantage could be achieved only through people, made it imperative for organizations to take a more strategic perspective about their people – the organization's human resources – planning both costs and investments.

Strategic analysis of people-related business problems

HRP now serves as a tool to provoke thought and discussion. Combined with other activities – such as strategic planning processes – it also becomes part of a process to determine long-term objectives and courses of action. The main thrust of HRP is to solve what Schuler and Walker (1990) describe as 'people-related business issues'. Rather than research the environment and trawl for likely issues, HRP picks up the issues that are at the heart of the business, such as acquisition, decentralization, empowerment, internationalization or technology, and investigates their human resource management implications.

HRP therefore requires a strategic approach to the recruitment, development, management and motivation of the people in the organization, in the context of a pressing business issue. It is a systematic process of linking human resource practices with business demands in order to improve an organization's abilities. It establishes the plans, courses of action and targets for the range of policies needed to enable the organization to influence the management of its human resources.

Two stances have been taken on HRP in relation to its strategic role. Writers such as Dyer (1986) and Walker (1980) argue that specific human resource activities are derived and then tailored to match or 'fit' the organization's strategic objectives. HRP plays an essentially reactive role. Others have argued that HRP can play a more central and proactive role and may be involved in the strategy formulation process itself (see, for example, Lengnick-Hall, 1984, Tichy et al., 1982).

Managing the what and the how

As HRP has adapted to a changing business environment it has led to shorter planning horizons, less complicated forecasting techniques and greater involvement of line management (Greer et al., 1989). The most common reasons for carrying out a human resource plan are to develop staff, avoid shortages of qualified personnel and provide information for decision-making. The most frequently used forecasting techniques are succession planning and replacement charts, personnel inventories, supervisor estimates and non-statistical formulae. HRP is therefore evolving into a decentralized line management function and is no longer the sole prerogative of centralized personnel or corporate planning departments. Personnel specialists and external advisers are therefore taking on a consultative role. A survey carried out on behalf of the Institute of Personnel Management (Cowling and Walters, 1990) shows that 60 per cent of personnel managers still see HRP as their responsibility. In fulfilling their role personnel managers have to provide two sorts of input: advice on what to do, and on how to manage the process.

Background to the case

The case that follows reveals a number of important issues in terms of both 'what to do' and 'how to manage' the HRP process. It is based on an assignment with the object of assisting a decentralized line management function to create an HR plan and reflects many of the points made in the introduction.

The case is set in the information technology (IT) department of Engindorf plc, a large multinational engineering and manufacturing organization. The department employs staff in a number of European locations, although the two largest sites are in the UK and Germany. There are over 1,000 information technology staff employed in three main operations: Commercial Systems, Computer-aided Engineering (CAE) and Data Processing and Communications.

Engindorf plc was undergoing a range of complex changes in its business strategy, technology and human resource management. Confronted with overcapacity in Europe, it had developed strategies to cut costs and bring products to the market more rapidly. The response included improving quality, raising margins, reducing fixed costs, pursuing joint ventures and investing in human resource management. Information technology had shown itself to play a major role in this strategic change. In response to the Japanese threat there had been a twelvefold increase in the number of robots used in manufacturing. Product development was carried out on a network of over 300 computer-aided design (CAD) work stations. Within the last ten years the amount of product design based on CAD had increased from 8 per cent to 90 per cent. Programme lead time for new products had been cut by two months, and four months had been taken off the design cycle.

In the mid-1980s a study by IT consultants had recommended that Engindorf plc should leverage its strategic opportunities by investing in information technology. There followed a sustained period of growth in IT resources in support of corporate strategies. By the late 1980s the central people-related business issue was how to continue to resource effectively an IT department which was now adding value to, and playing a central role in, the organization's business strategy.

The situation

Changes within the IT department

The IT department was led by Ian Davies. He had been IT director for six years and in that time had established his own business planning function. His department had undergone rapid change. The technologies managed, such as computer-aided design/computer-aided manufacturing (CAD/CAM), computer-integrated manufacturing (CIM) and networking, had become extremely complex. Moreover the role of the function had changed significantly. When Ian first arrived the department employed large numbers of people in data-processing operations, but the role now was to provide an information management service.

There had been a reduction in the number of people employed in data-processing operations but a large increase in the number of people employed in commercial systems and computer-aided engineering (CAE). The skills and competences needed by the IT managers had changed in line with the new role.

Not only was the management task more complex, but the IT department had also grown in size quite dramatically. The head-count had nearly doubled in five years. This growth had been spread fairly evenly across all the European sites. In order to resource the growth in head-count, the department undertook a large-scale graduate recruitment programme. The IT department had a policy of developing its own talent. Rather than recruit on the open labour market the department recruited graduates from a number of disciplines and then developed them. The numbers of graduates recruited each year had consequently also been growing. Last year eighty graduates had been recruited into the function. The bulk of the recruitment interviewing was done by IT managers. The process was eating into very limited management time. It was, however, seen as an essential task.

A few years ago a retention problem had developed with the graduates. Turnover rates increased from 10 per cent to 21 per cent. In order to address the problem a number of initiatives on team building, career development and employee involvement had been taken. A 'fast track' system had been set up in which the early part of graduate careers was actively managed. Graduates were rotated through a number of projects in the first two years of their career. The turnover rate had dropped again, but there was now a perception among managers that the IT graduates were being promoted far more quickly than before, perhaps too quickly.

The department now had nearly twenty different human resource initiatives. Information technology managers had progressively taken on responsibility for recruitment and marketing activities, appraisal reviews, promotion boards and a host of other arrangements. There were numerous pressures on management time. The department was run with very tight management ratios. As overall numbers had increased, the proportion who were on management grades had fallen from 30 per cent to 18 per cent. It was not known how this compared with the rest of the industry.

The IT director's agenda

In reviewing these changes Ian Davies had concluded that he was no longer constrained by technology. He was constrained by the organization culture, organization and people issues. Given the changed role of the department and the greater emphasis on management skills, he needed to feel confident that, in the broadest sense, he could resource his department so that he could deliver on the business strategy.

Within this resourcing issue Ian Davies had a number of pressing concerns. The first was that he had to improve levels of productivity. The business plan dictated that there must be a 10 per cent increase in productivity over the next two years. A large investment had been made in 'fourth generation' programming languages, and this new technology was expected to bring about the increased productivity. If it did not, extreme pressure would be placed on his budgets and he would find it hard to justify a higher head-count.

A second concern was the level of dependence on external contractors. Many of the skills and much of the specialist knowledge to meet the demand for services in the mid-1980s had not been available internally. Contractor use had grown to very high levels, and there had been a consequent drift of skills away from in-house staff to the contractors. He suspected that many of the key business and technological skills were now embedded in the contractor work force. Given the increasing strategic importance of his department, he wanted those skills in-house. That meant progressively replacing external contractors with internal staff. He had set a two-year deadline for this process to be completed. Could it be done?

Aims of the HR plan

It was clear to Ian Davies that he had to take a more strategic approach to the management of his staff in order to make a number of difficult decisions. It was imperative for him to establish his priorities in the human resource management sphere. John Martyn was the business planning manager within the IT department. His function had been made responsible for producing annual business plans. This process was now successfully established, and Ian Davies decided that John Martyn's function should now produce a human resource plan in conjunction with the annual business plan.

The IT department had attempted to produce an HR plan three years before. It had not been professionally managed and had been criticized for jumping straight into the perceived human resource issues and assuming the solutions. The IT director wanted a thorough job, with John Martyn gathering and analysing only appropriate data. He instructed Martyn to take on the task, making it clear that there was to be a strong empirical bias in the HR plan. Ian Davies agreed the following aims for the plan with John Martyn:

- Produce a stand-alone plan document that would form one of three linked planning documents (the other two being the business/IT strategy, and the technology strategy).
- Provide an objective assessment of the existing human resources.
- Outline the current approaches to their management.
- Identify the range and scope of the problems associated with that management.
- State the agreed approaches necessary to address the problems.

Head-count has grown by between 11 per cent and 13 per cent per annum since 1985

The UK recruitment market consists of straight graduates — aged 21 years — in computing and other disciplines

The German recruitment market consists of postgraduates aged around 25–26 years

Recruitment practices in the UK and Germany follow the same stages of first interview, second interview, psychometric testing, job offer

Demographic projections show a fall in the number of graduates in both labour markets by 1993

Salary surveys indicate that initial graduate pay rates are broadly competitive. Management grade pay rates are just below the average for software houses

Graduate recruitment numbers last year (1990) stood at eighty in the UK and forty-two in Germany. A handful of staff were recruited across other European sites

Graduate careers are managed by Tutor Groups. These now involve 120 staff and have been used to address twenty-one issues

Three years ago the IT department started to recruit increasing numbers of female graduates

The proportion of graduate recruits who are women was 26 per cent and 29 per cent in the UK and Germany respectively

A new career break scheme for women returners has been introduced across the whole of Engindorf plc.

IT careers in Engindorf plc progress through three technical grades, into a management grade, and finally senior management

An employee survey in 1985 identified the need for more job rotation. Over 100 job rotations within grades were achieved in 1990

The number of managers on foreign service assignments (UK to Europe, Europe to UK, etc.) doubled from 1988 to 1990

The Central Personnel Department has a representative who is responsible for employees within the IT Department

The majority of recruitment, career development and training decisions and actions are carried out by IT line managers

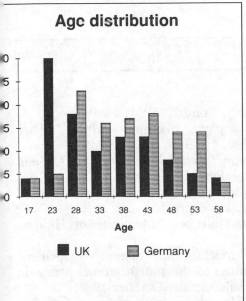

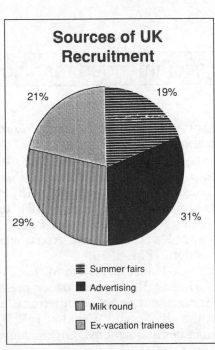

27

Whilst the original attempt had not been entirely successful, it had been a start. Flipping through its pages and pulling together other documents, John Martyn was able to glean a number of pertinent facts and snippets of information (see Figure 27.1).

Activity brief

You are John Martyn. As the business planning manager you are responsible for delivering the human resource plan to the IT director. The date is November and you are about to run a briefing meeting with your staff in the business planning function. Before you run the meeting you need to complete the following tasks:

1   Who would you involve in the HRP process, why, and what would be their respective roles?
2   In line with the aims of the HR plan, generate a list of all the possible areas that could be investigated.
3   Select *four* of the areas outlined in question 2 for inclusion in the HR plan. For *each one* describe:

   (a) Why you should collect data on this topic.
   (b) What types of data should be collected.
   (c) How you would justify the benefits of analysing the data.

4   What would be the main project management problems that you would anticipate?

Recommended reading

BRAMHAM, J., *Human Resource Planning*, London, IPM, 1989.
COWLING, A., and WALTERS, M., 'Manpower planning – where are we today?' *Personnel Review*, 19, 3, 1990, pp. 3–8.
DYER, L. (ed.), *Human Resource Planning: Tested Practices in five US and Canadian Companies*, New York, Random House, 1986.
GREER, C., *et al.*, 'Adapting HRP to a changing business environment', *Human Resource Management*, 28, 1, 1989, pp. 105–24.
INCOMES DATA SERVICES, *Recruitment*, European Management Guides, London, IPM, 1990.
LENGNICK-HALL, C. A. and M. L., 'A Model for the Strategic Management of Human Resources', paper presented to the fourth annual Strategic Management Society Conference, Philadelphia, October 1984.
SCHULER, R. S., and WALKER, J. W., 'Human resources strategy: focusing on issues and actions', *Organizational Dynamics*, 18, 2, 1990. pp. 4–20.

TICHY, N., *et al.*, 'Strategic human resource management', *Sloan Management Review*, 23, 2, 1982, pp. 47–61.

WALKER, J. W., *Human Resource Planning*, New York, McGraw-Hill, 1980.

WALKER J. W., 'Human resource planning; 1990s style', *Planning*, 13, 4, 1990, pp. 229–40.

Case 28

Innovation in human resource management: Venture Pressings Ltd

David Preece

This case study focuses upon some of the innovations in human resource management policies and practices which have been made by a new joint venture company located on a greenfield site.

Background to the case

Venture Pressings: origins and development

Venture Pressings Ltd (VPL) was formed in February 1988 as a £40 million fifty-fifty joint venture between Jaguar Cars (which has subsequently become part of the Ford Motor Company) and GKN Sankey. The board of the new company has seven members, one being VPL's general manager, the other posts being split equally between Jaguar and GKN Sankey directors. It is in the process of becoming the sole supplier of all Jaguar's main body panels, essentially the quality-critical outer 'skins'. It is located on a greenfield site on the outskirts of Telford in Shropshire, some thirty-five miles away from the nearest Jaguar plant at Castle Bromwich, Birmingham. The factory has been constructed out of the shell of what was previously a GKN Sankey tractor factory. The building and site have been extensively refurbished and equipped with entirely new services, such as telecommunications, drainage and a new high-perimeter wall, blocking the factory off from the nearby plants.

It is intended that the plant will be capable of producing 80,000 car body panel sets per annum on a three-shift, five-day-a-week basis or, alternatively, 60,000 panel sets per annum on a two-shift, five-day-a-week basis. The total work force planned for when full production is achieved is just over 300. This target was originally set for late 1991 but, in the light of the depressed state of much of the motor manufacturing sector in 1991, including Ford and Jaguar, is not now likely to be achieved until some time later.

Company mission and objectives

GKN Sankey's prime objective in its joint ownership of Venture Pressings is to reap a return on its investment. On the other hand, Jaguar's motives are of a more strategic nature: the company is looking to secure its supply line of key body panels of a high and consistent quality level. This reflects the nature of the competition in Jaguar's product market, where quality is a central element in gaining and maintaining market share. Hitherto its main competitors have been specialist German car manufacturers, but Japanese companies are beginning to move into this luxury/high performance segment, and it is known that quality will be emphasized, along, no doubt, with delivery, cost and 'lean' production. (For discussion of the latter see Womack *et al.*, 1990). It seems reasonable to assume that VPL's owners will wish to have some influence over the company, as well, perhaps, as Jaguar's new owners. The *nature* of such influence needs to be understood in the wider external context of Jaguar's (as the part owner and sole customer of VPL) and Ford's world-wide operations, economic and competitive positioning, and financial viability.

VPL's general manager acknowledges the above, although emphasizing that Venture is run as an 'arm's-length', stand-alone company; he observed that:

> We are owned by two big groups and, therefore, we have to step in line and accommodate their requirements from a financial point of view, and from a policy point of view, and we certainly would not do anything in this company that would put conflict between VPL and GKN Sankey or Jaguar and VPL – we would not do that. So, we're stand-alone within the rules that were set down within the early years.

What about VPL's mission? The following is an extract from its mission statement:

> Venture Pressings Limited aims to develop a business which will rank alongside the leading manufacturers of automotive body pressings worldwide. Our paramount objective is to produce quality products which will achieve the maximum possible customer satisfaction.
>
> Our company will seek continual improvement in its products and services, ensuring that the business produces a satisfactory return to both shareholders, and, in return, receives their continued commitment. To achieve this aim all employees will play a major part. Mutual trust and co-operation at all levels will lead to long term job satisfaction.
>
> We recognize that people are our most valued resource, and with that belief consider the following principles will be of value to all:
>
> • To build a company with common terms and conditions of employment with which we can identify and to which we are all committed.

- We accept the responsibility to provide leadership and training to develop the effective contributions of all employees by the expansion of individual capabilities.
- We recognize that all employees have individual contributions to make but that these contributions can be most effective within a team working environment.
- In all actions we will have a flexible approach and will not be restricted by traditional ways of working.
- We want information and ideas to flow upwards, downwards and across the company . . .

The situation

The development of human resource management policies and practices

The human resources plan for 1990 has as its aim for the Human Resources Department:

> To develop initiatives and strategies that take advantage of the unique opportunity presented by a greenfield site situation, to adopt the very best methods of human resource management and thereby support the achievement of VPL business objectives.

This was translated into the following HRM objectives:

- The creation of a highly skilled, flexible and quality-conscious work force.
- The expansion of employees' capability to the maximum of their potential.
- The development of effective leadership and team-building techniques.
- The provision of competitive reward and benefit systems and appropriate occupational care mechanisms.

The human resources manager has the primary responsibility for developing and implementing initiatives in this area. He is a member of the executive committee of VPL and reports to the director general manager, who in turn is a member of the non-executive board of the company. It was the general manager who in fact played the leading role in the project team which planned and inaugurated VPL. The human resources manager was the second appointee. These two people, with the help of an executive recruitment consultancy, set about recruiting the managers of the newly formed company. 'Headhunting' was part of the recruitment strategy. Subsequently the two managers took the initiative in staffing their own departments.

The human resources manager is continuously involved in developing and introducing new procedures, practices and responses to events and initiatives, with a view to 'keeping up the momentum'. Some indication of what has been achieved to date can be gleaned from an observation of the engineering manager:

> Within the motor industry the majority of your time is spent on dealing with people problems. Here, the majority of your time is spent on dealing with technical problems, in getting the job done, as opposed to the ramifications of 'If you did it, what would be the people problems that you'd get?' You don't have to worry about that.

Industrial relations

A single union agreement was signed in May 1988 with the General Municipal Boilermakers' and Allied Trade Union (GMBTU). As well as giving sole recognition to the GMBTU, it provides for a company council to be established as a forum for discussion and consultation. The council, which consists of four management nominees and six employee representatives, is also responsible for negotiating pay and terms and conditions of employment. The agreement commits all employees to flexibility and mobility and makes provision for pendulum arbitration by an agreed external arbitrator in the event of failure to reach agreement over pay and/or conditions in the council or through conciliation. The arbitrator is invited to decide in favour of one side or the other, and his or her decision is binding. No industrial action is to take place whilst any matter is in the process of resolution.

The following extract from the 'working practices' section of the agreement with the GMBTU indicates how this underpins the HRM objectives and plan. Under 'General Principles' we find:

> To ensure maximum utilisation of facilities and manpower, the Company, employees and the Trade Union agree:
>
> - To complete flexibility and mobility of employees and to this end employees will undertake work or will undertake training for all work required by the Company. Employees will train other employees as required
> - To the introduction, after full consultation, of technological practices, processes and procedural changes to improve productivity, which may alter manning levels and the range and mix of work tasks.
> - That manning levels, methods and work arrangements will be determined by the Company, using appropriate industrial engineering and manpower planning techniques.

Remuneration

In order to attract managers with the desired experience, expertise and attitudes, the company pays above average motor manufacturing rates. Rates of pay for non-managerial/non-technical employees were influenced by the 'going rate' in the local area, from where the great majority of employees were recruited (approximately 75 per cent having come from within a ten-mile radius of Telford). All categories of labour, up to and including team leaders, have their rates of pay negotiated on their behalf by the company council on a two-year cycle.

Manufacturing and production technology

The plant has nine production lines, incorporating fifty-three presses of up to 1,400 tonnes operating capacity. Two of these press lines have a total of fourteen materials-handling Comau robots, which transfer body panels between presses without the need for manual intervention. This is the first press shop in the UK to install such robots. A tool transfer programme began in December 1989 with the release of dies from Karmann in Germany. Subsequently dies began to be released from the Rover Group, Swindon, in August 1990. It was these companies who had previously done the Jaguar press work, using, on their premises, dies belonging to Jaguar. There had been concern at Jaguar for some time about the quality of the press work, although it must be said that many of the dies had been in use for some considerable time. The tool transfer programme was planned to be complete by January 1992.

The presses themselves have been transferred from two GKN Sankey plants and have been extensively refurbished, including the fitting of new electrical control systems and the incorporation of computer software, facilitating statistical process control through continuous monitoring. The Comau inter-press robots installed on the two automatic press lines allow flexible handling of a variety of body panels through component interchange by 'mid-air' transfer of panels between presses. There is a main toolroom for all major and minor die modifications and refurbishment, and two satellite toolrooms are located in manufacturing cells supporting minor service operations. The £4 million investment in inter-press robots will enable the production lines to produce over 300 panels an hour at maximum output.

Deliveries of steel from three European suppliers are controlled by a 'just in time' system. Particular attention has been given to scrap volume, with an automatic underfloor conveyor system serving four of the main production lines.

Job design and working practices

The core concept in manufacturing work design is that of production cells. Production workers are allocated to a team consisting of between eleven and seventeen people, headed by a team leader. The latter reports to a cell manager, who is responsible for two or three teams on a given shift. The cell managers report to the production manager (see Figure 28.1). Although cell members have, or develop, certain specialist skills, they all have broader responsibilities, being expected to take on a range of tasks as required by manufacturing requirements, including, for example, the cell maintenance workers doing production jobs. Provision for this is, as we have seen, incorporated in the agreement with the GMBTU.

When some particular expertise located in one cell is needed by another, team leaders can negotiate direct between themselves to share the expertise. Weekly meetings are held within the cells in specially designed team communication areas (where, *inter alia*, vending machines are located) to discuss cell work and performance and events in the company more generally. There is an extensive training programme for all cell members. The pay grading structure was designed to incorporate and encourage the flexibility and mobility referred to above. The wider employment contract has been drawn up along similar principles.

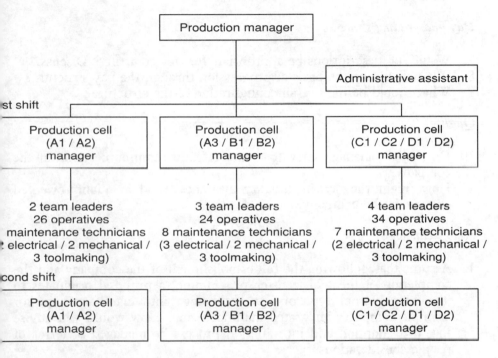

Figure 28.1 The production department structure at Venture Pressings

Activity brief

Recruitment and selection

1   Briefly outline what you consider to be the key elements of a recruitment and selection procedure for the following jobs: (a) manufacturing cell operative, (b) manufacturing maintenance technician, (c) manufacturing team leader, (d) manufacturing manager.
2   Would you expect any particular problems in recruiting any of the above employees? If so, provide details.
3   Why do you think top managers at VPL were given primary responsibility for recruiting their own staff?

Training and development

4 Outline briefly what you consider to be the key elements of a training and development programme for the following jobs: (a) manufacturing cell operative, (b) manufacturing maintenance technician, (c) manufacturing team leader.
5 How might the above staff be welded into an effective team?
6 What do you think is meant by the term '. . . a highly skilled . . . work force'?

Pay and grading structure

7 Would job descriptions be appropriate for this company? Discuss.
8 What should be the basis of progression through the pay structure?
9 What should be the overall configuration of the structure?

Quality

10 How might managers try to create effective communications in the company?
11 How might they create 'quality awareness' and a 'quality-oriented culture' in the company?

New technology

12 Assume that, following the full establishment of the company and the completion of the tool transfer programme, a proposal originates to introduce another type of new technology into manufacturing, for example computer-integrated manufacturing. How would you advise that this adoption and introduction process be managed in terms of people considerations?

Industrial relations

13 Why might VPL have opted for a single-union deal?
14 Should VPL management actively encourage employees to join the GMBTU with a view to getting as high a union density as possible? Give reasons for your response.
15 It was noted that Jaguar, in helping to set up VPL, were concerned to have a reliable supply of body panels. How have VPL tried to ensure that this will happen and what sensitivities do they have?

Flexibility

16 The achievement of functional or task labour flexibility is a key objective of VPL management. What are the particular elements of the company's internal and external contexts which underpin this?
17 Can you see any 'impediments' to the achievement of extensive functional flexibility?

Recommended reading

BEAUMONT, P., and TOWNLEY, B., 'Greenfield sites, new plants and work practices', in V. HAMMOND, (ed.), *Current Research in Management*, London, Frances Pinter, 1985.

BREWSTER, C., and CONNOCK, S., *Industrial Relations: Cost Effective Strategies*, London, Hutchinson, 1985.

CONNOCK, S., *The HR Vision: Managing a Quality Workforce*, London, IPM, 1991.

DANKBAAR, Ben, 'New production concepts, management strategies and the quality of work', *Work, Employment and Society*, 2, 1, 1988.

FRENCH, W., and BELL, C., *Organization Development: Behavioral Science Interventions for Organization Improvement*, Englewood Cliffs, N.J., Prentice-Hall, 1984.

OLIVER, N., and WILKINSON, B., *The Japanization of British Industry*, Oxford, Blackwell, 1988.

PETTIGREW, A., (ed.), *The Management of Strategic Change*, Oxford, Blackwell, 1988.

PREECE, D., *Managing the Adoption of New Technology*, London, Routledge, 1989.

STOREY, J., and SISSON, K., 'Limits to transformation: human resource management in the British context', *Industrial Relations Journal*, 21, 1, 1990.

WHIPP, R., *et al.*, 'Culture and competitiveness: evidence from two mature UK industries', *Journal of Management Studies*, 26, 6, 1989.

WOMACK J., *et al.*, *The Machine that changed the World*, New York, Rawson, 1990.

WOOD, S. (ed.), *The Transformation of Work: Skill, Flexibility and the Labour Process*, London, Unwin Hyman, 1989.

YEANDLE, D., and CLARK, J., 'A personnel strategy for an automated plant', *Personnel Management*, June 1989, pp. 51–5.

YEANDLE, D., and CLARK, J., 'Growing a compatible IR set-up', *Personnel Management*, July 1989, pp. 36–9.

Case 29

Total Quality Management?
Metaphorics plc

Carole Brooke

This case study will help you to understand the concept of Total Quality Management (TQM) and to recognize the problems which can arise in its implementation, especially in relation to 'British' organizational culture. Although the focus of the exercise is on cultural change in a service industry, the issues it raises concern the utilization of human resources and are applicable to the successful management of personnel in all sectors of business. One of the most important lessons to be learnt is that successful change is dependent not simply upon altered work processes and techniques but also upon an appropriate training programme which maximizes the contribution and motivation of staff at all levels in the organization.

Background to the case

A history of quality management

Achieving quality in a business context has been the subject of many books and articles over the years. In the UK service sector, however, the need to demonstrate quality has recently become a much more pressing issue. The reasons are various, including the opening up of competition through the single European market, the formidable performance of the Japanese, an economic recession and increased expectations of customers as a result of technological developments.

Businesses are having to be more responsive to customer need, indeed, to anticipate such need, and to take advantage of opportunities ahead of the competition. Thus a proactive, dynamic and flexible organization is required. However, these traits would seem to challenge the traditional British culture, which has tended to be bureaucratic, risk-averse and reactive. Organizations recognizing this problem have been searching for an aid to culture change. Total Quality Management has been heralded as one of the most valuable routes to success in this respect.

The Japanese are generally considered to be expert in the practice of quality management. Ironically, it was the Western world that introduced them to the idea. This is usually attributed to the American, Deming, in 1947. Although the UK and Europe were aware of the desirability of a total quality programme, it was felt to be too expensive to implement properly. It could be argued that this failure to recognize the longer-term benefits was a symptom of short-termist investment practices. In the meantime the Japanese adopted and adapted our quality concept to suit their own culture, with the result that they have become a strong and impressive competitor. This has been a major trigger in forcing the UK to reconsider its original reservations.

What is Total Quality Management?

What does Total Quality Management, as it has come to be known, really mean? The suggested reading will help to broaden your understanding but some basic principles are outlined below.

The simplistic definition of quality has always been to get the product right first time, on time and to budget. TQM implies much more. Whereas this definition centres on bald and ambiguous objectives, the 'what', TQM emphasizes the 'how'. It signals a move away from quality control as the responsibility of quality inspectors or quality control managers to quality as the responsibility of *everyone* in an organization. The customer becomes anyone for whom a service is provided. In other words, not just people outside the organization but its own employees too. This means that *quality becomes a people issue*. Only through the commitment of all employees will an organization achieve its quality goals. It is for this reason that TQM and its application within a business context should be of prime concern to all personnel managers.

The situation

This case is based on research conducted in one of the largest service-sector companies in the UK, hereafter referred to as Metaphorics plc. It is a multi-site concern and its computing division alone, which is based at headquarters in London, employs thousands of people.

The research was conducted at project level within the computing division and focused on a group of thirty analyst programmers in the software development department. This team was producing a system which would help the company's accountants (positioned in commercial outlets throughout the country) to utilize information relating to the fixed assets of the company. It was thus a prime example of service provision for internal customers.

Introducing a TQM philosophy into Metaphorics plc

A major programme of TQM had been introduced into the organization by senior executives. The process had taken three years to date, and was about to be relaunched the following year. The concept of relaunch was compatible with the TQM notion that employees need to be continually reacquainted with the quality principle in order to ensure continued commitment.

Prior to TQM the culture had been similar to that of the civil service and was fairly typical of the conservative aspects of UK culture. One of the main vehicles for TQM implementation was a set of manuals. These 'TQM guides' set out in detail the basic philosophy of TQM and presented a framework within which all employees should conduct their work.

The long-term objectives of the quality strategy (as stated in the guides) were to:

- Enable staff to do an effective, value-added and satisfying job.
- Make continuous improvement a routine task.
- Provide staff with the understanding to work with and towards the company's goals.
- Put staff in touch with their customers in order to provide them with direct feedback on the results of their efforts.
- Maximize the potential contribution of all employees.

The TQM guides were written by Metaphorics' own staff and distributed to all project managers, including the manager of software development, with a message from the chairman which expressed the importance of the new techniques. This was the first occasion on which staff at lower levels had had the opportunity to see the documentation. The TQM programme had been rolled out across the organization in a top-down way, and the primary impetus for its adoption had come from the written commitment of the top executives.

In applying TQM in this way Metaphorics plc had failed to involve staff in the strategy and to appreciate that TQM was essentially about people. It was, therefore, ironic that the following Chinese proverb should have appeared in one of the guides:

> Tell me and I will forget;
> Show me and I may remember;
> Involve me and I will understand.

Implementing the TQM methodology in the computing division

TQM was introduced in the computing division at two levels. The first was at project management level. In the old-style culture the quality of software had been based on a project management methodology devised in the 1970s by an outside consultancy firm. It therefore had a long history of use, and most staff felt comfortable with its application. It broke computer system development down into the seven stages of: feasibility study, initiation of project, specification of user needs, system design, system development, installation, and operation.

As part of the TQM programme a new project management methodology was devised by staff from within Metaphorics, and all project managers were expected to ensure that it superseded the old method. Once again, this was done in a top-down fashion, all projects being issued with documentation which outlined the new format. It identified ten stages in the system development 'life cycle': business survey, feasibility study, initiation of project, specification of user needs, specification of system, internal design, system construction and testing, installation, post-installation review, and maintenance and modification.

The role of analyst programmer in the software development team began at the stage of specification of user needs. At this point they needed to agree what was required of the new software system with the users (the accountants). However, they did not do so directly. Representatives of the finance department had been appointed by senior management to liaise with the team on behalf of the accountants. Finance Department were selected to do this because they were responsible for the work of the accountants and were located in a nearby building.

Once user requirements had been agreed, work commenced on developing the software in accordance with the rest of the stages set out in the new TQM methodology. However, the work did not progress smoothly. On a number of occasions the requirements which had been agreed with the finance department had to be changed because the accountants complained that they did not meet their expectations. Staff blamed the extra link in the communication chain, saying that it inevitably increased the chances of error, misinterpretation and delay.

The second level of TQM implementation involved two well known techniques for designing software systems and writing the computer code itself. Analysts were responsible for designing the system. The technique they were expected to use for the purpose was called logical structured design methodology (LSDM). It dealt with the user requirements and a design framework for the software product. The programmers were responsible for translating this design into computer code. The technique which they were expected to apply was called Jackson structured programming (JSP). Both LSDM and JSP were well established in the business world and were written by outside agencies.

The staff viewpoint

Staff expressed uneasiness about TQM at all levels of its introduction into the company. Although they were enthusiastic about the general principles, their top executive was still associated with the old-style culture, and they found it difficult to envisage the senior management as being totally committed to the new philosophy.

Three years seemed a long time in which to introduce major change and it was feared that, as a result, the impact of TQM would be lost and absorbed into the old-style culture. In expressing personal reservations, one individual cited an example of how this already appeared to be happening. The individual noted a tendency towards Total *Quantity* Management, with the emphasis on specific rules and procedures rather than qualitative issues of culture change and the raising of quality awareness in general.

This loss of impact was also evident at the lower levels of TQM application. At project management level inconsistency of approach was encouraged by the fact that manuals for both the old and the new methodologies were still in circulation. Since there was an overlap between the two anyway, and as staff felt happier using the old method, the TQM version was often neglected.

In addition to this ambiguity, the detailed nature of the TQM version had several effects deemed negative by staff: lack of flexibility, increased documentation and extended time scales. Nor was it clear how existing projects, which had been initiated under the old project management system, could be incorporated into the new TQM framework.

At the level of analysis and programming, LSDM and JSP were thought to have similar drawbacks to the project management method. In requesting the production of detailed documentation as a routine part of software development the consultancies which created LSDM and JSP had intended to simplify the later stages of software maintenance and modification. (The principle being that it is easier to make changes in something created by someone else when the steps in its production have been fully recorded.) However, staff saw it as introducing unnecessary time delays in developing the initial product. In addition, experienced staff felt that their skills were being undermined by the detail which they were supposed to follow.

Training for TQM

A one-off workshop was available on the general philosophy of TQM rather than on the documented methodologies, and those staff who had attended thought it very useful. Nevertheless, they felt that often the theory was not practised once people were back in the workplace.

Managers were responsible for providing general TQM training for their immediate subordinates, and in this manner it was cascaded down the organization to all staff. The top management had formed a team of employees (deemed conversant with TQM) from across the organization to act as liaison officers, and they helped to organize the workshops.

The Computing Division had its own training and development unit which advised on specialist training. However, training in LSDM and JSP was manual-based. The personnel division was entirely separate, although it did contain a section which was dedicated to servicing the computing division. Its role was to influence the training for managers, including training in project management techniques, and training for all new recruits. Even so, it was the line managers who actually made recommendations for the training of individuals.

29

Activity brief

Ensure that you have understood the main aims and objectives of TQM and then complete the following exercises.

1   Identify the barriers to introducing a TQM philosophy at corporate level within Metaphorics plc, using examples taken from the case.
2   How could these barriers be removed?
3   Specify in more detail the contribution which the training and development unit and the personnel division could make and the role to be taken to ensure the success of TQM.

Recommended reading

COLLARD, R., *Total Quality: Success through People*, London, IPM, 1989.

GILES, E., and WILLIAMS, R.,'Can the personnel department survive quality management?', *Personnel Management*, April 1991.

HODGSON, A., 'Deming's never-ending road to quality', *Personnel Management*, July 1987.

OAKLAND, J. S., (ed.), *Total Quality Management*, Proceedings of the Second International Conference, London, 14–15 June 1989.

ULLAII, P., 'The psychology of TQM', *Managing Service Quality*, 1, 2, January 1991, pp. 79–81.

WILLIAMS, A., *et al.*, *Changing Culture: New Organizational Approaches*, London, IPM, 1989.

WITCHER, B., and WILKINSON, A., *Total Quality Management in the United Kingdom*, DUBS Occasional Paper 9072, Durham University Business School, 1990.

Case 30

Acquisition management at Able Engineering Ltd

Ivor Roberts

This case concerns a firm which, as a result of declining orders, becomes the subject of an acquisition by another firm. The focus of the case is on managing the human resource repercussions of the acquisition.

Background to the case

Able Engineering is a medium-size manufacturing company located in a west London suburb. Family-owned for the fifty-three years of its existence, the company has developed a reputation for producing hydraulic test units for use in testing aircraft systems in both the civil and military aviation fields. Much of its production is based on specialist work for the Ministry of Defence (MoD), with a high level of quality control being the requirement for retaining the prized MoD recognition status without which no company can be awarded a government contract.

The board of the company consists of Charles Griffin (sixty-three), chairman, Robert Griffin (forty-two), managing director, Jim Kelly (fifty-seven), works director, Bob Hope (fifty-six), sales director, and Barry Henderson (fifty-two), finance and administration director (Figure 30.1). The majority of the shares are held by the chairman and managing director, with the other three directors holding a nominal 500 ordinary shares each.

The company occupies a somewhat disorganized site in west London which has had various extensions added during the last twenty years as business has expanded, but the limits of such expansion have been reached. The factory staff of eighty-two is made up of working supervisors, skilled technicians, fitters, machine operators and a well organized apprentice scheme (Appendix 30.1). The remaining sixty staff consist of designers, draughtspeople, quality control and test inspectors, general administrative staff and speciality sales staff (Appendix 30.2).

During the last five years the chairman has suffered from increasing ill health and has been unable to spend much time in his office, leaving the day-to-day running of the company to his son, Robert as managing director, who has little technical knowledge (although he possesses a degree in Business Studies, and is a local councillor). The remaining directors have long periods of service with the company and have seen it grow steadily over the years, mostly owing to MoD contracts.

Since 1986 the civilian airline orders have declined, as have the MoD orders, mainly owing to the impact of new high technology on aircraft design and the complexity of their systems, which the sturdy test trolleys of Able Engineering cannot service, not having kept pace with the demands of the industry. New, smaller trolleys have been produced, both in the UK and in the USA, and the market has moved away from the company because of its failure to update their design.

The company is particularly concerned at the changing nature of the defence industry, related to a growing understanding between the superpowers of the West and the Eastern Bloc countries. The consequent reduction in the conventional forces of both groups has already had a significant impact on government defence thinking as the need for conventional equipment diminishes. Whilst existing contracts will be honoured, the long-term projections indicate that government spending on defence will progressively reduce over time, and this will have a negative effect upon companies which, historically, have regarded the supply of military equipment as a major revenue factor within their business plan.

Able Engineering has a long history of defence contracting, and the planned reduction of government spending will have a major impact on the business in terms of production requirement and profit. It is not alone

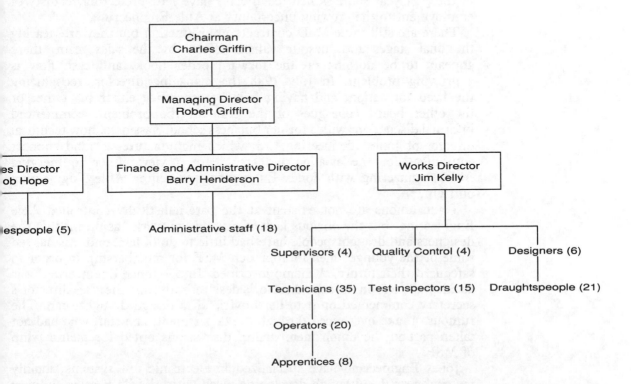

Figure 30.1 Able Engineering: the organization structure

275

in its concern, for many similarly sized companies have been engaged in the defence industry almost exclusively for many years, and the industry is already expecting major redundancies and perhaps the closure of some companies.

Strategic plans will have to be reviewed in depth, and forward projections revised, particularly where they concern areas of defence supply which are still open to tender. Competition between firms still actively engaged in defence manufacturing will therefore intensify, perhaps reducing price structures to the point where there is very little margin left and bringing in its wake a requirement for very tight cost controls. In the case of Able Engineering, with so much reliance on defence supply and a declining civil airline order book, there must be a major review of the market and much discussion of the identification of new markets for the company's product range. Time, however, is perilously short.

The situation

July 1988

The lack of orders has had a significant impact on the work force in respect of almost zero production bonuses, once an integral part of earnings, and in the past year some skilled technicians have left, preferring security of employment to the growing uncertainty at Able Engineering.

There are still three MoD contracts in production but they are nearing the final stages and, despite valiant efforts by the sales team, there appears to be nothing on the forward order book, and cash flow is a growing problem. In July 1988 the managing director, recognizing the need for action, and having failed to convince either his father or the other board colleagues of the scale of the problem, commenced informal discussions with a former business school classmate, now technical director of Jones Engineering Ltd, which manufactures ground support equipment for the aviation industry, with a view either to merging Able Engineering with Jones Engineering or selling Able Engineering outright.

Trade unions are non-existent at the paternalistically controlled Able Engineering, but the obvious lack of new design work has meant that the designers and draughtspeople have had little to do of late, and this has led some of the younger men to approach MSF for membership in order to safeguard their future. A memo inscribed 'Info – Jones Engineering' was accidentally left on the sales director's desk recently, and the sales director's secretary commented on it to her boyfriend, a design draughtsman. The rumour of take-over raced through the department, and staff who had not taken part in the union membership discussions opted for membership of MSF.

Jones Engineering have specialized in electronic test systems, mainly for civil aircraft, although developing work with Middle Eastern military customers over the last two years. In addition, they have developed support systems for a whole range of aircraft requirements, e.g. passenger steps, catering support vehicles and towbars for aircraft movement. They do not, however, have an MoD contract designation. If they could obtain one it would open channels into a wider market for their total range of products.

September 1988

By September 1988 the grave financial situation at Able Engineering had brought reluctant agreement from the rest of the board to formal take-over talks with Jones Engineering (Figure 30.2). Although the board of Jones were particularly interested in gaining control of the Able company, specifically for the acquisition of the MoD contract recognition status, they took time in deciding their approach strategy:

- To allow the cash-flow situation at Able Engineering to bring the company into receivership, allowing low-cost acquisition but risking loss of MoD status.

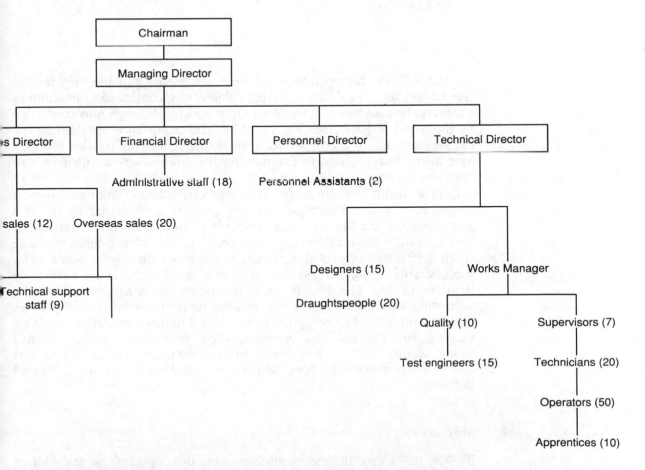

Figure 30.2 Jones Engineering: the structure before the take-over of Able

- To guarantee retention of MoD status by buying the business from the family, but obviously at higher cost.

After some consideration the board opted for the second option and gained full agreement to acquisition from the board of Able Engineering – the whole transaction being completed by the end of December 1989.

Jones Engineering immediately announced the intention of relocating Able to the Jones site in West Drayton, where there was plenty of room for development, and offered employment to a limited number of skilled staff from the design team, plus two supervisors, twenty-three technicians and operators, eight apprentices and six administrative staff. None of the board would be required, and generous offers were made for the shares held by the family and other directors, plus compensation for termination of their service contracts, all of which were accepted.

Jones Engineering are highly successful, with a positive cash flow and a thrustful management style, resting heavily upon clear objective-setting and result achievement. Trade unions do not exist, nor are they encouraged. A manager was seconded from the production division to oversee the run-down of the west London site and the transfer of staff and equipment to West Drayton.

March 1989

By March 1989 this operation had been completed and the original site cleared and sold to a developer. Able Engineering continued to function as a separate trading name on the West Drayton site, although now controlled by the board of Jones (see Figure 30.3). The importance of retaining the two separate trading identities (recognized throughout the aviation industry over many years) related to maintaining the established customer base of both companies.

General facilities such as the car park, canteen and administration of wages, invoicing and banking, buying, etc. are now shared by the two companies, as are the sales and marketing effort and production units. The hydraulic products occupy one complete side of the main machine shop, whilst the electrical products are located on the opposite side, sub-assembly being carried out in a new workshop, again shared by both companies. The two design departments retain separate identities, occupying adjacent offices, whilst coming under the control of the Jones technical director. The reception of the Able Engineering staff at the West Drayton site was not well planned. They were shown the space they would occupy and left very much to their own devices, having to sort out their equipment and files, which were piled up in the area allocated to them.

May 1990

By May 1990 very distinct rumblings were developing from the staff of Able Engineering, now isolated from their new owners and feeling like 'second-class citizens' in an alien world. The direct, objective-oriented style of management of the Jones directors was proving something of a culture shock and, coupled with the rather offhand attitude of their new colleagues, added to a growing feeling of discontent.

The board were keen to gain full recognition from the MoD (already retained with the Able Engineering products) for their own range of electrical ground support products. Discontent could seriously affect this plan should word of it reach the ears of the MoD officials. A full investigation was immediately put in hand, and recommendations were required from the enquiry team within a month.

All the Able Engineering staff at West Drayton had been retained because of their wide product experience. This meant that they had considerable market potential within the aviation support industry, and many began to explore new employment prospects. In fairness to Jones Engineering, they had tried to smooth the path by integrating the Able Engineering staff into their wage structure, but the discontent continued to grow, despite improved wages.

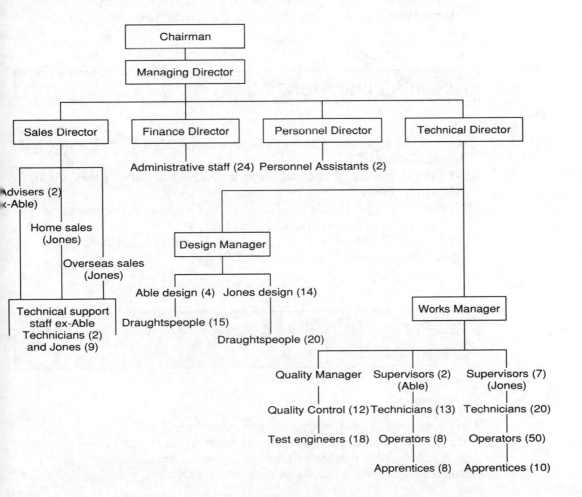

Figure 30.3 Jones Engineering: the structure after the take-over of Able

30

1   What information should the employees of both companies have been given regarding the acquisition of Able Engineering?
2   How and when should management convey such news to employees?
3   What should have been the main areas of consideration for the acquiring company (a) in the initial decision, and (b) in decisions after the acquisition?
4   In terms of the transfer of staff from Able Engineering to Jones Engineering, comment on the most effective ways of ensuring fairness, as related to age, service level and sex, in arriving at the required numbers.
5   What were the main problems for the acquired company?
6   What should be the long-term strategy for the two companies?

Recommended reading

CARNALL, C., *Managing Change in Organisations*, New York, Prentice Hall International, 1990.

LUFFMAN, G., *et al.*, *Business Policy: an Analytical Introduction*, Oxford, Blackwell, 1987.

MCILWEE, T., and ROBERTS, I., *Human Resource Management in the Corporate Environment*, Huntingdon, Elm, 1991.

TORRINGTON, D., and HALL, L., *Personnel Management: A New Approach*, Hemel Hempstead, Prentice Hall, 1991.

Appendix 30.1 Able Engineering Ltd production staff

Supervisors

Tony Johnson (32), test shop, fourteen years' service.
David Freed (61), assembly, twenty-three years' service.
Albert Zelouf (49), machine shop, twenty-seven years' service.
Graham Briggs (37), paint shop, nine years' service.

Technicians – thirty-five men

Age	No.	Service	No.
21–35	11	1–5 years	4
36–50	4	6–10 years	11
51–60	16	11–20 years	11
61+	4	21+ years	9

Fitters – fifteen men

Age	No.	Service	No.
21–35	4	1–5 years	1
36–50	5	6–10 years	8
51–60	4	11–20 years	3
61+	2	21+ years	3

Operators – fourteen men, six women

Age	No.	Service	No.
21–35	4	1–5 years	nil
36–50	12	6–10 years	6
51–60	2	11–20 years	7
61+	2	21+ years	7

Apprentices – eight men

Age	No.	Service	No.
18–20	4	1–5 years	8
21–35	4		

Transfers to Jones Engineering

Supervisors: Tony Johnson, test shop, and Albert Zelouf, machine shop.
Technicians: Fifteen.
Apprentices: Eight.
Operators: Eight.

Appendix 30.2 Able Engineering Ltd monthly paid staff

Design department – six men

Age	No.	Service	No.
21–35	2	1–5 years	1
36–50	1	6–10 years	nil
51–60	2	11–20 years	4
61+	1	21+ years	1

Draughtspeople – twenty-one men

Age	No.	Service	No.
21–35	7	1–5 years	4
36–50	6	6–10 years	7
51–60	3	11–20 years	3
61+	5	21+ years	7

Quality control – four men

Age	No.	Service	No.
21–35	nil	1–5 years	nil
36–50	1	6–10 years	1
51–60	2	11–20 years	1
61+	1	21+ years	2

Test inspectors – six men

Age	No.	Service	No.
21–35	nil	1–5 years	1
36–50	1	6–10 years	2
51–60	1	11–20 years	2
61+	2	21+ years	1

Sales staff – five men

Age	No.	Service	No.
21–35	1	1–5 years	nil
36–50	3	6–10 years	nil

| 51–60 | nil | 11–20 years | 2 |
| 61+ | 1 | 21+ years | 3 |

Administrative staff – seven men, eleven women

Age	No.	Service	No.
18–20	4	1–5 years	7
21–35	7	6–10 years	5
36–50	3	11–20 years	5
51–60	1	21+ years	1
61+	3		

Transfers to Jones Engineering

Design department: Four.
Draughtspeople: Fifteen.
Quality control: Two.
Test inspectors: Three.
Sales staff: Two.
Administrators: Six.

Case 31

Organizational Development and change: introducing flexible working groups in a high-tech environment

Thomas Garavan and Michael Morley

This case study is set in the context of a high-technology work environment, and explores some of the issues involved in organizational change and development at different levels, with particular reference to the introduction of flexible working groups at the production level. It examines both the system and the value changes that accompany a job restructuring intervention, and allows the reader to observe, in a concrete manner, the human resource implications of this type of change.

In-depth interviews were used to collect the data, and all interviews were conducted on site. Because of the nature of the information being sought, the respondents had to be selective with respect to what information they could divulge. Thus some of the areas were discussed in general, as opposed to specific, terms, forcing the authors to draw certain inferences.

Background to the case

Leeway Ltd, a unionized organization with headquarters in the United States, is a leading manufacturer of computer systems and associated equipment. Founded in the 1970s, the company has been actively involved in building computer networks for more than fifteen years. The company operates in highly competitive circumstances, and its external environment is both complex and dynamic. The company appreciates that organizational change is necessary in order to remain a market leader.

In the past Leeway has come to recognize the need to become a more employee-centred organization. While it started out as what might be termed 'organic' in nature, a number of negative features have manifested themselves in the course of time:

- Many layers of supervision.
- Large growth in the number of technical specialists and support staff.
- A growth in the number of procedures and rules, leading to considerable inflexibility.
- Poor general decision-making, with little or no input from employees.
- A fall-off in the level of innovation.
- Poor communications and duplication of activities.

Overall, the organization was 'out of tune' in terms of what was being demanded of it by the external environment. The negative features combined to form what the company labelled the 'traditional organization' (see Figure 31.1), one not conducive to high levels of performance and effectiveness.

The situation

The move to a cluster-based organization structure and flexible working groups

Following a series of meetings at various levels in the organization, a number of features of a 'new organization scenario' were identified. These may be described as follows:

- Greater optimization of human and technical resources.
- Implementation of a philosophy whereby human assets are to be viewed as resources to be developed rather than as expendable spare parts (agents not objects).
- The achievement of optimum task groupings, and multiple broad, flexible skills.
- The promotion of ownership and responsibility lower down the organization, and the utilization of internal controls and self-regulating sub-systems and groups.
- The achievement of a flat organization structure and a participative management style.

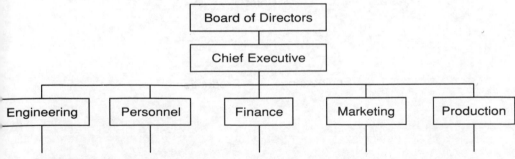

Figure 31.1 Traditional organization structure

- The encouragement of innovation and intrapreneurship.
- A highly proactive stance in relation to the external environment.

After much discussion with the key 'stake holders', including managers and employees, these characteristics were accepted as underlying the new philosophy required by the organization. The company therefore formulated a number of specific objectives for the programme, designed to:

- Change the overall organization structure in an attempt to increase participation.
- Implement new work structures and practices over a three-year period, aimed at improving cost-effectiveness in the use and development of human resources.
- Bring about an improvement in productivity and product quality.
- Engender group-based commitment to the business as a whole.
- Bring about maximum flexibility and mobility.

These objectives, combined with a number of driving forces, prompted the move to a 'cluster' structure (see Figure 31.2). These forces for change included:

- The organization had become larger and more bureaucratic in the way it functioned.
- There had been an increase in the number of managerial and statistical controls to guide members of the organization.
- The large amounts of technology and automation resulted in relatively simplified, deskilled jobs.

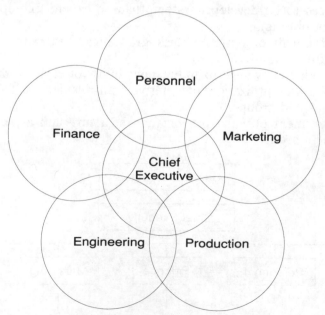

Figure 31.2 The new cluster organization structure

- Conditions in the external environment (increased competition and falling prices leading to pressure to reduce costs).
- The demands by workers for increased participation and equity.

It was felt that the overall organizational change should commence at the top and be driven down through the organization.

Leeway had a number of options open to them in relation to the changes that could have been introduced at lower levels in the organization. However, they were trying to achieve both a system change (structures, including changes in jobs/tasks) in conjunction with a complete value change (including the development of participation and product ownership). It was concluded that the introduction of flexible working groups was the most appropriate option to take.

Planning and introducing the restructuring system

The company opted for internal rather than external change agents. The actual time scale, from the generation of the concept to the operation of the pilot group, spanned three years. Figure 31.3 presents the key phases in implementing the flexible working groups.

The change agents selected for introducing the new production system were the production manager and the human resources manager. Both received strong top management support at all times. These managers, as project leaders, were members of a cross-functional steering committee which was established to evaluate the production process then in operation and to make recommendations for an alternative system, ensuring that any changes in the system facilitated the achievement of both business and employee needs.

The committee concluded that a redesign was required, in line with current thinking on the organization and management of the production

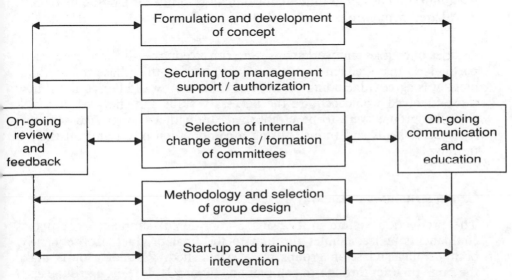

Figure 31.3 Key phases in the introduction of flexible working groups

function. The committee was consultative in nature, seeking as it did the opinions of all those who were going to be affected by the changes. In arriving at these recommendations for a new system it noted a number of problems with the traditional production process.

- The production process resulted in a relatively large volume of waste, and the lead time to complete a product (through assembly, to test and final assembly) was above the industry average.
- The standard of 'housekeeping' was low and the work-in-progress inventory too high.
- There was a need to reduce set-up and change-over times and to lower the rejection rate.
- There was a need to devolve more power throughout the whole organization by driving information and knowledge down in an attempt to increase overall loyalty and commitment.

A new innovative, all-encompassing job restructuring system was proposed. Rather than being based on the narrow concept of the job itself, it was based on the concept of the skills an employee brings to the group of which he/she is a member and the jobs/tasks he/she performs within the group. In facilitating group production, it focuses on the person and his/her full range of skills.

However, gaining acceptance of the concept took longer than expected, primarily because the groups would only survive given the proper climatic conditions, which involved a complete value change. Flexible working groups will flourish where the following conditions apply:

- Respect and trust between individuals.
- Open communication systems.
- Visible commitment to quality at all levels.
- Commitment to and funding for human resource development (HRD).
- Shared responsibility and authority.

A series of courses and workshops were run to educate all those concerned, particularly management and supervisors. During this phase the methodology was agreed, including the type of skills that would be required, how those involved would acquire the necessary skills and the area in which the pilot groups were to be established. Individuals were then screened for specific skills and trained, using a combination of on and off-the-job training.

Group structures at Leeway

The production system at Leeway is considered complex, as it makes components and assembles through to the final product. Consequently, both parallel and scion groups were established. **Parallel groups** make the same product through to completion (Figure 31.4). **Scion groups** each make a different family of products through to completion (Figure 31.5).

All groups are made up of members who possess a series of individual skills and experiences. The key players in a group are:

- The core group members.
- The support group members.
- The group leader.

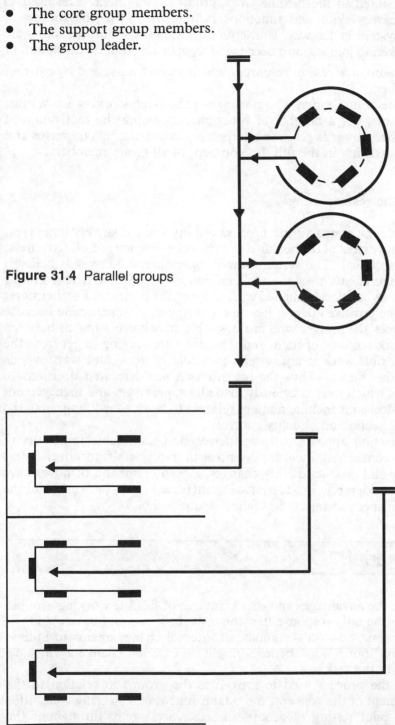

Figure 31.4 Parallel groups

Figure 31.5 Scion groups

31

The core group members are chosen on the basis of specific individual and group characteristics. Accurate assessment of these individual and group characteristics is an essential element in the process of selecting those most suited to the flexible work group environment. The need to co-operate across skills and functions is fundamental to the success of the group system at Leeway. Consequently, support group members are normally asked to join a group because of a particular skill qualification, or perhaps because of access to resources which are not possessed by existing group members.

Finally, the group leader, who possesses a thorough working knowledge of the business, has a number of functions, including the motivation of group members towards achieving common goals, building consensus and morale and assisting in the full development of all group members.

Results of the restructuring

Clearly, while the restructuring process did involve a relatively large cost, the nature and extent of the benefits, in terms of efficiency and effectiveness, need to be specified. The system now in operation at Leeway is believed by the change agents to assist the creation of satisfied, efficient groups whose interests are closely aligned with those of the business. Furthermore, because of the positive effect it has on employee involvement, and because it is employees themselves who are best able to achieve a match between what the work requires of them and what they are seeking to get from the work, the flexible work group system, particularly, goes some way towards facilitating this match. Thus the organization has delegated decisions to these groups which were previously made by supervisory and management staff. Such decisions include matters relating to work scheduling, material ordering, inspection and quality control.

Job satisfaction appears to have increased. Quantifiable indicators of satisfaction considered include absenteeism rates, staff turnover rates, productivity and product quality changes. Absenteeism and turnover have decreased considerably. Productivity has increased by 14 per cent, and the number of inspection rejects has fallen dramatically.

Activity brief

1 Evaluate the advantages and disadvantages of flexible working groups. Are they the only response that the organization could have made?
2 What is your view on the choice of internal change agents to initiate the intervention? What benefits might an external change agent have brought to the task?
3 Analyse the process used to introduce the groups in relation to the development of the concept, the establishment of a steering committee and the pilot testing of groups in select areas only throughout the organization. What other approaches could Leeway have taken?

4   What implications do flexible working groups have for the role of the supervisors and their training?
5   Typically, what skills need to be developed when an organization's work force is reorganized into flexible working groups? What implications does this have for the delivery of training generally?
6   While the company identified the initial benefits attached to the introduction of flexible working groups, how would you ensure that the benefits were on-going? Also, what might be the additional HRM implications of introducing such changes?

Recommended reading

BUCHANAN, D., 'Job enrichment is dead: long live high performance work design', *Personnel Management*, May 1987.
BUCHANAN, D. A., and McCALMAN, J., *High Performance Work Systems: the Digital Experience*, London, Routledge, 1989.
CASE, T. L., *et al.*, 'Internal and external change agents', *Leadership and Organization Development Journal*, 11, 1, 1990.
LEIGHTON, P., and SYRETT, M., *New Work Patterns: Putting Policy into Practice*, London, Pitman, 1989.

Case 32

The Organizational Development implications of financial stringency: Dorefleet Social Services Department

Philip Frame

Organizational Development in times of financial stringency

This case gives the opportunity to consider the Organizational Development role of personnel managers in organizations which are experiencing financial stringency.

The Social Services Department of the borough of Dorefleet is in crisis. The department's three management teams have, largely as a result of their different sub-cultures, responded in different ways to the requirement that they cut their budgets. The resulting conflict threatens the organization's continued effectiveness.

In financial hard times, organizations focus on retrenchment strategies, that is, reducing expenditure, including expenditure on human resources. With this focus, the principal task of the personnel department is to devise and operate redundancy procedures, or some alternative, which will reduce the organization's spending on staff. But those who remain with the organization are usually ignored.

This case provides an additional and equally important focus for personnel professionals: what they can do within the organization to ensure that it continues to operate in an effective and efficient manner. Thereby it encourages consideration of the types of support that can be offered to managers coping with 'hard times' and, more generally, of Personnel's role as a developer of human resources.

Finally, the case will help develop understanding of the role a personnel professional can play in Organizational Development.

Defining Organizational Development and sub-cultures

Organizational Development is defined as purposeful and managed organizational change. It aims both to initiate change and to help employees cope with change. Usually it is associated with growth and the organizational problems which result. It has an equally important function, though, in times of no growth or reduced growth. Firstly, it can help restore a degree of equilibrium to an organization's human relations when they have been profoundly disturbed by a crisis such as that described in this case. It can help, for example, to reduce conflict. Secondly, it can assist individuals and groups in coming to terms with harsh reality and in deciding what can be achieved in the new circumstances.

The concept of sub-culture used in this case is derived from the model of organizational culture suggested by Schein (1985). Sub-culture means the 'taken for granted' ways of thinking, behaving and attaching value which are shared to a greater or lesser extent by members of a working group. These norms develop over time to provide an effective means of task management. Only in times of crisis such as that due to massive environmental or organizational change, as is evident in this case, do they become the subject of debate, often because they are no longer effective to cope with new and threatening circumstances. The aspects of sub-culture which are of particular significance here are management styles and definitions of the management role.

The Social Services Department

Dorefleet is situated on the boundary of a run-down inner-city area and a more prosperous suburban residential area in a large northern city. Dorefleet Social Services Department is responsible for providing all personal social services to the borough's residents. It has three major client groups: children at risk, the elderly and the handicapped. Services are provided either in the community, e.g. at clients' homes, or in residential and day-care establishments. The range of activities is extremely wide, and includes home helps and meals on wheels, residential care, therapy, counselling and legal action.

As the provision of many services is required by law, the department has little choice in determining what it will or will not provide. Recent legislation has, in fact, increased the range of services the department has to provide. It works closely with other council departments, the local offices of government departments, a variety of aid agencies, both public and private, and the local courts.

The department is structured into four divisions (see Figure 32.1). Two of them, Fieldwork and Residential, are major service providers; these divisions manage respectively the community-based and the establishment based provisions identified above. Co-operation between the two divisions is essential if clients are to be provided with an effective service. Each division has its own management team, which co-ordinates activities and establishes procedures. A support role is played by the remaining two divisions, Finance, and Research and Development. The personnel function is located within the latter division.

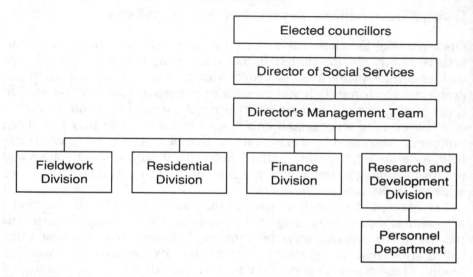

Figure 32.1 The organizational structure of Dorefleet Social Services Department

Overall management of the department is the responsibility of the Director of Social Services, supported by a group of five senior managers and including the senior managers of the Fieldwork and Residential divisions. Together, they comprise the Director's Management Team. It is this team, together with those of the Fieldwork and the Residential divisions, which are the subject of this case study.

The situation

The financial crisis
The council is controlled by Labour. Various external environmental pressures, including changes in central government's funding policy and a fall in Dorefleet's revenue associated with the community charge (poll tax), have resulted in the authority having to provide services with less money. As a result, councillors have instructed all departments to reduce their expenditure in the current financial year by 3 per cent and their projected expenditure for the coming financial year by 5 per cent. There was, though, a degree of uncertainty about the council's position, in that the percentage reduction had been changed on a number of occasions. Indeed, the decision to retrench had, at one point, been reversed and then reinstated.

Decision-making time was limited, especially in relation to the current financial year. Little or no guidance on the basis of which decisions were to be taken was provided, though a policy of no redundancies was agreed. Apart from that, the ruling party agreed to 'stand by our election pledges'.

The Director of Social Services instructed both the Fieldwork and Residential management teams to review spending and come up with the requisite reductions. Again, no guidance of a specific nature was given. Reference was made, though, to the protection of life-preserving rather than life-enhancing services. Additionally, managers of each division were encouraged to suggest reductions in the other.

On two occasions, then, the two divisional management teams produced a response, though in one case the response was seen to be less than adequate. Each team recommended savings in both their own and in the other division. The director's management team used these as the basis of its own recommendations to councillors.

Money was to be saved, it suggested, by increasing charges for some services and instituting them for other services which had previously been 'free' to clients. Major savings would result from a 'managed vacancy element', that is, not filling posts which became vacant. The councillors considered these cost reduction areas in a document entitled 'Savings in Social Services'. Following a lengthy debate, which resulted in modifications to the recommendations submitted, they voted it through.

In the event the Social Services Department lost less than was anticipated. For more than the first half of the coming financial year there was adequate funding; the remainder of the year, though, was much less certain. In contrast, the human costs of the exercise were considerable.

Human costs resulted from the different responses to expenditure reduction exhibited by the department's three management teams: the Fieldwork, the Residential and the Director's Management Teams. The response of each team, and the team sub-culture on which it was based, are elaborated below.

The Fieldwork management team
Initially, this group of twelve middle managers, led by a senior manager, produced some recommendations; they were below the required 3 per cent cuts in current expenditure. Subsequently they refused to prioritize their services. Instead they suggested a 5 per cent reduction across the board in their own division, and reductions in the Residential division too. They expressed very strong opposition to financial reductions of any kind. They voiced this both within the organization, that is, to their peers in the Residential division and to senior management, and to elected members and the press. On a number of occasions labour was withdrawn. For example, they took part in a 'day of action' which involved highlighting their opposition to the reductions and their effect by taking part in a demonstration. A Fieldwork office was closed for a day and clients were referred to councillors for assistance. In another Fieldwork office no client case files were removed from the filing cabinet for a number of days because the post of filing clerk had been left unfilled as part of the 'managed vacancy element'. Client services were thus disrupted.

For this the division was heavily criticized by both middle and senior management. In turn, Fieldwork managers were highly critical of both these groups for obeying instructions. One likened this response to that of Eichmann, the Nazi war criminal: just like him, some people were 'following orders', regardless of the consequences. Additionally, they were scathing of senior management for not providing any guidance or establishing any priorities of service. Thus relations between this team and the Director's Management Team were said to be at an 'all-time low', as were their relations with the Residential management team.

When the financial position became clear, as set out in the document entitled 'Savings in Social Services' referred to above, they discovered that their division had not lost as much as had been feared. Fieldwork managers then changed their response from overt and vocal resistance to withdrawal from reduction-related tasks, such as restricting services and financial monitoring. As one of their number said, 'We're sick of it; if we keep quiet, it might all go away.'

The Fieldwork management team's sub-culture

Traditionally, the Fieldwork management team subscribe to management by consensus, both as a means of managing their staff and as a preferred style within the team. They strongly value a democratic and participative style. Consultation took time, though, and as a group they were not especially effective in either reaching decisions or doing so speedily. Team meetings were characterized as 'rambling, long-winded and lacking a sense of direction'. On the other hand, 'everyone has their say'. Whilst this style continued during the financial crisis, there was growing awareness that it was less than effective – 'We need to make some decisions!' – and that something had to be done to change the way in which the team's process was working.

Professionally, the Fieldwork division was recognized as a centre of excellent practice at the national level. Managers in the division thus had a well developed perspective on what had been, and what should continue to be, provided to clients. Fieldwork managers believed their division's task was to 'continue to meet unmet need'. It was not their job to recommend reductions or to prioritize services formally in any way, that is, decide who was not to be helped or determine what services were no longer to be provided. They had never been required to do so in the past when the service had been expanding. Some team members felt, though, that they had some responsibility in this area: 'If we don't decide to [establish priorities] someone else will, and we'll have no control.'

The members of the team were unversed in the ways of financial management. There was no budgetary control; none had been necessary in the past, when the message had been 'Spend, spend, spend: the council will pay up.' Some managers were negative about financial management – 'It's the last thing I'm interested in.' Some saw it as being in opposition to their role as professional social workers, but others suggested that training of some sort was a prerequisite of their beginning to exert financial control.

The Fieldwork division, including the Fieldwork management team, was unionized. Their union had a policy of non co-operation with cut-back management, though what this policy meant in practice was felt to be unclear by some Fieldwork managers.

In conclusion, it was clear that differences of opinion on what was the right thing to do was resulting in a breakdown of the team's usual method of operating. Also it was leading to staff demoralization and lack of motivation.

The Residential management team's response

The eight managers of the Residential division responded to the task as instructed. They came up with the requisite percentage sums, and went some way further: they identified larger savings which could, if necessary, be made. Reductions in the Fieldwork division were also recommended. They did not engage in any form of resistance activity, nor voice their opposition to expenditure reductions. Whilst commenting that it was not an easy task, they nevertheless did it. They were highly critical of their Fieldwork peers for responses that were characterized variously as 'childish', 'unprofessional', 'political', 'unrealistic' and 'selfish'. In contrast, they were uncritical of senior management for failing to provide task guidance or establish priorities.

The Residential management team's sub-culture

The team were able to routinize the crisis because they were experienced in financial management and had existing systems which ensured that control was exercised. On a monthly basis, spending was reviewed in the light of the budgetary allocation, and appropriate action was taken. To do so was regarded as part of their job, not as problematic. Indeed, it was a key aspect of the team's sub-culture.

As a group they valued direction, or being told what to do, both in their relations with their staff and with the senior manager in charge of their team. A number characterized themselves as 'benign despots'. Consultation and participation were of little significance. 'It takes so long', 'In some cases you need to take action, not talk' are typical comments on this issue. Thus as a group they were able to reach decisions speedily, under the direction of their team leader, and to value action of this sort positively.

The Residential division was just beginning to grow professionally. In comparison with Fieldwork, though, it was significantly underdeveloped. The Residential division was not unionized to any significant degree: union policy was, therefore, not especially relevant. Rather, the team's job, as professional managers in the public service, was 'to follow orders and not to get involved in the issues'. Senior management, then, defined the management tasks for this group. Whilst as individuals they might have negative views on expenditure reductions, it was not their job to voice opposition; that was the role of elected members. To do otherwise, as their Fieldwork peers had done, was unacceptable. They were, on the other hand, concerned that the deterioration in inter-divisional working relations would adversely affect the service that was offered to clients.

The Director's management team's response

The team believed in locating 'decisions on saving as close to the ground as was possible', hence their open instructions to the two divisional management teams. These, they assumed, could and should be followed without too much difficulty. They did not believe that it was up to them to determine priorities of service, or to revise the department's strategy in view of less money being available. That was the job of the elected councillors. The team, in fact, rejected a proposal to prioritize the services the Social Services Department offered. They were, according to the director, 'at the mercy of councillors: our priorities may not be the same as theirs'. Because of this, engaging in 'sophisticated criterion-setting exercises was useless'.

A number of working parties were set up to investigate 'high-spending' areas, but they produced little that was of practical use. At the same time, the director's management team agreed to save money by keeping vacancies open: this became known as the managed vacancy element. In drawing up their recommendations, however, they decided to 'protect' the Residential division. This division was felt to have been underfunded in the past and was therefore less able to sustain saving than the Fieldwork division. This priority was not made explicit to middle managers.

The Director's management team's sub-culture

The team was not an effective arena for policy-making or decision-taking. Meetings seldom had an agenda; items for discussion were announced by the Director of Social Services. Discussion documents were circulated just before a meeting or at the meeting itself, leaving little time for detailed consideration. Meetings were heavily controlled by the director. In relation to the financial crisis, he strongly believed that 'things were not as bad as they're made out to be; it's only a question of moving money about from one budget head [category] to another. Things are all right as they are.'

Traditionally, long-term or strategic issues were seldom considered; according to the director, the team 'got side-tracked with nuts-and-bolts issues', that is, day-to-day matters which were of minor concern. As a team it provided little direction to the department. Indeed, one team member likened the department's management to 'a doughnut; it's got nothing in the centre'. Privately a high degree of discontent was expressed by senior managers about the team's lack of direction and effectiveness. Such concern, though, was infrequently raised at team meetings.

Generally, it avoided issues of strategy and service priority by denying that it had any power, and continued to do so despite the financial crisis. Instead it assigned the task to its middle managers. At the same time it was incapable of managing the different responses by divisional teams outlined above. Managing diversity or understanding the bases of difference was not seen as significant. Rather the team expected the Fieldwork management team to respond as their Residential peers had done. That they had not done so was 'explained' in terms of individuals' personal and political values, and was roundly condemned.

In conclusion, there was a degree of dissatisfaction within the director's management team about its role in 'managing' the crisis, summed up by the following remark: 'It was chaos, an exercise based on hearsay and gut-level reactions: we can't afford to go through it again.'

The need for action

The Social Services Department's personnel manager was aware of some of the issues identified above, from informal contact with various senior and middle managers and from stories which were in circulation. She had been present at a joint meeting of the Fieldwork and Residential management teams when each team had recommended reductions in the other division's resources. The conflict and acrimony apparent then had made a lasting impression. Feelings were running high. At the same time there was a general air of despondency around the organization, a feeling of demoralization and fear of what the future would hold.

Some action was essential to improve the working relations between the various teams, so as to ensure that an effective service continued to be provided. In addition, the personnel manager was interested in expanding her own role into the Organizational Development area. But what could she do and what sort of risks were involved?

Activity brief

Take the role of the personnel manager and members of her team in answering the following questions.

1 Read the case and note the ways in which team sub-cultures affected responses to financial 'cuts'.
2 What can be learned from this case about the effective introduction of organizational change?
3 How would you discover the sub-culture of a group?
4 Identify specific intervention opportunities for the personnel manager in this case: identify which managers are involved and what action you might take. You may find it useful to consider these matters under the following headings: individual, intra-group (within a group) and inter-group (between groups).
5 Now establish an action priority list, based on the intervention opportunities identified, of what is more important to change and what is less so. Whilst this will ultimately be a matter of professional judgement, you should consider what support for change is evident in the text, and what sorts of change it applies to. Finally, you should consider the degree of likely success or failure involved in each type of intervention.
6 In small groups, exchange the results of your work and agree one target for an intervention. You need to justify your selection by reference to the text, and by your assessment of the risk involved.
7 Prepare a ten-minute oral presentation which details the results of your group-based work.

32

Recommended reading

HARDY, C., *Strategies for Retrenchment and Turnaround*, Basingstoke, de Gruyter, 1990.

LESSEM, R., *Managing Corporate Culture*, Aldershot, Gower, 1990, chapter 4.

SCHEIN, E., *Organizational Culture and Leadership*, San Francisco, Jossey-Bass, 1985.

Students are expected to draw on their learning to date, particularly input from Stage I concerning both *organizational culture* and *the environment*, and current teaching on *employee development*. They need to consider what range of activities are open to them. In addition, students are invited to draw upon their own experience both as an initiator of, and subject for, developmental activities.